Westview Special Studies on Latin America and the Caribbean

The New Cuban Presence in the Caribbean
edited by Barry B. Levine

The Caribbean area projects an image—not entirely accurate—of instability, and it is within that context that the United States and Cuba, the region's chief protagonists, struggle.

This book explores in detail the history and nature of Cuba's influence in the Commonwealth Caribbean, Mexico, and Central and South America, as well as its relations with revolutionary movements and communist parties throughout Latin America. The authors place Cuba's Western Hemisphere contacts within the wider framework of the island's involvements with the Third World (especially Africa) and the Soviet Union. The meaning of the new Cuban presence becomes clear in the authors' analyses of the limits to that presence and the way the United States should respond to it.

The special issue of *Caribbean Review* on which this book is based has been described as "a round-up not only of Cuban involvement, but U.S. involvement as well . . . [that] articulates a political card game of scary proportions being played in what was once known as an American lake." *The New Cuban Presence in the Caribbean* provides a much expanded, completely revised study of the dynamics of Caribbean international politics, using Cuba's activities in the region as a focal point.

Dr. Levine is professor of sociology and anthropology at Florida International University. From 1965 to 1972 he was a member of the faculty at the University of Puerto Rico. Among his publications are *Problemas de desigualdad social en Puerto Rico* and *Benjy Lopez: A Picaresque Tale of Emigration and Return.* He is cofounder and editor of *Caribbean Review.*

The New Cuban Presence in the Caribbean

edited by Barry B. Levine

Westview Press / Boulder, Colorado

Westview Special Studies on Latin America and the Caribbean

Published in 1983 in the United States of America by
Westview Press, Inc.
5500 Central Avenue
Boulder, Colorado 80301
Frederick A. Praeger, President and Publisher

Library of Congress Cataloging in Publication Data
Main entry under title:
The new Cuban presence in the Caribbean.
(Westview special studies on Latin America and the Caribbean)
"Based on a special-topic issue of *Caribbean Review,* with the same title"—Pref.
Includes index.
1. Caribbean Area—Foreign relations—Cuba—Addresses, essays, lectures. 2. Cuba—Foreign relations—Caribbean Area—Addresses, essays, lectures. 3. Cuba—Foreign relations—1959- —Addresses, essays, lectures. I. Levine, Barry B., 1941- . II. Series.
F2178.C9N48 1983 327.7291 83-5870
ISBN 0-86531-538-8
ISBN 0-86531-567-1 (pbk.)

Printed and bound in the United States of America

Contents

Preface

This book is based on a special-topic issue of *Caribbean Review,* with the same title, that won for the journal several important honors—among them finalist status in the 1980 National Magazine Awards where it was characterized as "a round-up not only of Cuban involvement, but of U.S. involvement as well . . . [it] articulate[s] a political card game of scary proportions being played in what was once an American lake." *The New Cuban Presence in the Caribbean* now provides in book form a completely revised and much expanded study of the dynamics of Caribbean international politics, using Cuba's activities in the region as the focal point.

The origin of the idea for this book dates back to July 1979, when I attended Carifesta, the biannual Caribbean arts and cultural festival, which was held that year in Cuba. Many images, not all consistent, date from that trip. One image is of the distrust with which the United States has been viewed by Third World intellectuals. To the extent that any debate was heard in Havana at all it was whether the Third World was to accept Cuban ideology or resist it. Put more sharply, it was clear that Third World intellectuals had become reluctant to think of the United States as a society worth trying to emulate. When Havana presented its arguments it did so on a Caribbean-nation-to-Caribbean-nation level. And Havana's aid when made at this regional level had unanticipated benefits: Third World countries, for example, that send their students to study medicine in Cuba are much less likely to suffer the brain-drain casualties that occur when such students train for medicine in the First World. I had hoped to articulate some of these ideas in the special-topic issue.

Carifesta was held amid a phenomenon that had, for all the hostility between the United States and Cuba, been taken as quite normal: the return of more than 100,000 exile Cubans to visit family and friends. Exiles, no longer referred to as *gusanos*, had become members of *la comunidad*. This mass interaction between the two parts of the Cuban nation seemed to be the capstone of an impending rapprochement between the United States and Cuba: Castro talking amiably of U.S. President Carter, the permitted exit of dual citizens, the release and flight of political prisoners, agreements on hijacking and fishing rights—all this suggested that some diplomatic changes were in the making, notwithstanding the Cuban military involvement in Africa.

The Sixth Nonaligned Nations Conference held in Havana during September 1979 and Castro's appearance before the United Nations in October further demonstrated apparent diplomatic advances being made by Cuba. Most Caribbean nations do not have an articulate foreign policy, much less such diplomatic flair. The U.S. reaction to all this, expressed as concern over the presence of a Soviet brigade on Cuban soil, made clear that something was indeed worrying the United States. But the Soviet brigade issue never seemed to hold water. Clearly what was worrying the Americans was the new Cuban presence in the Caribbean.

Cuban geopolitical activity, however, began to demonstrate vulnerability quite unexpectedly. In December 1979 Panama admitted the shah of Iran as a favor to the United States. In January 1980 the Soviet Union invaded dirt-poor Afghanistan; the new ruler—while still in Moscow—publicly thanked the Soviets for their efforts and added that if needed, he would ask the Cubans to come and help also! And the Cuban government, rather than vote against the Soviets, or even abstain, voted with them against the United Nations' condemnation of the invasion. Cuba had been made to pointedly feel the squeeze between its loyalty to the Soviet Union and its loyalty to any principles of nonalignment. The Third World took notice, and Cuba thereupon lost the United Nations Security Council seat that it had tried so diligently to win.

These changes took place between the time I had asked the original contributors to produce their articles and the time that the special-topic issue of *Caribbean Review* was published. Even greater changes have taken place since that time. Omar Torrijos of Panama and Eric Williams of Trinidad and Tobago died in office; Nicaragua's ousted strong man, Anastasio Somoza Debayle, was assassinated in exile in Paraguay; Puerto Rico's Luis Muñoz Marín and Venezuela's Rómulo Betancourt, two great Caribbean democrats, died in retirement. Yugoslavia's president, Marshal Josip Tito, an important voice in the Nonaligned Nations Movement, died, as did Leonid Brezhnev, who as leader of the Soviet Union had built up the Soviet military capacity that allowed the Castro government the luxury of its overseas involvements. A plethora of elections has been held throughout the Caribbean. Jamaica's incumbent prime minister, socialist Michael Manley, was defeated at the polls by a capitalist contender, Edward Seaga. The U.S. president, Democrat Jimmy Carter, was defeated by Republican Ronald Reagan. El Salvador's incumbent leader, U.S.-backed Christian Democrat José Napoleón Duarte, was defeated by a rightist coalition coordinated by Roberto D'Aubuisson in an election that was overwhelming in its high degree of voter participation in the midst of civil war. Ten thousand Cubans stormed the Peruvian Embassy in Havana seeking asylum. One hundred twenty-five thousand Cubans left the island for exile in the United States via the ragtag flotilla from Mariel. Guerrilla warfare flared up once again in Central America.

Fortunately, the contributors to this book are superior craftsmen. Even given the incredible turns of events, their chapters, written and revised—some at least twice—during the volatile happenings, demonstrate singular understanding of the nature of Caribbean politics. They reveal a political card game of extraordinary deftness involving players of great awareness, an awareness that includes an understanding that social reality is subject to constant redefinition, that what looks like ideological superiority one day may become an ideological hindrance the next. For—unlike the card game—what looks like a good deal in one hand may not be in another when the rules of the game suddenly have changed.

Seven of the chapters presented here appeared in the original issue and have been rewritten; another appeared in a previous issue of *Caribbean Review* and also appears here in revised form. The first chapter has been added to provide an introduction to the Caribbean context within which Cuba's activities have unfolded; chapters on Cuba's relations with Mexico, Venezuela, and the Latin American communist parties fill in previous voids in the analysis; two interpretative chapters on Cuba's relations with the USSR and on the exportability of the Cuban model have also been added in the interest of completeness of analysis.

The book follows the editorial policy of *Caribbean Review.* We have often described that policy as "crossed swords," a deliberate attempt to avoid homogeneity of opinion and to seek a diversity of perspectives. As a consequence, the reader should find himself in a situation in which he will not be able to agree with all of the articles incorporated in this book. Precisely in that spirit of intellectual debate, I had hoped to be able to incorporate a revised version of Norman Matlin's "The Myth of Mastery—A Decision Analytic Critique of 'The New Cuban Presence in the Caribbean.' " Matlin's critique of the original issue appeared in the Fall 1980 issue (Vol. 9, no. 4) of *Caribbean Review.* The unhappy pressures of time and space unfortunately prevented that critique, and responses to it, from being included here.

Barry B. Levine
Florida International University
Miami, Florida

1
Geopolitical and Cultural Competition in the Caribbean—An Introduction: Cuba Versus the United States

Barry B. Levine

The Caribbean is an area of abundant variety: There is diversity in economic styles, political institutions, religious preferences, language and ethnic traditions, racial and emigrant origins, and cultural and artistic manifestations.[1] It is also an area of conflict and change. There are border conflicts among neighboring states,[2] conflicting interpretations of the law of the sea,[3] and much domestic civil strife, including coups, civil wars, and revolutions.[4] Many of the leaders who have given the region its political flavor have within recent years departed from the scene.[5] This cultural plentifulness, institutional divergencies, and social conflict and change provide the backdrop for earnest efforts to influence the course the area's nations are to take. It is in conjunction with these efforts that explanations are offered to justify positions taken in the battles that storm the region. One such explanation sees many of the battles as those between two geopolitical Titans clumsily trying to clobber their antagonists in the name of this or that pantheon of gods; another sees various battles as those between fractious nationalists playing on the fears of past enemies and current prejudices. In the course of presenting these arguments, in one context or another, the Caribbean is portrayed distinctly, its divisions are presented differently, and the battles brewing within the area are characterized diversely.

One portrayal of the Caribbean sees it as the Caribbean archipelago. In addition to the islands of the greater West Indies, the mainland states of Guyana, Belize, Suriname, and French Guiana fall within this definition, as do settlements on other parts of the coasts of Central

America and northern South America. Its peoples share long histories of colonialism and dependence, have large numbers of Africans in their populations, have experienced the dominance of slavery and the sugar plantation in their earlier economies, and are essentially immigrant-descendant in their demographic makeup. Today, the Caribbean archipelago has some 32 million inhabitants and a combined gross national product of about $47 billion annually.

Because the countries and territories of the archipelago share to some degree a series of experiences, the archipelago is the favorite definition of the Caribbean by those analysts who use cultural explanations of events occurring in the region, explanations based on common roots and identities. But as culture binds, it also divides, and many divisions based on cultural distinctions and alliances skewer the archipelago, divisions that often align one or another culture with societies outside the region. Thus, for example, French-speaking islanders may feel a greater affinity with mainland France than they do with nearby Dutch-speaking islands, and Dominicans may feel greater ties with Spanish-speaking countries of the Caribbean or South America than they do with the French-speaking Haitians with whom they share the island of Hispaniola.

Another portrayal of the Caribbean sees it as the Caribbean basin. The basin includes the nations, territories, and settlements of the archipelago plus Mexico, the five Central American republics, Panama, Colombia, and Venezuela (all, except El Salvador, "washed by the Caribbean Sea"). Geographically coterminous with an environmentalist's definition of the Caribbean, the basin includes all the sensitive passageways to and through the area: the Panama Canal, the Yucatán Channel between Mexico and Cuba, the Windward Passage between Cuba and Haiti, the Mona Passage between the Dominican Republic and Puerto Rico, the passages between the various Windward and Leeward islands. These lanes control the coming and going of maritime commerce, particularly oil, and lately even of boat people. The basin has a population of 168 million persons and an annual combined gross national product of $257 billion.

Because the countries and territories of the basin share to some degree geographic characteristics as well as proximity, the basin definition of the Caribbean is the favorite of those analysts who use geopolitical explanations of events occurring in the region, explanations that focus on the strategic importance of geographic proximity. The rivalries and interventions, from within the area as well as from without, all induce anxiety in nations of the Caribbean basin, each concerned over the political consequences of its neighbor's activity. Thus, geopolitical explanations may be offered in bilateral or regionwide circumstances. Strategic alliances bind as well as divide the countries of the basin into ideological blocs and spheres of influence. Contemporary geopolitical definitions portraying the Caribbean as a basin derive a unity from common though antagonistic concerns for what is happening in the area.

One finds today geopolitical definitions dividing the basin into adherents of the left and the right, of socialist and capitalist ideological camps. Each side sees the area as unified by virtue of the threat to stability posed by the other: by U.S. imperialism or by Soviet-style totalitarianism. Elaborate constructions justify each position and attempt to delegitimate the opposing one. Whereas one side sees the threat of terrorist wars of liberation, the other sees the threat of destabilizing attempts at counterrevolution. Each side faults the goals and accomplishments of the other's economics; each side accuses the other of having surrogate nations act on its behalf; each calls the other names, attributing rationality to its claims and hypocrisy to those of its opponent. The result is a kind of ideological geopolitics whose explanations are proferred by antagonists who, for all the hostility toward each other, and even in moments of extreme polarization, do, however, share reciprocal perceptions of the Caribbean as a target of contentious diplomatic and strategic concerns.

Prior to the initiation of the 1982 war over the Falkland Islands the ideological geopolitical definition of the Caribbean as a basin prevailed with both right and left, capitalist and socialist—perspectives arguing for the unity of the Caribbean in terms of a need to defend against perils purported to be common to all in the area—communism in the one case, imperialism in the other. With the onset of the South Atlantic hostilities, such arguments seemed with disarming ease to be rapidly replaced by cultural ones. The Caribbean was not a battleground of right and left but of Anglo and Latin: the same actors, but now with new allies and new enemies. And then, amid loud protestations that the new cultural explanations would prevail, the ideological geopolitical explanations once again resurfaced. The ease with which the transition from one mental set to another was accomplished should sensitize observers to the apparent functional interchangeability of these alternatingly useful interpretations, as well as make one distrustful of their use.

Neither geopolitical nor cultural explanations are by themselves "correct" in any normative sense, but each is used for specific purposes and to articulate if not justify and legitimate specific interests. In other words, the definitions of "the Caribbean," like the "explanations" for events within the Caribbean, presented in the act of pursuing allies or damning enemies, are socially constructed. Sociocultural definitions are diachronic; geopolitical ones, synchronic. One is in terms of that which is believed to have been historically given, the other in terms of current interpretations of international political interests, an agenda for a promised future. Although both styles of interpretation take liberties with the discrete realities of the social worlds of the Caribbean, the participants find it useful to think of or to portray the region as in some sense a manifestation of either some underlying level of anthropological being or, alternatively, as a consequence of the interaction of political forces. But not only do nations group themselves together, or divide themselves from each other, on the basis of either geopolitics or culture, but these two alternatives also intertwine. Thus, nations will frequently invoke ethnic identifications in attempts to achieve geopolitical goals,[6] or geopolitical concerns may reinforce sociocultural linkages.[7]

On the Historical Differentiation of Definitions

Within a half century after the Spanish arrived in the Caribbean, the area became a battleground for outside powers. Attracted by the mineral wealth Spain was exporting to Europe, the French, English, and Dutch fleets raided Spanish settlements. The Dutch settled the Guianas and Curaçao and other islands; the English settled Barbados, Nevis, Montserrat, and part of St. Kitts. As Spain's power declined it began to lose territories: The French took over the western part of Hispaniola, the English, Jamaica and the Caribbean coasts of Central America. European geopolitics replicated itself in the Caribbean as various islands changed hands. The Caribbean in the sixteenth and seventeenth centuries was an area where, internationally, the geopolitical divisions were, in fact, the sociocultural ones.

The seventeenth, eighteenth, and nineteenth centuries saw the transformation of Caribbean economies from small-scale subsistence and farming to plantation agriculture for export—especially sugar, but also tobacco and coffee. In Central America, Indian populations were forced to meet the new demand for labor. But in the archipelago, where the Indians did not survive, various kinds of labor-repressive mechanisms combined to import labor, including indentured servants from the ports of Europe, slaves from Africa, and "coolie labor" from India. Sugar then began a decline in most of the Caribbean, but precisely at this moment it took hold in the Spanish islands. There, slavery and additional labor-repressive mechanisms, such as compulsory work laws, were utilized.

The nineteenth century witnessed the decline of Spanish authority in the region and the rise of two Caribbeans: a Hispanic Caribbean operated as a U.S. sphere of influence and an English-speaking Caribbean still part of the British Empire. It was at this time that international geopolitical definitions and sociocultural ones began to be differentiated.

During the 1820s the countries of Central America and Mexico, Colombia, and Venezuela gained their independence from Spain. In 1823, U.S. President James Monroe issued the Monroe Doctrine prohibiting European recolonization of the Americas: Geopolitics was to take precedence over any reversion to a political articulation of cultural links (especially Hispanic links[8]). In 1898, the battleship *Maine* was destroyed in Havana harbor, initiating the Spanish-American War. After the war, the United States annexed Puerto Rico and by virtue of the Platt amendment to the Cuban Constitution reserved the right to intervene militarily in a Cuba newly independent from Spain. Under the approving eye of U.S. President Theodore Roosevelt, Panama seceded from Colombia in 1903; the United States leased the Canal Zone and built the Panama Canal. Between the two Roosevelts U.S. intervention reached its peak. U.S. forces occupied, for different lengths of time, parts of Cuba, the Dominican Republic, Haiti, Mexico, and Nicaragua.

The beginning of the twentieth century, which encompassed the crash of the world price of sugar in the 1920s and the Great Depression of the 1930s, saw the rise in the Hispanic Caribbean of some of the region's most notorious patriarchs (Venezuela's Juan Vicente Gómez, 1908–1935; Cuba's Gerardo Machado, 1925–1933; the Dominican Republic's Rafael Leonidas Trujillo, 1930–1961; El Salvador's Maximiliano Hernández Martínez, 1931–1944; Guatemala's Jorge Ubico, 1935–1941; and Nicaragua's Anastasio Somoza García, 1937–1956). Officially, U.S. policy toward the region changed with President Franklin Roosevelt's Good Neighbor Policy in 1933. The Panama Canal treaty was unilaterally made more favorable to Panama, the U.S.-imposed Platt amendment to the Cuban Constitution was dropped, and the United States no longer openly claimed the right to intervene. The surrender of this claim was somehow interpreted by the United States to mean that it needed to support the patriarchs of the day, a neat geopolitical accommodation to sociocultural differences, an accommodation for which the United States is still blamed.

Reactions to the economic crises of the 1920s and 1930s were different in the colonies of the British Caribbean—the results there were widespread riots that spanned the West Indies. Out of the disorders strong labor unions emerged. And it was with these labor unions at the core that, first, democratic political processes and, then, the movements toward self-government came about in the British colonies. Labor leaders became the principal political leaders (Grantley Adams in Barbados, Vere Bird in Antigua, Robert Bradshaw in St. Kitts, Alexander Bustamente and Norman Manley in Jamaica, among them). They pushed for the end of colonial government, the adoption of adult suffrage and representative political institutions, and eventually, self-government. Representative government came in the late 1940s and early 1950. In the late 1950s the short-lived West Indies Federation was formed, and then, beginning in 1962, independence was granted, one by one, to those former colonies of Great Britain that requested it (a process that is still going on as even the smallest of the islands ask for independence).

The Autumn of the Patriarch[9]

Recent leadership in the Caribbean has been for the most part talented and democratic. The initial stages of modernization have demanded that the new leaders play the combined roles of educator, culture promoter, and political coordinator.[10] Examples of this enlightened leadership include Eric Williams in Trinidad and Tobago, 1956–1981; Norman Manley in Jamaica, 1940–1962; Luis Muñoz Marín in Puerto Rico, 1948–1961. These leaders have been followed by a more technocratic group of administrators no less committed to democratic institutions; leaders such as Errol Barrow and Tom Adams in Barbados; Roberto Sánchez Vilella, Rafael Hernández Colón, Luis A. Ferré, and Carlos Romero Barceló in Puerto Rico; Antonio Silvestre Guzmán and Jorge Blanco in the Dominican Republic; Michael Manley and Edward Seaga in Jamaica; and George Chambers in Trinidad and Tobago.[11]

But the Caribbean also witnessed a second round of patriarchal dictators: Fulgencio Batista in Cuba, 1952–1958; Marcos Pérez Jiménez in Venezuela, 1952–1957; the sons of Somoza García, Luis Somoza Debayle, 1956–1967, and Anastasio (Tachito) Somoza Debayle, 1956–1979, in Nicaragua; François (Papa Doc) Duvalier, 1957–1971, and his son, Jean Claude (Baby Doc) Duvalier, 1971–present, in Haiti; and Forbes Burnham in Guyana, 1964–present. Eric Gairy in Grenada, 1967–1979, followed the patriarchal style and applied it to democratic politics. For all their staying power, however, the patriarchs have consistently aroused resentment and resistance. A particularly interesting example of this was the mysterious Caribbean Legion.[12] Founded by antidictatorial exiles, including José (Don Pepe) Figueres (who was to be president of Costa Rica, 1948–1949, 1953–1958, 1970–1974) and Rómulo Betancourt (who was to become president of Venezuela, 1959–1964), under the sponsorship of Guatemalan President Juan

José Arevalo (1945–1951), it mounted unsuccessful attacks against the dictatorships of Somoza García in Nicaragua and Trujillo in the Dominican Republic. Later, Figueres, Betancourt, and Puerto Rican Governor Luis Muñoz Marín formed an alliance of the democratic left, attacking by diplomatic means Somoza, Trujillo, Batista, and subsequently, Fidel Castro.

The responses of both the ideological left and the ideological right refer to purported economic bases underlying the impulses for change; but in fact the possibilities of change have rested, more often than not, on the displeasure engendered by the patriarchal style of regimes whose very nature in the context of the modern world has undercut even their minimal legitimacy. Colombia, Venezuela, and the Dominican Republic today have regimes that grew out of resistance to old-fashioned bossism; but so too do Cuba, Nicaragua, and Grenada. Many of the area's problems are political, not economic; certain kinds of political structures invite revolution. Patrimonialism sooner or later generates the seeds of its own destruction.

Thinkers as diverse as French political theorist Jean-François Revel and Mexican novelist and diplomat Carlos Fuentes have pointed to this political aspect. Revel, referring to "*caudillismo* and corruption" in Latin America, has argued that much of the region

> is a projection of Europe . . . the "bad" Europe of coups d'etat and civil wars, of military adventurers and demagogic chieftains, of corruption and injustice, of pseudo-revolutions and bloody repression. . . . The underdevelopment of Latin America stems from its problem, a problem of the self-poisoning of the political culture.[13]

Fuentes, following Max Weber, has characterized this style of governance as patrimonialism,

> a condition brought on by the confusion of all public and private rights in favor of the chieftain and his clan of relatives, favorites, sycophants, and hangers-on. Patrimonialism—the right of the *conquistador*—precludes competent administration or economic planning. It is based on obedience and whim, not law. This state of things requires a standing army—thugs, mercenaries, death squads, responsible to no law save that of the caprice of the ruling clan.[14]

In 1959, Fidel Castro and his guerrillas successfully ousted the intensely disliked, prototypically patriarchal Cuban dictator, Fulgencio Batista. Castro stood up not only to the patriarch but also to the United States, which had supported the entrenched strong man. The

Castro revolution in Cuba, more than any other recent series of events, shattered the belief in U.S. supremacy in the Caribbean, the belief that the Caribbean is an "American lake." If early on Castro drew international support because of his nationalism in defiance of the United States, he shortly thereafter secured additional support through his ability to cross geopolitical swords by adopting the opposing international ideology, allying with the United States's antagonist, the Soviet Union. Castro more than any other hemispheric leader has been able to sometimes marry, sometimes alternate, successful cultural and geopolitical opposition to the United States.

For many observers, Fidel Castro represents not the end of the patriarchal *caudillo* tradition but rather its continuation. But for others, it is Castro's commitment to modernization, regardless of ideological perspective, that marks him as different from the patriarch. Whether Castro hid his Marxist-Leninist colors until he achieved power or once having achieved power decided to appropriate for his own purposes the ideological frame of reference of the Marxists is a question of much debate. What is no longer in dispute is the fact that since the early 1960s, the Caribbean has been more and more drawn into East-West ideological geopolitics. For some, Castro's rise represented a hopeful alternative; for others, it represented a menacing one. For some, the superimposing of the East-West ideological map upon the political cartography of the Caribbean ultimately meant greater opportunities to play one side off against the other; but for others, this superimposition upon the culturally and socially distinct nations of the Caribbean would ultimately mean fewer opportunities, for henceforth all individuality and innovation would be judged in massive terms little tolerant of subtlety.

The New Cuban Presence in the Caribbean

The success of the Castro revolution forever changed not only Cuba but the Caribbean as well. It will take future historians years of research to unravel the extent of the Cuban nation's enormous influence on the development and direction of the Caribbean—the influence of both Cubas on the Caribbean, for the revolution split the island society geopolitically into a Cuba of the left and a Cuba of the right. The Cuba of the right, the Cuba of the exile, concentrated in Miami but not limited to it, has spread out to all the shores of the basin with the establishment of intra-Cuban, inter-Caribbean communication links and economic patterns, a web of business connections. These Cubans generate international trade rather than offer cross-boundary gifts of aid. Appropriately, they have become known as the Phoenicians of the Caribbean. The Cuba of the left, island Cuba, the Cuba of ideological plentifulness and economic meagerness, has even more visibly spread out across the Caribbean and beyond. But the forays of these Cubans have been diplomatic and military rather than economic—they offer gifts of aid rather than sources of trade. To continue drawing parallels from the Mediterranean, these venturers have become the Spartans of the Caribbean.

Although the Caribbean is not the poorest of the poor, or to use Trinidadian novelist V. S. Naipaul's caustic phrase, "the Third World's Third World," it suffers a full range of economic scarcities. When Fidel Castro came to power in 1959 the development model then in vogue was the so-called Puerto Rican model. Puerto Rico had maintained its colonial tie with the United States but with a twist, best described as "imperial development."[15] Whereas the United States controls the ultimate prerogatives of sovereignty of culturally distinct Puerto Rico, it has been obliged to promote the economic and social development of the island as a condition of that arrangement. "Operation Bootstrap" invited U.S. capital to come to the island to create jobs for Puerto Ricans via a series of inducements, such as tax incentives, inexpensive labor, and inclusion within U.S. tariff walls. By virtue of the colonial link, Puerto Ricans freely migrate to the continent in search of additional jobs. The Puerto Rican model has worked as a transfer economy, accepting increases in personal income throughout the social structure, with scant regard for the development of an economic infrastructure that would allow for a degree of economic independence.

Although some aspects of the Puerto Rican model have been adopted elsewhere in the Caribbean (notably, the inducements to foreign capital to invest to create jobs—what has been called "industrialization by invitation"[16]), other aspects cannot be adopted (notably, the citizen's right to migrate to the mainland). Beyond that, the Puerto Rican model rekindles animosity toward the United States, given the history of U.S. intervention in the area. For many in the Caribbean, the trade-off of legitimate Puerto Rican nationalist goals to achieve economic gains invalidates the whole model. Castro's attempt to combine nationalism and socialism is thus seen as an alternative model for development.

A clear example of a plebiscitarian state, without competing internal constituencies, Cuba has rather easily and dramatically changed policy at Castro's direction. In the period immediately after the revolution serious efforts were made to industrialize the island, first eliminating capitalism and then attempting to incorporate Soviet-style socialism. A second stage saw a retreat from attempts at rapid industrialization in favor of a return to efforts to develop sugar. The economy at this point was to be propelled by moral incentives along the lines proposed in the mid-1960s by Ernesto (Che) Guevara. The third and current stage, begun in the early 1970s, maintains the concentration on the development of sugar but gives up the Guevarist emphasis on moral incentives in favor of a return to Soviet-style centralized planning.

Revolutionary Cuba boasts successes in the distribution of services such as literacy, health care, and education. But Cuba retains many of the dependencies that it had before the revolution, albeit with a different partner. Before the revolution 75 percent of Cuba's exports went to and 65 percent of the island's imports came from the United States; today the island sends 72 percent of its exports to and brings in 60 percent of its imports from the Soviet Union.[17] The island remains overwhelmingly dependent on sugar for the bulk of its foreign earnings, a dependency that becomes painfully obvious with the sharp swings of the world sugar market, on which some 45 percent of the crop is sold. The rest of its sugar is sold to the Soviet Union and Eastern European countries at between two and five times the market price. Cuba's other traditional crop, tobacco, has also been beset by problems, so much so that the island has had to import unprocessed tobacco to maintain its exports of cigars. Nickel production, another mainstay, cannot be increased until plant capacity is increased; it still depends on plants built before the revolution. Some 75 percent of the output is purchased by the Soviet Union, also at prices set artificially above the market price. In February 1982 Cuba announced laws designed to encourage foreign capitalists to invest in joint ventures with the Cuban government under conditions that ironically compete more than favorably with "industrialization by invitation" programs elsewhere in the Caribbean. More than 97 percent of Cuba's oil needs—about 250,000 barrels daily—are supplied by the Soviet Union. In 1982 Cuba paid $12.80 per barrel, approximately one-third the OPEC (Organization of Petroleum Exporting Countries) price and even below what other COMECON (Council for Mutual Economic Assistance) countries are asked to pay. The total Soviet subsidy, including soft loans, cheap oil, and high prices for sugar and nickel, amounts to between $3 and $4 billion per year.

If Cuba's economic picture has been miserable, its successes in the international arena have been remarkable. Given its size, population, and level of economic achievement, one would expect Cuba either to be too insignificant or to be too absorbed internally to have become an important international actor. Cuba before Castro had no foreign policy of note; Cuba since Castro has become a significant international force.

When Fidel Castro and his guerrillas came down from the Sierra Maestra on January 1, 1959, they were flush with the enthusiasm of willful actors who had just changed the world. Castro's immediate program was nationalistic and vocally anti-U.S. but was not yet intertwined with the Soviet Union. It was not until mid-1960 that Cuba and the USSR opened diplomatic and trade relations. After a series of escalating and retaliatory economic sanctions by each government, the United States and Cuba severed diplomatic relations in January 1961. In May the U.S.-backed Bay of Pigs invasion to overthrow the Castro government was thoroughly defeated. At the end of 1961, Castro, who just prior to the Bay of Pigs invasion had declared Cuba to be "socialist," declared that he was and always would be a Marxist-Leninist. In January 1962 Cuba was suspended from membership in the Organization of American States. By this time, the Soviet Union had made a major military commitment to arm Cuba, and in October 1962 the world witnessed the nuclear brinkmanship of the Cuban missile crisis. Soviet leadership had decided to install strategic atomic missiles on Cuban soil. When they were discovered, the United States confronted the Soviet Union; Khrushchev agreed to their removal from the island, and Kennedy agreed not to invade.[18]

During the early 1960s, Cuba supported guerrilla groups in Bolivia, Colombia, Peru, and Venezuela in South America and in Guatemala and Nicaragua in Central America. By 1967, the year in which Ernesto (Che) Guevara died in Bolivia, these movements were all but wiped out. Cuban support for these groups was at odds with the Soviet Union's policy of supporting the traditional communist parties in these countries, on the grounds that the so-called revolutionary conditions were not yet "ripe." Relations between the Soviet Union and Cuba were near the breaking point in 1966–1967.[19] Soviet willingness to exert pressure by slowing down delivery of oil in the late 1960s produced, in turn, a willingness by the Castro government to consider bringing its strategy more in line with that of the Soviet Union.

During the 1970s, the Castro government adopted more conventional methods of government-to-government relations. Cuba was able to normalize relations with many of the nations of South America, with Panama and Costa Rica (on the consular level) in Central America, and in the archipelago, with Jamaica, Guyana, Barbados, and Trinidad and Tobago. In 1975 the Organization of American States lifted its proscription on member states' interacting with Cuba. In states labeled as "progressive," such as Jamaica and Panama, or as "liberal-democratic," such as Mexico and Costa Rica, Cuba has dissuaded the radical left from attempting to overthrow the regimes. No such strategic restraint was shown toward pro-U.S., anticommunist regimes.[20] The end of diplomatic isolation was accompanied by all sorts of technical exchanges: Cuba began to regularly send abroad teams of medical doctors, agricultural experts, teachers, and other technicians. In addition, flocks of students from the Third World were sent to Cuba for education. In 1976, Cuba was designated to be the future host, and Castro the future chairman, of the Nonaligned Nations conference.

In the early 1970s Cuba began sending military training missions to Africa. The critical act in this new phase of Cuban international relations occurred when Cuba sent forces, at one point totaling 19,000 men, to Angola, thousands of miles from its shores, to support one of three guerrilla factions seeking to rule an Angola to be freed from Portugal. Cuban troops with Soviet logistical support won the conflict for the Popular Movement for the Liberation of Angola and today remain in Angola as a guarantor of Angolan independence. Cuba in 1978, at the behest of the Soviet Union, sent some 15,000 troops to defend Ethiopia from defeat by Somalia on the Horn of Africa in a strange war that originally saw the Soviet Union and Cuba supporting Ethiopia's antagonists, the Somalis and Eritreans. Cuba has had some kind of military and technical presence in more than a dozen African countries, totaling more than 40,000 advisers, all in the name of "proletarian internationalism."

For fifteen years no government was overthrown by force in the Caribbean. In 1979, Grenada and Suriname were subjected to coups, and the Nicaraguan revolution ousted the Somozas. The civil wars in El Salvador and Guatemala heated up considerably. Cuba had in the late 1960s given up on the use of force in the region. But now, with the experience gained in Africa, it appeared to have returned to that strategy in the Caribbean, and with some success. The U.S. government under Carter had made overtures toward Cuba concerning a rapprochement between the United States and Cuba. Before such overtures became crystallized, the Americans once again became worried. Carter claimed the discovery of a Soviet brigade in Cuba. This issue surfaced and then faded. What the Americans were really worried about was the new Cuban presence in the Caribbean: new allies in Grenada and Nicaragua, a new friend in Jamaica, potential trouble in the Eastern Caribbean and even in the French islands. To some observers, Castro's success was the result of his well-coordinated ideological geopolitics; to others, it was the coming together of events whose outcomes were not that well coordinated.

Castro's successes coincided with his hosting of the Nonaligned Nations conference. He seemed invincible. But shortly thereafter the Soviet Union invaded Afghanistan; 10,000 Cubans sought asylum in the Peruvian Embassy in Havana; 125,000 Cubans chose exile via the

Mariel exodus. Castro's Jamaican ally, Michael Manley, lost an election to pro-Western Edward Seaga. Panamanian strong man Omar Torrijos backed away from Cuba because of the direction of the Nicaraguan revolution; Torrijos's death and the subsequent change of government put Panama even further to the right. Relations with the Andean countries deteriorated—in the case of Colombia, markedly so when that government discovered Cuban support for insurgents. A supposed "final offensive" in El Salvador, fueled in part by Cuban arms, evaporated, and the Salvadoran people turned out in massive numbers to elect a coalition further to the right than the then-governing junta. As one scholar has put it, "Cuban foreign policy has been strikingly unsuccessful since late 1979, breaking the pattern of success achieved during the previous decade."[21] To some observers, Castro's lack of success was the result of the United States's well-coordinated ideological geopolitics; to others, it was the coming together of events whose outcomes were not that well coordinated.

The Caribbean Drama and the United States

As the British have been giving up their colonial role, as U.S. dominance has been challenged in the Hispanic Caribbean, the area is once again in flux. The Caribbean today reminds one of the sixteenth and seventeenth centuries, when the area was also a battleground for competing powers. Soviets and Americans; Cubans, Venezuelans, and Mexicans; Canadians, French, and Germans (East and West); social democrats and Christian democrats; revolutionaries and reactionaries; businessmen and Black Power advocates, among others—all are attempting to influence events. The revolution in Nicaragua, the civil wars in El Salvador and Guatemala, the coup in Grenada, even the coup and attempted countercoups in Suriname have all recently been couched in terms of a hemispheric geopolitical battle of global significance and origin.[22]

The 1980 U.S. presidential contest took place in an ambiance of malaise concerning U.S. capacity to execute clear and favorable foreign policy objectives. On the one hand, Carter had redefined the objectives to more idealistic ends; on the other hand, Iran, Afghanistan, and the Mariel exodus symbolized the feeling that the United States had become impotent, no longer able to influence international events even concerning projects of undeniable worth. As a consequence, if one contemplated the Caribbean and the recent coming to power of the Sandinista government in Nicaragua, the success of the New Jewel Movement in Grenada, and the tense election in Jamaica between socialist incumbent Michael Manley and capitalist challenger Edward

Seaga, as well as the continuation and escalation of the hostilities in El Salvador and Guatemala, it appeared that the Carter policies, with their emphasis on human rights, were ineffectual.

Indeed, Jeane Kirkpatrick, who was later to be appointed by Ronald Reagan to be U.S. ambassador to the United Nations, argued that once the fragile order in many Third World societies is undermined, then it is difficult for authority to be restored, thus opening the way for Marxist takeovers.[23] The consequence of her position, adopted by the Reagan administration, is to tolerate authoritarian governments rather than risk their replacement by totalitarian ones. This distinction between authoritarian and totalitarian only polarizes the situation. For to accept the authoritarian *caudillo,* the patriarch, is to leave people with no alternative but to be willing to risk totalitarianism in order to overcome patrimonialism. Thus, to many in the Caribbean, Maurice Bishop looked better than Grenada's oddball Eric Gairy, and the Sandinistas better than Nicaragua's Somozas.

By 1982, the geopolitical swords were unsheathed. The Americans saw a Soviet-Cuban threat, and the radical left, a U.S. threat. U.S. Assistant Secretary of State for Inter-American Affairs Thomas O. Enders argued:

> Today the peace and security of the Caribbean Basin are deeply threatened . . . by a web of political violence, economic collapse and Cuban support for subversion. . . . Timing the move to exploit . . . vulnerabilities, Cuba has mounted a campaign to establish Marxist-Leninist dictatorships in both Central America and the Caribbean. Beginning in 1978, Fidel Castro redoubled his efforts to discredit Basin governments, ridicule democracy and glorify armed violence.[24]

By downgrading the importance of human rights in U.S. foreign policy, by conceptually forcing all the area's ills into a Cuban-Soviet funnel, by being willing to accept patriarchal governments, the Americans set up a mirror image to the Castro-Soviet geopolitical projection.

If the one is willing to denigrate electoral democracy, the other is willing to demote human rights; if the one is willing to accept totalitarianism, the other is willing to accept authoritarianism; if the one argues that "true" nonalignment can be achieved only by alignment with the Soviet bloc, the other argues that any attempts at rapprochement with the self-proclaimed socialist countries of the region are efforts that would finally benefit Marxism-Leninism; if the one sees the Argentine and Salvadoran juntas as surrogates for the United States, the other sees Cuba, Nicaragua, and Grenada as surrogates for the Soviet Union.

It is important to remember that geopolitical models get their unity by the projection of a regionwide threat and the creation of merely partisan institutions that attempt to (but, of course, cannot) breach the geopolitical gap. This allows for additional possibilities for other actors in the region. Indeed, it is within the wide area created by the polarization of the U.S. and Cuban positions that other interested actors battle for influence in the Caribbean: some to oppose the polarization, others to adopt "middle" positions to suit particular purposes. Thus, for example, during the escalation of fighting in El Salvador, Mexico joined France in recognizing the Salvadoran guerrillas as a political force with the avowed purpose of abstracting the conflict from the geopolitical war of ideologies into which it was placed.[25] Mexican President José López Portillo went so far as to try to mediate between Cuba and the United States to tone down the polarization.[26]

Similarly, the war over the Falkland/Malvinas Islands, couched as it was in nongeopolitical terms, provided opportunities for interested parties to escape previously self-imposed ideological restrictions. Thus, Venezuela, for example, used the moment to re-approach Cuba, with which relations had deteriorated as a consequence of the events that led up to the Mariel exodus. Almost as a reaction to the de-emphasis of sociocultural links that was a concomitant to the overbearing emphasis on geopolitics, post-Malvinas posturings were couched in terms of competing cultural links. In such terms Venezuela appealed to Cuba to refrain from supporting Guyana in the Guyanese-Venezuelan dispute over the Essequibo region in the interest of *Bolivarismo,* "the common spirit of the hemisphere's Spanish-speaking nations."[27]

There is no indication that the two main antagonists will attempt to defuse today's geopolitical polarization. But unless they both do so the conditions for that polarization will remain. And under such conditions there is always present the danger that, short of outright victory, one side not only will create the other but will also end up deserving the other.

Notes

1. To demonstrate the abundant variety of the Caribbean, consider the following: The Caribbean is populated by Africans; East Indians; creole descendants of immigrants, as well as more recent expatriates, from Spain, Britain, the United States, France, the Netherlands, and Portugal; Amerindians; Chinese; Javanese; Syrians; Lebanese; and Jews. It contains many locally defined ethnic groups such as the poor Redlegs of Barbados, the Black Caribs of Belize, and the Maroons (descendants of runaway slaves) of Jamaica, as well as the "natives" of St. Barthélemy, who follow the remnants of a Norman

culture frozen centuries ago. The Caribbean puts forth a seemingly unlimited variety of racial combinations: Mulattoes (African and white), Mestizos (Amerindian and white), Zamboes (African and Amerindian), "Dooglas" (African and East Indian), "Chinee-Creoles" (African and Chinese), among them. Its peoples speak a babel of languages: Spanish, English, French, Dutch, Hindi, and Javanese; a whole host of pidgins and patois such as Creole, Papiamentu, Sranantongo, and Sarnami Hindostans; native tongues such as those of the Chibcha and Maya-Quiche groupings—all in a wide range of accents and slangs. Religious preferences in the area go from the Christian (including Roman Catholicism and the full panoply of Protestant sects), Islamic, and Hindu faiths—to Amerindian animist practices; to African-derived cults like *vodun* in Haiti, *santería* in Cuba, Shango in Trinidad, *espiritismo* in Puerto Rico; to locally-produced beliefs such as Pocomania and the Rastafari movement in Jamaica, as well as that of the Miteños in Puerto Rico. The geographies of the region's countries differ widely: Cuba is thirteen times the size of Puerto Rico, which, in turn, is thirteen times the size of St. Lucia. Caribbean economies differ: Cuba is communist, Grenada and Nicaragua claim to be socialist, Puerto Rico and Trinidad are capitalist; Jamaica's main export is bauxite, Cuba's sugar, El Salvador's coffee, Trinidad and Tobago's petroleum. The Trinidadian government is relatively wealthy and lends money, Jamaica's is relatively poor and borrows it. Martinique has a relatively high per capita gross national product, Haiti a miserably low one. The politics of the region differ: Barbados, Costa Rica, and the Dominican Republic are democracies; Cuba, Haiti, and Grenada are dictatorships. The relationships of the region's entities to their colonizers are different: Haiti and the Dominican Republic are independent; Puerto Rico and the Netherlands Antilles have associated statehood relationships; the British Virgin Islands are dependencies; Martinique and Guadeloupe are integrated into the French political structure. Militarily, Cuba is quite powerful, with an enormous standing army and militia, Costa Rica has neither army nor militia. Even its demographics differ widely: Life expectancy at birth is only 51 years in Haiti, 74 years in Puerto Rico; Barbados and Puerto Rico are overcrowded, Guyana and Nicaragua have low population densities.

2. There are disputes between Guyana and Venezuela, Colombia and Venezuela, Colombia and Nicaragua, El Salvador and Honduras, Guatemala and Belize, and Haiti and the Dominican Republic.

3. Such as between Venezuela and Colombia, Venezuela and Trinidad and Tobago, and Cuba and the Bahamas.

4. Such as riots in Panama in 1964, Jamaica in 1968, and Curaçao in 1969; the "youth-cum-military" rebellion in Trinidad and Tobago in 1970; and revolutions, civil wars, and coups in Cuba (1959), the Dominican Republic (1965), Grenada (1979), Suriname (1980), and El Salvador and Guatemala today.

5. Among them Puerto Rico's Luis Muñoz Marín; Venezuela's Rómulo Betancourt; Trinidad and Tobago's Eric Williams; Panama's Omar Torrijos; and Nicaragua's Anastasio Somoza Debayle.

6. Thus, in the border dispute between Venezuela and Guyana both parties have appealed to Cuba for help to achieve their goals: Venezuela on the basis of cultural identity with Cuba, Guyana on the basis of ideological identity.

7. Witness, for example, the near unanimous support by the West Indian countries for Great Britain in the Falklands/Malvinas conflict as a consequence of their abhorrence of the use of aggression in settling disputes, an abhorrence that derives from their own vulnerable military circumstances. On this point, see Anthony P. Maingot, "The Falklands for the Falklanders," *Miami Herald,* April 25, 1982.

8. Anthony P. Maingot has reminded us that the United States accepted, however reluctantly, not only the British but also the French presence in the Caribbean. See his contemporary analysis, "Perceptions, Power Politics and Foreign Policy. The U.S.A., Venezuela and Cuba," paper presented to the Conference on Latin American Foreign Policies, Chile, September 20–24, 1982.

9. The reference is to the novel by the same name by Colombian novelist Gabriel García Márquez.

10. Gordon K. Lewis, "The Politics of the Caribbean," in Tad Szulc, ed., *The United States and the Caribbean* (Englewood Cliffs, N.J.: Prentice-Hall, 1971), p. 12.

11. For an analysis of the health of democratic institutions in the Caribbean, see the special-topic issue of *Caribbean Review,* "The Status of Democracy in the Caribbean," Vol. 10, no. 2 (Spring 1981), as well as Don Bohning, Juan Tamayo, and Bernard Diederich, "The Springtime of Elections," *Caribbean Review,* Vol. 11, no. 3 (Summer 1982):4ff.

12. See Charles D. Ameringer, "The Thirty Years War Between Figueres and the Somozas," *Caribbean Review,* Vol. 8, no. 4 (Summer 1979):4ff.; and "The Tradition of Democracy in the Caribbean," *Caribbean Review,* Vol. 11, no. 2 (Spring 1982):28ff.

13. Jean-François Revel, "The Trouble with Latin America," *Caribbean Review,* Vol. 8, no. 3 (Summer 1979):15.

14. Carlos Fuentes, "Farewell Monroe Doctrine," *Harper's,* Vol. 263, no. 1575 (August 1981):32.

15. Barry B. Levine and Ralph S. Clem, "Imperial Development: The Cases of American Puerto Rico and Soviet Georgia," in *Comparative Studies in Sociology,* Vol. 1 (1978):319–336. See "Puerto Rico at the Turning Point," a special-topic issue of *Caribbean Review,* Vol. 9, no. 3 (Summer 1980), for a discussion of the cultural consequences of the Puerto Rican model of development.

16. The term is from Lloyd Best, "Black Power and Doctor Politics," *Caribbean Review,* Vol. 2, no. 2 (Summer 1970):5–7.

17. Data in "Mother Russia's Son," *Economist,,* Vol. 283, no. 7242 (June 19, 1982):95–96.

18. Jorge I. Domínguez has argued that there are a total of three understandings between the United States and the USSR concerning Cuba: "The

first and most important understanding dates from 1962. The Soviet Union withdrew strategic nuclear weapons from Cuba in exchange for the understanding that the United States would not invade Cuba to overthrow its government. The second understanding, reached in 1970, was based on the U.S. expectation that the Soviet navy would not use Cuban ports as bases for strategic operations. The third understanding, reached in 1979, was the result of a Soviet promise not to send combat troops to Cuba in the future and the Soviet assertion that its military personnel in Cuba at the time were there principally for the purpose of training Cubans." *U.S. Interests and Policies in the Caribbean and Central America* (Washington, D.C.: American Enterprise Institute, 1982), p. 8.

19. Jiri Valenta, "Soviet Policy and the Crisis in the Caribbean," in H. Michael Erisman and John D. Martz, eds., *Colossus Challenged: The Struggle for Caribbean Influence* (Boulder, Colo.: Westview Press, 1982), pp. 52–53.

20. Ibid., p. 57.

21. Domínguez, *U.S. Interests,* p. 10.

22. See the special-topic issue, "The New Geopolitics," *Caribbean Review,* Vol. 11, no. 2 (Spring 1982).

23. Jeane Kirkpatrick, "U.S. Security and Latin America," *Commentary,* Vol. 71, no. 1 (January 1981):29–40. Her example of the unintended consequences of human rights policy is Nicaragua. For an opposite viewpoint, using Panama as an example, see Robert A. Pastor, "Our Real Interests in Central America," *Atlantic Monthly,* Vol. 250, no. 1 (July 1982):27–39.

24. Thomas O. Enders, "A Comprehensive Strategy for the Caribbean Basin," *Caribbean Review,* Vol. 11, no. 2 (Spring 1982):10.

25. See Barry B. Levine, "The French Connection: Two Views of Their Latin American Policy," *Caribbean Review,* Vol. 11, no. 2 (Spring 1982):46ff.

26. See Wayne S. Smith, "Dateline Havana: Myopic Diplomacy," *Foreign Policy,* no. 48 (Fall 1982):157–174. Smith, former chief of the U.S. interests section in Havana (1979–1982), argued that it was the United States that refused to negotiate.

27. Juan O. Tamayo, "Venezuela Decides to Play Cuban Card," *Miami Herald,* August 4, 1982.

2
Cuba and the Commonwealth Caribbean:
Playing the Cuban Card

Anthony P. Maingot

In a footnote that in a different context would have been in the text, K. S. Karol related somewhat humorously his attempts to reach Cuba from Jamaica during the Bay of Pigs invasion. "Our futile maritime adventures," he recalled, ". . . taught me something about the unholy fear Cuban ideas inspired in the Caribbean."[1] In the course of preparing for the trip he had dealings with both the Cuban consul and the U.S. consul general. The former, Alfonso Herrera, occupied a room on the second floor of a "dusty old house" and performed single-handedly all the tasks of the consulate. Karol had the clear impression that the times—and the Cuban's lack of resources—were such that his influence in Jamaica was extremely small.

The U.S. consul general, on the other hand, enjoyed luxurious accommodations both in the office and at home. This consul general had previously been in the Belgian Congo where, to hear his wife tell it, the Belgians had done a splendid job. Jamaica he felt was different, and he appeared deeply concerned about the island's social unrest; it was, he claimed, reaching alarming proportions. "According to the Consul," Karol recalled, "the blame was entirely Alfonso Herrera's; it was only since the arrival of 'that revolutionary agitator' that the normal peaceful tenor of Jamaican life had become explosive."[2] Karol, who had seen the poverty in the island, remembered having difficulty containing his laughter.

By the late 1970s the unholy fear of Cuban ideas had become not only more intense but also more widespread. Had Karol visited Jamaica then, he might have hesitated to laugh at stories of Cuban involvement. Rather than a dusty second-floor room, the Cuban mission in Kingston was now an impressive complex—complete with radio-transmitting antennas similar to those of their U.S. and British counterparts. The Cuban ambassador—not infrequently the center of political controversy—presided over an ever-increasing network of Cuban activities in health, education, construction, agriculture, tourism, sports, and some would maintain, politics. And so it was in much of the rest of the Caribbean.

In Guyana, where the Cuban mission takes up nearly half a city block, Cuba's multiple involvements had long been the talk of Georgetown. Across the sea in tiny Grenada, Cuba was represented at the highest level; it had the only resident ambassador on the island, an island where there was virtually no trade with Cuba, no Cuban citizens to represent, or any of the other traditional reasons for such high diplomatic representation. That ambassador would preside over a growing Cuban presence. Cuban doctors arrived, some 15 of them, as did fishing trawlers and instructors; and on November 18, 1979, Prime Minister Maurice Bishop told a rally that he expected 250 Cubans to start building a new international airport. As he had only just been in Canada seeking funds for a feasibility study for that same project, local surprise was understandable. Some Grenadians began to say that if it were only the fourteen bulldozers, six scrapers, twenty trucks, and thousands of tons of cement and steel that had arrived, it would have been all right. Rumor had it that there were three truckloads of Cuban arms hidden somewhere on the island. What was not rumor were the new "military zones," which were off-limits, and the presence of numerous military advisers; these were quite visibly on site. Today Grenadians laugh at the "Chilean connection" of Eric Gairy: three homesick Grenadian policemen training in Chile and two crates of guns that apparently were never opened and that certainly have never been seen publicly before or after the coup d'etat.

This network of Cuban diplomats and involvements comes under the aegis of the Caribbean section of the Cuban Ministry of Foreign Affairs. Unlike so many of the U.S. diplomats sent to the area, these Cubans are professionals to be reckoned with. In Barbados (which has refused to allow a resident Cuban mission despite having diplomatic relations since 1972) high government officials have a healthy respect for Cuban intelligence. They will note, for instance, that the man who heads the Caribbean desk in Havana was formerly posted in Guyana and before that was an important Directorio General de Inteligencia (DGI) agent, and that the Cuban ambassador to Jamaica during the late 1970s was also a high-level DGI officer, well briefed in Jamaican and Caribbean affairs. Such was the Caribbean perception of Cuban skill and expertise in the late 1970s that in the Netherlands

Antilles one heard that the Cuban Caribbean section had correctly predicted the outcome of mid-1979 elections in Curaçao, when even *antillano* pundits were at a loss to do the same.

It was not surprising, therefore, to hear moderate Caribbean leaders such as Antigua's Vere Bird warn the Venezuelans that Cuban "intervention" was spreading everywhere in the area, aiding and abetting new radical groups in each island. Such warnings were eagerly received as Venezuela's relations with Cuba deteriorated and its interests in the Caribbean increased during this period.

How much of all this Caribbean perception of Cuban involvement and power was real? Clearly there was in the decade 1970–1980 at least a surface unity among the area's new Marxist-Leninist groups. This could be seen, for instance, at the public launching of Jamaica's communist party, Trevor Munroe's Workers Party of Jamaica (WPJ), formerly the Worker's Liberation League. In attendance were delegates from the communist parties of the USSR, Britain, Canada, the United States, and Cuba; in attendance from the English-speaking Caribbean were Guyana's People's Progressive party and Working People's Alliance, the Barbados Movement for National Liberation, Grenada's New Jewel Movement, St. Vincent's Liberation Movement, and St. Lucia's Worker's Revolutionary Movement.

To see Cuban machinations behind this unity, however, is to ignore the long-standing ties among Caribbean radical groups—ties that predate the Cuban Revolution and that, more often than not, are the result of specific and independent decisions on each island.

Be that as it may, it would be a mistake to underrate the significance of the political and ideological role defined by the Cubans and the capacity of their intelligence and diplomatic corps. Art, science, sports, music—and everything else—were parts of this political thrust into the Caribbean. For instance, the Cubans astutely, albeit sincerely, understanding the crucial importance of race in the Caribbean, took full advantage of the points built up by their popular and commendable anti–South African policies and actions. Less sincere yet still effective was the quite explicit use of black Cubans as diplomats in the Caribbean. An island where fewer than 25 percent of the people are black and where few of these have achieved important positions in the Revolutionary Government, Cuba managed to be represented nearly exclusively by blacks in the Caribbean. It was not surprising to note, therefore, the number of West Indians who believed Cuba to be a black Caribbean state. Unlike the Americans, who have played the racial diplomatic game since the beginning of their Caribbean contacts, the Cubans have the advantage of playing this racial angle while also emphasizing class and class conflict as the basic units of struggle. Such a strategy allows a fundamentally pragmatic approach to the area's complex politics in which issues of race and class interact in a bewildering fashion.

During the 1970s, then, the Cubans were clearly on the move in the Caribbean. Yet, despite this phenomenal expansion of the Cuban presence since Karol's Jamaican experience, it would be a mistake to conclude that the Cubans had it then—or have it now—all their own way in the Caribbean. In part but not exclusively, this is due to U.S. power in the area. There are other factors limiting Cuban policy and action. An important one is that the Cuban involvement is being played as a "Cuban card," quite skillfully manipulated by some Caribbean politicians toward less than ideologically pure ends. The Cuban card is used as political leverage in some instances, as a protective shield in others, and in more and more cases as a straw man.

In the cases discussed here the Cuban role was fundamentally that of providing a mantle of revolutionary legitimacy to regimes that had both achieved and retained power through less than revolutionary means. And as every card has two sides (the other side is the actual or potential use of this same Cuban presence as a straw man), it is amazing how frequently some Caribbean politicians used and use both sides of this card. Some did so successfully; on others the tactic backfired dramatically.

The down-to-earth savvy of many West Indian politicians is not to be minimized; they first tasted power during colonial days and still have a hearty appetite for it. It can be argued in fact that few areas of the world have more enduring practitioners of what Rexford Tugwell called "the art of politics" than does the Caribbean.

Whether it is the old, traditional politician who stays in power by playing on the primordial attachments of race or religious fundamentalism, or the young "revolutionary" seeking socialist modernization through extra-constitutional means, they all face one dilemma: how to retain power in societies that are politically complex, restless and eager for better days, yet hardly revolutionary. The fact is that the masses in the English-speaking Caribbean tend to be politically radical but sociologically conservative. Call it "false consciousness," "fear of freedom," or whatever, they are a difficult lot to satisfy. Obviously the first task of those who would govern, whether they be conservatives or radicals, is to stay in power, and the Cuban card, played on both its sides, has proven to be of considerable value.

Jamaica and Cuba

During much of the 1970–1980 decade, the English-speaking Caribbean divided into three distinct camps: those openly pro-Cuba

(Jamaica, Guyana, Grenada); those retaining diplomatic relations with Cuba but privately critical of its role (Trinidad and Tobago and Barbados); and those openly hostile to Cuba and the "leftist trend." St. Vincent's Milton Cato and Antigua's Vere Bird were the most outspoken leaders among the latter group.

As good as any player of both sides of the Cuban card was Jamaica's Michael Manley, an adept political practitioner in both national and international arenas. The multiple transformations of this erstwhile conservative son of Norman Manley are in the best tradition of political artistry. Brought back from England in the early 1950s to do battle with the left wing within the People's National party (PNP)—the so-called 4-Hs—Manley successfully cleaned out the radical elements from both the party and its labor branch.[3] As his father faded from the national picture, Michael began to transform his image as a conservative and partisan union leader into one of a more flamboyant charismatic figure of national dimensions. He became the bearer of two religious traditions: "Joshua" to the Bible-reading Christians, to the large number of Rastafarians he became the man with the "rod of correction," a reference to the imperial walking staff given to him by Haile Selassie, which made its appearance at political rallies. With it Manley would teach his opponents "proper manners," an allusion to strict and old-fashioned theories of child rearing. This was in the first metamorphosis.

The second was his socialist phase. In this phase, neither the biblical references ("comrade" has replaced Joshua) nor the rod of correction was still relevant to Manley's new politics, the politics of "principle." In fact the noun "principle" became the most common word in Manley's political vocabulary. Clearly he understood what is today axiomatic in political sociology: that expedient interests are more constant than principled interests and that in a conflict between the two, you always place your bet on expediency. Thus, we heard Manley say that his relations with Cuba were "principled relations"; his support for Cuba's right to have Soviet troops on its soil was based on "a single matter of fundamental principle"—that the Cuban people wanted them. Yet, his support for independence for Puerto Rico was based on the Nonaligned Movement's "principles"—even if the people do not want it. He was of course in favor of the U.S. Navy's moving out of the islands of Vieques and Culebra, not because the majority of Puerto Ricans want it but because it is a logical extension of his "principled" stance on Puerto Rican independence. It is clear that Manley understood that absolute and inflexible adherence to principle is the policy of political fools or fanatics, and he was manifestly neither.

Manley knew that outright communist movements had never fared well in Jamaica. This was seen in the defeat of the Marxists within the PNP in the early 1950s as well as the fiasco of Chris Lawrence's Community Party of Jamaica of the 1960s. This is not surprising: Both the major Jamaican parties emerged from trade union movements and both have been traditionally polyclass in composition from the inception of party politics and responsible government; both have been geared toward control of the state machinery—as tends to be the case in two-party systems. Both understood the circular operation of state patronage: Power is dependent on patronage, continued patronage on continued power; patronage increases as the widening and deepening of power increases. In a political system such as this, third parties are for the disaffected, the alienated, or the ideologically "pure," all of whom, in the final analysis, are equally irrelevant in the distribution of power in parliamentary systems.

Aside from this element of raw politics, there has been and still is the additional fact that there is in Jamaica a deep-rooted fear of communism among both the urban and rural masses, as repeated surveys by Carl Stone indicate.[4] As a consequence, both parties traditionally have cast their programs in populist tones, the approach historically favored by those who cater to popular grievances but fear the trap of excessive ideological dogma. How, then, to explain the shift to the left in Manley's second term (1976–1980)? The first thing to note is that this shift was more demonstrable in rhetoric than in actual programs or policies. But whether rhetorically or through actual policies, the shift responded to a series of complex changes that ran the gamut from urban growth and unemployment to a new generational struggle within the PNP.

Within the party the leftward thrust came from a group of young PNP politicians clearly led by Dr. D. K. Duncan, widely recognized as the party's best urban strategist. Although the young radicals within the PNP seemed to be committed to socialist principles, they were nevertheless more interested in power. Were this not the case, many of them would have had a logical place in Dr. Trevor Munroe's Worker's Party of Jamaica. Ex–Rhodes scholar Munroe, a tireless organizer who, without any particular mass or labor union base, consistently preached many of the "principles" that Manley had to play politics with, often managed to capitalize on rhetorical support from the PNP's left. This support, however, could never be too overt, given the anti-communism of the masses of the PNP and of many of the party front-benchers. One such was Finance Minister Eric Bell, who in early 1978 made it clear in the Jamaican House of Representatives that "if any member of the People's National Party is a communist and avowed to be a communist then they are entitled to be expelled."[5]

In the context of Jamaican politics during Manley's second term, the Cuban card came into play in the following fashion: It allowed Munroe to stick to Marxist ideological principle both in speech and in practice; Manley's intraparty opponents to emphasize these principles in speech while calling for the party to assert them in action; and Manley himself to assert the principles rhetorically. In other words, by providing legitimacy to all who asserted radical "principles" the Cuban "presence" blurred the distinction between theory and practice, an abandonment of the Marxist emphasis on praxis but one that nevertheless served all involved in the short term.

The point, of course, was that it served Manley even better because at any time he could play the other side of the card, which asserted that communists do not belong in the party and should therefore be either expelled or silenced. It is quite evident that this is what happened to the Youth Wing of the party in 1977. This ability to play both sides of the Cuban card was especially convenient as the Cubans did not seem to be put off by it (at least not publicly). So that the PNP—and by implication the system within which it functioned—continued to enjoy the support of the Cubans regardless of which way the card was played. This Jamaican case was in keeping with Cuba's policy of supporting friendly regimes no matter whether these are opposed by Marxist forces internally. Jamaica was no different from Spain, Peru, or Mexico in this regard. In exchange for this support, the Cubans benefited from Jamaica's (and Manley's) very real prestige in Third World circles and not a few developed countries. The Cubans thus have learned that it pays to support friendly noncommunist regimes rather than putting all their bets on small communist parties with little chance of coming to power.

It is an arrangement that suits both parties and that, by the way, need not affect North American multinational interests too adversely. The continued profits of the bauxite sector and parts of the tourism industry, even while the Jamaican economy as a whole was (as of 1977) in a downward spiral of low productivity, unemployment, and inflation, stand as witness to that.

It was not only that the Jamaican economy was showing a real growth rate of minus 13 percent for 1974–1977 (compared to plus 20 percent for 1969–1973), for in some ways this could be attributed to external causes such as the increase in oil prices. More worrisome because they reflected purely internal causes were drops in productivity, notably in the agricultural sector. According to Food and Agriculture Organization (FAO) figures, dry beans, corn, and rice all showed substantial drops in output per acre during 1975–1977 (as compared to 1969–1975). Most disastrous of all was the brain drain, which even the Jamaican National Planning Agency called a hemorrhage of high-level manpower.

To what extent were the educated fleeing from actual revolutionary change? Interviews with some of the 15,000 Jamaican "exiles" in Miami in 1979 indicate that they were fleeing not from socialism but rather from unchecked crime, shortages of all kinds, and a general sense that no one was managing the economy. They saw it as a case of rhetorical radicalism gone berserk—their view of the Cuban role was likewise tinged with cynicism.

They pointed with incredulity to the fact that Jamaica was now importing milk from a country, Cuba, where milk was rationed and that received grants of milk from the FAO—milk produced originally in the United States. They noted that the dozen-odd general practitioners sent by Cuba were hardly substitutes for the mass exodus of Jamaican medical specialists.[6] One source calculated that there were left on the island only thirteen dentists with specialized training, including one periodontist and one orthodontist.[7] The University of the West Indies Medical School was increasingly staffed with Indian medical professors, the Jamaicans and other West Indians having left in droves. And all this in a society where no socialist measures had been taken against the medical profession.

Far from being a socialist society, Jamaica during the second Manley period was rather what economists call a "transfer society": Resources were drawn from the few productive sectors and used up in an effort to acquire existing resources for others. In other words, more valuable resources were used to produce less valuable resources. The political advantages of such a system are obvious, but these are necessarily short-term as, economically, transfer policies result in a negative-sum game for the society as a whole. But in the short-term the political advantage was maximized by the Cuban connection. It facilitated the rationalization that all this was a consequence of a "revolutionary process." Such a process preempts any "ordinary" criteria of performance measurement or comparison with "nonrevolutionary" societies (such as Barbados) that, with fewer resources, were managing at that same time a respectable pace of growth and development. Again, the Cuban connection operated as a sort of smokescreen covering up deficiencies and incompetence of all kinds. It was a significant element in the ability of the middle-class leadership of the PNP to defend its administrative performance with a degree of credibility it otherwise would have lost much sooner than it did. But lose it would. The two-term mandate now traditional in Jamaican politics was up in 1980, and the PNP had little tangible to show. It lost the elections by the biggest margin in Jamaican history. In democratic, pluralist politics (such as Jamaica's) the Cuban card tends to lose its value much sooner than it does in dictatorial systems (such as Grenada's).

Grenada and Cuba

The coincidence between Cuban interests and the interests of radicalized middle-class groups bent on holding on to state power is clearly evident in Grenada. Grenada ranks with Haiti among the poorest of Caribbean societies. Its poverty has been only mildly ameliorated by the proximity of the neighboring island of Trinidad, which has traditionally provided an outlet for excess population as well as a source of remittances, an important part of Grenada's economy. Not surprisingly, relations with Trinidad have always been an important issue in Grenada's politics. All that changed when on March 13, 1979, some forty-five men (apparently using arms smuggled in from the United States) carried out the first coup d'etat in West Indian history. The victors, all members of the New Jewel Movement, promised a socialist revolution and even began talking as if they were in fact leading a social revolution. They were confusing middle-class relief at getting rid of Eric Gairy with support for socialist changes.

In fact the situation facing the Revolutionary Government of Grenada two years after the coup might be described as follows: Significant sectors of the peasantry continued loyal if not to Gairy personally at least to what is best called "Gairyism"—black peasant populism; the coalition of urban forces that formed the backbone of the anti-Gairy movement (churches, Chamber of Commerce, Rotary, Lions, labor unions—the so-called Committee of 22) was not much given to revolutions; the Civil Service was interested in paychecks and security; and the traditional political parties were eager for elections and suspicious of the young radicals in the New Jewel Movement who had tried their hands at electoral politics before without much success.[8] On the other hand, the new government enjoyed the support of the largely unemployed urban youth, clearly a sector to contend with, and to some extent, of some big businesses whose profits had not been affected and who were totally disaffected from the incompetence and venality of the Gairy regime. Not surprisingly, the Grenada Chamber of Commerce declared after the coup that it did not "anticipate any worrying changes in the methods and patterns of business or in the direction of government's fiscal policy."[9] Clearly, the chamber was basing its assessment on its acquaintance with the men involved rather than on the 1973 Manifesto of the New Jewel Movement, which called for a thorough socialist redoing of society.

Who, then, are these revolutionary leaders? One begins with one fact: The group that toppled Eric Gairy is fundamentally middle-class in origin. Prime Minister Maurice Bishop was about five years old in 1950 when Eric Gairy returned from the oil fields of Aruba to begin the anticolonial drive. Bishop is a graduate of Presentation College in Grenada and read for the law in London. He is clearly a member of the island's small but stable middle class. So are Bernard Coard, Ken Radix, and others in the regime. Richard Jacobs, Grenada's first ambassador to Cuba, and since mid-1982 to the USSR, although a citizen of Trinidad and Tobago, belongs to a prominent middle-class family that covers the Eastern Caribbean. This educated and well-traveled elite shared middle-class Grenada's dislike of Gairy, and he returned the favor.

Bishop once told an interviewer that he remembered Gairy's identifying and then rejecting him when he was nominated in the early 1960s to a commission of inquiry by the students of Grenada Boys' Secondary School. This incident probably had more social than political overtones, reflecting the strained relations between Gairy and his middle-class antagonists. Not surprisingly, Bishop's middle-class values are already apparent in his positions. Note, for instance, how he concluded that, although freedom of the press is appropriate for the British, who can weigh the points of view and choose one, it is not so for Grenadians. His interviewer related his reasoning: "He said that in the situation of Grenada with backwardness, illiteracy, superstition, rumor mongering, certainly functional illiteracy, most people could hardly even fully appreciate the one statement in front of them. 'How are they going to sift up three and four?' he asked."[10]

Also note, for instance, Deputy Prime Minister Bernard Coard's answer to a question on elections: "We don't want to have only a 'representative democracy'—which means that once every five years for five seconds you go to the polls and mark your X having been given enough rum and corned beef at the local rum shop. . . . We call this 'five second democracy.' "[11] Interestingly enough it was against such very attitudes that Gairy originally led his anticolonial movement in the 1950s. But even beyond that, if we are to accept Bishop's and Coard's description of the Grenadian people we would have not only to agree with Marx's portrayal of the "idiocy of rural life" but also to conclude that in such a population no socialist revolution is possible. What is possible, of course, is authoritarian state capitalism, not by the people but for the people.

The actions taken during the first two years of the revolution clearly reflect the secular rationalism of this educated middle-class elite. First to be combatted were Obeah (black magic) and Rosicrucianism, both skeletons in Gairy's political closet. A section of the Rastafarian movement came next. But in addition to those holding to "superstitions" that had no place in a modern socialist state, others also had to fall in line. The only independent newspaper, *Torchlight,* was closed in 1979 on the pretext that it was largely foreign (Trinidadian) owned. In 1981 the government closed down as counter-revolutionary the totally Grenadian-owned *Grenadian Voice.*

That this authoritarianism suits well the nature of the radical middle-class leadership was the theme of a book by Archie Singham that not long ago was heralded as the most significant analysis of Caribbean politics in general and Grenadian politics in particular.[12] Singham identified two kinds of West Indian political heroes: the "middle class hero, and the hero who comes from humble origins." Singham's sympathies were clearly with the latter, and Eric Matthew Gairy was the prototype. But Singham had enough sociological perspicacity to note that "in spite of the differences in their class origins and their leadership style, however, these two types share certain similarities: they tend to develop personal organizations which are essentially authoritarian." Singham was perceptive in his call for more studies on the "anxiety-ridden" middle-class hero: "His ideology is usually populist: for him the rhetoric if not the content of Marxism or radical socialism fulfills a very useful role by enabling him to sustain the vicissitudes of politics in the light of the sacrifices he has to make."[13]

Be that as it may, there is good reason for the new Grenadian elite to be anxiety-ridden. As leaders of a political revolution, they have less time to deliver the goods than do leaders of social revolutions. The latter preside over populations mobilized for change and prepared to sacrifice for that change. The former have to first secure their political positions, all the while engaging in redistributionist policies, policies designed to placate or even redress a sense of injustice rather than restructuring an unjust system. The problem is that there is not much to redistribute in Grenada: Previous governments led a hand-to-mouth existence, and Gairy's past corruption and mismanagement virtually guaranteed the same for the New Jewel regime.

Here is where the Cuban card came into play. First, and most important, was the immediate and efficient short-term Cuban aid—enough in fact to secure two requirements: to shore up the regime politically through military and security (including intelligence) assistance, and to shore it up economically where it counted by providing jobs, health services, and technical advice. As noted above, so rapid were the Cuban moves that soon after Prime Minister Bishop visited Canada seeking funds for a viability study for a new international airport, he announced that some 250 men together with a great deal of machinery, cement, and steel, would arrive from Cuba to begin work on it. As other infrastructure projects were begun by the Cubans, the regime was freed to use its limited resources for what West Indians call "make work," public works employment on a piecemeal basis.

The Cuban connection also served to provide a mantle of revolutionary urgency for acts that were manifestly political: the closing down of the *Torchlight,* the banning of one branch of the Rastafarian movement, the suspension of students who led a protest, the arrest of opponents who were then held without formal charges, the sealing off of major areas for military reasons, and finally, the ridiculing of parliamentary politics as "five-second democracy." The Cuban card allowed Grenada's minister of security, Hudson Austin, to do all this and then explain: "There are still some people in the country who do not realize there is a revolution in the country."[14] Surely even the minister should have recognized that his words contained an empirical truth as well as a political rationalization.

Trinidad and Cuba

All this is of deep concern to the governments of Trinidad and Tobago and Barbados. In the April 30, 1979, "Memorandum of Understanding of Matters of Cooperation Between the Government of Barbados and the Government of the Republic of Trinidad and Tobago," Prime Ministers Eric Williams and Tom Adams took note of the "growing complexity of the security problems of the Caribbean region and agreed to consult from time to time thereon." Among the issues they identified as of particular concern to their countries were "terrorism, piracy, the use of mercenaries . . . and the introduction into the region of techniques of subversion." Not unimportant was the April 1979 publication of the Trinidad government's "White Paper on CARICOM [Caribbean Community and Common Market], 1973–1978," a pessimistic assessment, especially of Jamaica's and Guyana's roles in the common market arrangements. The two documents were an indication that oil-rich Trinidad was at least intimating a shift in its regional policies, to favor its friends and shun its enemies. Barbados's Adams was in the former category; Manley, Burnham, and the other Caribbean leftists were in the latter. Eric Williams was playing the negative side of the Cuban card—Cuban subversion and interference as straw man. Thus the Trinidad case is further illustration of the West Indian art of politics, for few Caribbean politicians were more astute at playing the Cuban card than Williams; he remained the master political artist of the area until his death in mid-1981.

In a real sense Eric Williams's legitimacy as a politician was from the beginning based on his reputation for personal independence, even rebelliousness—first from the Caribbean Commission (dominated by France, Britain, the Netherlands, and the United States) for which he worked, then as premier of autonomous Trinidad. During the years of the West Indies Federation, Williams led the battle for "unit participation" in foreign policy, refusing to surrender any powers in this area to the federal government. His background included the writing of a classic in Marxist historiography, *Capitalism and Slavery* (1944), and a consistent battle to regain major parts of the U.S. military base at Chaguaramas. Williams took good advantage of his reputation as a radical: He used it fundamentally to outflank the Trinidadian left represented within his party (the People's National Movement [PNM]) by C.L.R. James and outside it by the various leaders of the Oil Field Workers Trade Union (OWTU). When it was convenient, he played on the anticolonial angle.

In 1963 Williams warned a high-level Venezuelan delegation that unless a Venezuelan 30 percent surtax on goods from Trinidad was removed, he intended to initiate discussions in the United Nations on remaining colonialism in the Caribbean, "and he wished to indicate that included the 30 percent Antillean surtax, the importance of which should not be minimized."[15] Williams's attitude toward Latin America in general and Venezuela in particular was always ambiguous. His hope had always been to integrate the Caribbean archipelago. "Our stand on this," he wrote in 1968, "has always been crystal clear from as far back as January, 1962. . . . It was to work towards the formation of a Caribbean Economic Community, beginning with, but not limited to, the Caribbean Commonwealth countries."[16] Such an alignment, he argued, was warranted by a common history, geographical proximity, similarity of economic structure, and limited national markets.

In the early 1960s, however, Williams was not eager to push this idea far enough to include Cuba. In fact, it was the Cuban Revolution of 1959 that forced him to seek an understanding with Venezuela. Good relations with that nation—which is separated from Trinidad by only seven miles on the Gulf of Paria—made good ideological and national security sense. With Cuba's Castro and Venezuela's Betancourt locked in a battle with hemisphere-wide ramifications, Williams placed Trinidad on the side of Venezuela and anticommunism in a clear anti-Castro stance. Faced with increasing opposition from leftist forces that had become disappointed in his middle-of-the-road policies, Williams had his eye on events at home and on the guerrilla movement just across the Gulf of Paria. The appearance in 1963 in Trinidad of a newspaper that carried news of Venezuela's guerrilla movement, including a verbatim reprint of a Fuerzas Armadas de Liberación Nacional (FALN) statement,[17] indicated some degree of transnational contact and cooperation among radical circles. Williams wasted no time.

That same year, 1963, the first anniversary of Trinidad's independence, Williams chose *Le Monde Diplomatique* of Paris to take his first public stance on the Cuban issue. He portrayed the significance of Trinidad and Tobago as an independent country in the modern world as representing a confrontation in the Caribbean of the dominant points of view that faced the world of the day: (1) active partnership between government and investors in Trinidad and Tobago as against the state direction of the economy of Cuba; (2) a direct democracy superimposed upon a parliamentary tradition in Trinidad and Tobago as against Cuba's one-party state dominated by its *caudillo;* (3) the vision in Trinidad and Tobago of a Caribbean economic community with some sort of independent existence as against the submerging of the Cuban personality behind the Iron Curtain. By 1967 the anti-Cuban line in Trinidad's foreign policy had reached a high pitch.

On September 24, 1967, the position of Trinidad and Tobago vis-à-vis Cuba was put emphatically to the final session of the Twelfth Meeting of Consultation of Foreign Ministers of the Organization of American States (OAS):

> We have extended assurances to the government of Venezuela that we will not permit the soil of Trinidad and Tobago to be used for purposes of subversion against the democratic regime of the Republic of Venezuela. . . . We propose to take all necessary action within our community to avoid the danger of communist infiltration. . . . Finally, in the dispute between the government of Venezuela and the totalitarian state of Cuba, and in all the circumstances demonstrated at this Meeting of Foreign Ministers, we wish to state emphatically and unequivocably for public opinion in the Hemisphere and elsewhere in the world, we stand by Venezuela.

Again, only a few days later, on the occasion of Trinidad and Tobago's presentation on September 27, 1967, to the Twenty-Second General Assembly of the United Nations, the Trinidad and Tobago position on Cuba was made clear by its then minister of external affairs, A.N.R. Robinson:

> I cannot end this brief review of areas of tension over which my delegation is particularly concerned without reference to those states

> which indiscriminately seek by force to impose a pattern of government and of society on peoples outside of their borders. I refer particularly to the activities of the government of Cuba in the Western Hemisphere. I say to the representative of the government of Cuba: "Unwarranted intervention in the affairs of other states cannot but justify intervention in your own. Exporting revolution, be it remembered, is a two-edged sword."

In 1967 Trinidad imported TT$283,675,700 worth of goods from Venezuela (primarily crude for refining and re-export); TT$298,137,900 worth of goods was exported to the United States; total imports from Cuba were TT$100 and there were no exports to that island. These figures tell a story of Cuban isolation, both ideological and economic. For Williams, keeping Cuba at a distance was good politics. It helped mend fences with Venezuela, a major supplier of crude for the island's refineries, at the same time making his political moves against the left opposition in Trinidad easier.

By the end of the 1960s, however, Williams was preparing to use the other side of the Cuban card, the "positive" one. The shift began in 1969 with some ambiguous statements and positions. That year the Trinidad government recommended that "the door should be left open for the inclusion of Cuba into CARIFTA [Caribbean Free Trade Association]." There was no explanation of whether this meant with or perhaps after Castro. In his *From Columbus to Castro,* Williams noted for instance, that "Castro's programme is pure nationalist, comprehensible and acceptable by any other Caribbean nationalist." And in the field of race relations he saw Cuba as the only bright spot in the area. But Williams's old reservations were still there: "Cuba has illustrated the basic weakness of West Indian countries—the tendency to look for external props. But the real tragedy of Cuba is that she has resorted to a totalitarian framework within which to profoundly transform her economy and society. This is the real point about the essentials of the political system in Cuba today."[18]

The "Cuban Model," as he called it, was not recommended for the Caribbean. Yet in 1970, Williams used the occasion of his chairmanship of the Economic and Social Council of the OAS meeting in Caracas to call for "reabsorption" of Cuba into the OAS. Whether this was to counterbalance his call for the admission of Guyana (then locked in a border dispute with Venezuela) or an outright statement of conviction is difficult to tell. Two years later, Trinidad joined its CARIFTA partners in extending diplomatic recognition to Cuba.

It was not until June 1975, however, that Williams would make Cuba a central part of his foreign policy through a state visit to that island. "In this mighty effort to achieve greater Caribbean solidarity," he told the students of the University of Havana, "Cuba has a great role to play." The search, Williams stressed, was for the Caribbean's "fundamental unity and distinctive identity."[19] Williams was now prepared to admit the island of Cuba into his conception of the Caribbean archipelago. Naturally this had to be justified somehow, and Williams was effusive in his reasoning. "Cuba's progress," he wrote Fidel Castro, "is something that has to be seen to be believed."[20]

What explains this dramatic shift in Eric Williams's foreign policy? Part of the answer lies in the changed context of the Caribbean. The "subversive" threat seemed defeated on the island as well as in Venezuela. To Williams, a new threat was posed by what he regarded as Venezuela's improper designs on the Caribbean area generally and Trinidad and Tobago specifically. Two speeches made in 1975 give a picture of Williams's concern with Venezuelan moves.

In the first speech (May 1975) Williams attacked the notion that Venezuela was a Caribbean country ("I expect next to hear that Tierra del Fuego is") and pointed to "Venezuela's relations, territorial ambitions in respect of our area."[21] The second speech was delivered to his party's convention on June 15, just two days before his trip to Cuba (and to the USSR, Romania, and the United States, where he met with Henry Kissinger). In what amounts to one of the most scathing attacks by one Caribbean country on another during peacetime, Williams warned of Venezuela's "penetration" of the Caribbean, berated that country for its "belated recognition of its Caribbean identity," and chastised his CARICOM partners for falling for the new Venezuelan definition of the Caribbean (the "Caribbean basin") and leading a "Caribbean Pilgrimage to Caracas."[22]

The sources of Williams's irritation with Venezuela were many, and some were certainly legitimate. For instance, contrary to the provisions of the CARICOM charter, which calls for multilateral trade with nonmembers, Venezuela was encouraging bilateral deals. This was especially the case in bauxite and oil, both of which Williams had long wanted to dominate. But there were also differences regarding the law of the sea, objections to certain Venezuelan claims to islets in the Caribbean and to Venezuelan loans, tourism initiatives, and cultural "penetration" through scholarships. Williams expressed the fear that Caribbean and Latin American primary products were "jumping from the European and American frying pan into the South American fire" and that the net result would be the recognition of Venezuela as "a new 'financial centre' of the world."[23]

Despite the weightiness of any one of these issues, however, Williams's most detailed analysis was reserved for an inventory of his attempts to get a fishing accord with Venezuela, a long-standing controversy that, by 1975, Williams wanted to put to rest, stating that "one man can only take so much, and I have had enough. . . . As far as I am concerned, I have had my fill of this fishy business, and as Prime Minister I wash my hands of it . . . if we can't agree on fish, how can we agree on oil."[24]

The truth was that the fishing dispute had spilled over onto Trinidad's domestic political arena. It had become part of the racial political strife as the largely Indian opposition party, the United Labour Force (ULF), began to agitate for the rights of the predominantly Indian fishermen caught in the dispute with Venezuela. Williams felt that the Venezuelan government was siding with the Indians and thus interfering in internal Trinidadian politics. He feared that this was but a harbinger of what would follow once the question of oil in the ill-defined Gulf of Paria came up, as it no doubt would. It was time to play the positive side of the Cuban card on the international scene.

Williams gladly traded open praise for Cuba for Cuban neutrality in the struggle within Trinidadian politics, especially within the opposition party, in which a battle was unfolding between moderates and radicals. A radical victory could very well mean an end to the racial politics that was the best guarantee of continued power for Williams's black-based PNM. It paid off: In 1976 the ULF split, the radical faction remaining a clear minority isolated in every way. Once again, a radical group, not enjoying any mass base, had been outflanked by the traditional politician playing on the theme of friendship with Cuba. In this case, Venezuela adequately substituted as the straw man. In politics it is useful to have external enemies as well as friends; Williams knew how to manipulate both. After his death the PNM transferred power smoothly and proceeded to call an election in 1982, which it won handily. As the national budget for 1982 reached TT$10 billion, both Cuba and Venezuela faded as issues. Nothing had changed.

The Eastern Caribbean

During the 1970s, however, politics in the Eastern Caribbean islands took a turn that caused a shift in the policies of both Trinidad and Venezuela. A renewed anti-Cuban alliance, similar to what existed in the early and middle 1960s, was in the making.

By 1979 the islands of the Eastern Caribbean had clearly joined the ideological fray. The April 30, 1979, "Memorandum on Economic Cooperation Between Trinidad and Barbados" clearly illustrated the trends in the Eastern Caribbean: close links between oil-rich Trinidad and fast-growing Barbados, ranging from cooperation in defense and security matters, to support for the University of the West Indies, to energy. This was an obvious move to counter the activities of the "radicals" in the Eastern Caribbean. And they in turn responded.

The July 1979 Declaration of St. Georges (Grenada), signed by the prime ministers of Grenada, Dominica, and St. Lucia, was supposed to herald a dramatic shift in ideological orientation in the Eastern Caribbean. Bishop of Grenada clearly had the stellar role, followed closely by Deputy Prime Minister George Odlum of St. Lucia; a distant third was Oliver Seraphin from Dominica. Bishop and Odlum had previously revealed that they had met some ten years before on Rat Island, off St. Lucia, to plan a revolutionary strategy for the Eastern Caribbean. The Declaration of St. Georges was from all appearances the culmination of that process. With independence for St. Vincent approaching, that island was fully expected to join the "radical" alliance.

There can be no doubt that the political battle had been joined in the Eastern Caribbean. On the "radical" side were the young intellectuals, scions of the area's middle classes, and on the other, the aging veterans of the anticolonial movements, the labor-union-based politicians. Events in St. Vincent gave some indication of the way the battle went. It was predicted that the 1979 elections would be a toss-up between the traditional forces, which remained divided (Milton Cato's St. Vincent Labour party, "Son" Mitchell's New Democratic party (NDP), and Ebenezer Joshua's People's Political party—all three past premiers of the island), and the radical forces, recently united under the banner of the United People's Movement (UPM). This coalition joined one social democratic party (People's Democratic Movement) with two professing "scientific socialism," ARWEE and the Youlou Liberation Movement (YULIMO).

YULIMO was led by a white Vincentian, Dr. Ralph Gonsalves, at the time a professor at the University of the West Indies Cave Hill campus in Barbados. An intense and attractive public speaker, Gonsalves was representative of the new middle-class radicals of the region: impatient with parliamentary structures and procedures, moved by a profound conviction that they could provide better leadership than the old guard. The nearly eulogistic description of the radical UPM's principal leaders by *Caribbean Contact* is revealing: "A roll-call of UPM's principal leaders is like a who's who of St. Vincent's brighter and more dedicated sons and daughters. These include Oscar Allen, Simeon Greene, Dr. Kenneth John, Carlyle Dougan, E. Dougan, Y. Francis, Robbie FitsPatrick, Renwick Rose, Adrian Saunders, Caspar London, Tysel John, Mike Browne, and Dr. Ralph Gonsalves."[25] The election results, however, indicated that Vincentians were not yet ready for what Dr. Gonsalves called "a broad theoretical programme of socialist orientation." Cato's Labour party won eleven of thirteen seats and ex-Premier "Son" Mitchell's NDP won the remaining two. Cato had run on virtually one theme: "Stem the leftist tide." It paid off, at least for the time.

The postelection uprising of Rastafarians on Union Island in the St. Vincent's Grenadines and the quick dispatch of a Barbadian police contingent to assist the Cato government indicate that there might not be too many more Grenada-like surprises possible in the Eastern Caribbean, certainly not in St. Vincent.

Events in the other islands also showed that the euphoria surrounding the St. Georges Declaration was already on the wane by the end of the decade. Dominica's Oliver Seraphin, for instance, began to moderate his utterances to such a degree that one of his speeches in Miami, Florida (November 1979), received a standing ovation from some three hundred U.S. and Caribbean businessmen. Michael Manley, on the other hand, received merely polite applause from the same audience. Seraphin's pitch to the businessmen was in fact no different from Manley's: They both made an appeal for foreign capital.

In St. Lucia a real split developed between Prime Minister Allan Louisy and Deputy Prime Minister Odlum. What began as a promising alliance between reformist-minded members of the old guard, such as Louisy, and the radicals ended up in a bitter battle that immobilized the government for two years and cost it the elections in 1981, won by the conservatives. On the surface the split had to do with the Louisy government's harder line toward the Rastafarians and other dissident groups. In fact, it was a struggle for power, with Louisy apparently refusing to turn over the government to the radical wing as per a secret but widely known understanding. The mood in the Eastern Caribbean had shifted to the right, and Louisy shifted with it.

There can be little doubt that Odlum's position was weakened by his well-publicized links to the Grenadian leadership. His defense of the local Rastafarians, for instance, was seen as less than sincere given the Grenadian actions against one segment of their Rastas.

In St. Lucia, as in the rest of the English-speaking Caribbean, the Rastafarian issue has forced into the open certain contradictions of the radical position. Throughout the region, invariably opposition radical groups have joined their cause as part of the anti-establishment crusade. Once in power, however, these same groups "discovered" that the Rastas were an obstacle to the kind of secular socialist modernization these middle-class radicals desire. Certainly there are few Caribbean groups more alien to the regimented and clean-shaven Cubans than these grimy and tattered followers of the Lion of Judah. And so it is with so many of the other West Indian lumpen groups and practices—such as the puritanical Seventh-day Adventists, the animist believers in Obeah, and those who smoke ganja on the job.

Conclusion

In societies with very few resources and few opportunities for advancement and prominence, government and its bureaucracy offer remarkable rewards. Status is not only national, it is international: The United Nations and the Third World and the Nonaligned Movement provide forums for the articulate of even the smallest of nations. And if there is one thing that these radical sons of the islands' middle classes are it is articulate. A Michael Manley, a Maurice Bishop, or a Bernard Coard makes a good impression and stands in stark contrast to the ridicule reserved for some of the old leaders, such as Milton Cato or Eric Gairy. But while their informal revolutionary dress—*de rigueur* everywhere in the English-speaking Caribbean during the 1970s—contrasts dramatically with the excessive formality of such old-timers such as Robert Bradshaw, Ebenezer Joshua, or Norman Manley, the clothes cannot hide their middle-class backgrounds or European educations.

While the old-timers were organizing labor unions and political parties, these radicals were in Europe being educated in the various issues of the 1960s. Unable because of class and/or race to be integral parts of the Black Power movement, they nevertheless have deep-rooted and sincere sympathies with the large young, urban, unemployed lumpenproletariat. It is those lumpen sectors that Frantz Fanon felt would immerse themselves in revolutionary violence to emerge cleansed and liberated, ready to undertake the task of socialist modernization. But Fanon was talking about social revolutions in societies experiencing brutal colonization. In the Caribbean we have been witnessing political revolutions led by intellectuals with no mass base, without even significant labor union support. It is the revolution of youthful hope rather than street-wise experience, secular experimentation against primordial racial and ethnic attachments, abstract ideas of a New International Economic Order against populist promises of a chicken and a yam in every pot—all this in territories the European colonizers have been only too eager to be rid of.[26]

In this context the Cuban card has extraordinary value to the new elites; it extends the mantle of revolutionary legitimacy while providing the arms, intelligence, and training essential for grabbing power and keeping it. Clearly and predictably, as this analysis of the politics of the 1970s indicates, that mantle of legitimacy will show weak spots as it spreads over more and more Caribbean "revolutions." Because they are political movements, they respond more to the unique configurations of each territory rather than to any universal, class-based factors. The Cuban mantle has thus to cover a Burnham, a Michael Manley, and a Bishop equally. Consequently, if Bishop's counterparts in Guyana (with whom he shares ideological, intellectual, educational, and even class origins and proclivities), the university-professor-led Working People's Alliance (WPA), are oppressed by Burnham, Bishop can only keep silence.[27] Not only does he "owe" Burnham for his very early support of the revolution, he is also inhibited by Cuba's support for the Guyana government. Ironically, the defense of human rights in Guyana becomes by default a matter for liberal groups in Trinidad, Barbados, and the United States. Similarly, the repression of the Rastafarians in Grenada did not bring forth a protest from Manley's regime, which had made a big issue of its own support of Rasta culture.

By the end of the 1970s it was clear that the battle for the English-speaking Caribbean had been joined by all parties. It is still premature to concede victory to one side or the other. It is not premature, however, to note certain structural aspects of the battle.

Cuba announced that its growth target for 1980 would be a mere 3 percent. This compared to targets of 7.4 percent for 1978 and 6 percent for 1979. Clearly its inability to achieve anywhere near those goals led to a more realistic goal for 1980. To analyze the very candid speeches delivered during 1979 by both Fidel and Raúl Castro, however, was to understand that the island's sputtering economy could not achieve even the 3 percent goal in 1980. The performance in 1980 was little different than it had been during the past decade. At no time did Cuba offer the English-speaking Caribbean a viable economic alternative. To the political elites of this region of dependent and complementary economies, the Cuban card will necessarily continue to be a political one, not an economic or social one.

Radical Grenada can twice vote against United Nations resolutions condemning the Soviet invasion of Afghanistan, but it will seek its funding in Western Europe and Venezuela and coddle its private sector. The Cuban card allows the two actions to avoid appearing incompatible. But the Grenadians should know, as Manley discovered in Jamaica, that the Cuban card is very much a double-edged sword in the tumultuous political cultures of the English-speaking Caribbean. Because it is political—thus, not responding to any mass-based social or economic movements—it can be used in its positive and its negative sides by elites of all classes, skin colors, or ideological positions. Power, i.e., state control, is the operative value, the goal toward which Caribbean elites, new and old, bend their every effort. Cuban assistance in this endeavor is appreciated, but it involves a marriage of convenience. As occurs in such marriages, the rules can change at the most unexpected moment. And in this art of shifting political signals and changing rules, in the Caribbean Cuba has been and is dealing with some of the most skillful practitioners to be found anywhere today.

Notes

1. K. S. Karol, *Guerrillas in Power: The Course of the Cuban Revolution* (New York: Hill & Wang, 1970), pp. 19–20.
2. Ibid., p. 20.
3. For a fuller discussion of this point, see A. P. Maingot, "The Difficult Path to Socialism in the English-Speaking Caribbean," in Richard Fagen, ed., *The State and Capitalism in U.S.–Latin American Relations* (Stanford, Calif.: Stanford University Press, 1979), pp. 254–301.
4. These surveys have appeared periodically in the *Daily Gleaner* (Jamaica), January 30, 1978; and February 6, 1978. Carl Stone has also made the point in his study *Electoral Behavior and Public Opinion in Jamaica* (Mona: ISER, 1974).
5. *Weekly Gleaner* (Jamaica), April 10, 1978.
6. Interviews by the author with Jamaican "exiles" (Miami, Florida, August 1978).
7. *New York Times*, September 30, 1979.
8. Cf. A. P. Maingot, "Political Analysis and Contemporary History," in Peter A. Gonzales et al., eds., *Independence for Grenada* (St. Augustine, Trinidad: Institute of International Relations, 1974), pp. 21–35.
9. *Caribbean Insight,* Vol. 2, no. 4 (April 1979):4.
10. Interviewed by Alister Hughes and John Redman, *Caribbean Life and Times,* Vol. 1, no. 2 (December 1979):39.
11. *Miami Herald,* November 27, 1979.
12. Archie Singham, *The Hero and the Crowd* (New Haven, Conn.: Yale University Press, 1968).
13. Ibid., p. 152.
14. *Miami Herald,* October 16, 1979.
15. This section is more fully analyzed in A. P. Maingot, "National Policies and Regional Definitions: The Caribbean as an Interest Area," paper presented to the Conference on Contemporary Trends and Issues in Caribbean Affairs, Trinidad, May 23–27, 1977.
16. "Feature Address and Official Opening," in *Seminar on the Foreign Policies of Caribbean States* (St. Augustine, Trinidad: Institute of International Relations, 1968), p. 9.

17. *The Circle* (Port-of-Spain, Trinidad), Vol. 1, no. 11 (November 1963).

18. Eric Williams, *From Columbus to Castro* (London: André Deutsch, 1970), pp. 486, 510.

19. *Guardian* (Port-of-Spain, Trinidad), June 21, 1975, p. 1.

20. Ibid., June 24, 1975, p. 1.

21. Ibid., June 13, 1975, p. 9.

22. Ibid., June 18, 19, and 20, 1975 (all p. 1).

23. Ibid., June 20, 1975, p. 9.

24. Ibid., June 16, 1975, p. 1.

25. *Caribbean Contact* (Barbados), September 1979. The arbitrary and selective nature of radical sentiments in the Caribbean is patent in this weekly. Although financed by U.S., Canadian, and Western European monies, this weekly has been a vocal supporter of Cuba and of radical movements in the Caribbean—except Guyana, from where the editor was expelled.

26. That this situation of political rather than social revolutions exists in other parts of the Caribbean can be seen in the Suriname case. In February 1980 the junior army officers overthrew the elected government. In 1982 they took a sharp turn to the left, including very close ties with Grenada. A good analysis of the political nature of that revolution was given in March 1980 by the left-leaning *Latin America Report* (London). It lamented the absence of any revolutionary initiative, attributing it to "the absence of much social pressure." The *Report*'s 1980 analyses contain a plausible limit on the cause of a future change: "There is no pressure for real reform in such an environment, and little radical change seems likely to come from the new regime until the military either become disillusioned with their new cabinet, develop overweening ambitions, or face a social crisis." The shift left came without a "social crisis."

27. The brutal murder of Working People's Alliance leader Dr. Walter Rodney has focused new attention on the repressive regime in Guyana but has yet to bring the kind of censure or harsh words that Bishop seems to reserve for Prime Minister Tom Adams of Barbados, a leader of social democracy in the English-speaking Caribbean.

3
Cuba and Nicaragua: From the Somozas to the Sandinistas

William M. LeoGrande

The Somozas, vehement in their anticommunism, cast Nicaragua in the role of regional gendarme long before the victory of the Cuban revolution. When the United States undertook the subversion of the Arbenz government in Guatemala in 1954, Anastasio Somoza García opened training facilities for Castillo Armas's exile army, acted as intermediary for arms transfers from the United States, and provided an air base for the exiles' bombers.[1] Later in the decade, when the United States suspended military aid to Batista, Luis Somoza stepped in to sell him arms for use against Cuba's revolutionaries. Somoza was among the earliest and most vocal opponents of the revolutionary government that came to power in Cuba on January 2, 1959.[2]

With the victory of the revolution, Cuba became a haven for Latin American political exiles, many of whom proceeded to foment plots against their native governments. Some had the backing of the new Cuban government; some did not. Expeditions were launched against Panama and the Dominican Republic; others were planned against Guatemala and Nicaragua but never came to fruition. Somoza accused Cuba of mounting an abortive exile attack from Costa Rica in June 1959 and the OAS concurred, although the Cubans have consistently denied involvement.[3] Faced with an internal uprising in November, Somoza again held Cuba responsible and requested U.S. aid to fend off an anticipated expedition from the island. The Eisenhower administration dispatched a naval task force to patrol Nicaragua's coastal waters to prevent a "communist led" invasion of Central America, but no such invasion ever materialized.[4] Whatever the extent of Cuba's early support for the opposition to the Somoza dynasty, the animosity between the two regimes was never in doubt.

As the Cuban revolution moved to the left, U.S. hostility toward it grew to be as intense as Somoza's. When the United States endeavored to reenact the "Guatemalan solution" at the Bay of Pigs, Luis Somoza once again volunteered Nicaragua as a forward base of operations. The exile brigade of the Central Intelligence Agency (CIA) embarked for Cuba from Puerto Cabezas on Nicaragua's Caribbean coast, and the brigade's bombers flew sorties from a Nicaraguan airfield.[5]

The Bay of Pigs debacle did not dampen the Somozas' dedication to the Cuban exiles' cause. Both Luis and Anastasio (Tachito) repeatedly offered Nicaragua's cooperation in a new invasion attempt, urging the United States to mount one long after U.S. enthusiasm for such an endeavor had waned. From 1962 to 1975, Cuban exile leader Manuel Artime was allowed to maintain training camps in Nicaragua, and even after the camps were closed, Nicaraguan aid to the exiles continued, albeit more discreetly. Indeed, the Somoza dynasty's ties to the Cuban exiles transcended politics as a number of exile businessmen developed economic ties with the Somozas' business empire.[6]

While Nicaragua trained and armed Cuban exiles, Cuba trained and armed Nicaraguan exiles. The Frente Sandinista de Liberación Nacional (FSLN) was founded in 1962 in Havana by a group of Nicaraguans long active in the revolutionary opposition to the Somoza dynasty. Throughout the 1960s, FSLN members received both arms and training in Cuba. The amount of Cuban aid was circumscribed, however, by the FSLN's small size (it numbered fewer than fifty) and by its inability to establish a guerrilla *foco* against the well-trained and well-equipped National Guard.[7]

During the late 1960s when Cuban foreign policy was in its Tricontinental phase, Cuba provided substantial material support to virtually every guerrilla movement in Latin America, no matter how weak or minuscule that movement happened to be. By 1968, however, the repeated failures of Latin American guerrillas—particularly the death of Che Guevara in Bolivia—prompted a change in Cuban policy. Based upon a new assessment that conditions were not ripe for revolution in Latin America, Cuba reduced its material aid to guerrillas. Instead of attempting to end its hemispheric isolation by promoting revolution, Cuba began to pursue a diplomatic strategy of normalizing relations with those governments willing to ignore the existing Organization of American States (OAS) sanctions. This strategy was such a success that in 1975 the sanctions were relaxed.

For Cuba to continue providing any significant material aid to Latin American revolutionaries would obviously have undermined the new diplomatic strategy. Thus, during the 1970s, guerrillas received only minimal support from Cuba. The FSLN, still with fewer than 100 members in 1977, was no exception to this new policy. Arms aid was apparently halted and the training of FSLN cadres was greatly reduced.[8] Diminishing material aid did not, however, signify diminishing solidarity. Cuba remained a refuge for Nicaraguan exiles and for Sandinistas freed as a result of various FSLN military actions. In 1970, when four Sandinistas (including FSLN founder Carlos Fonseca Amador) were released from prison in Costa Rica in exchange for a hijacked airliner, they were given refuge in Cuba. Again in 1974, when fourteen Sandinistas were freed in Nicaragua as a result of the FSLN's famous Christmas party raid, they sought asylum in Cuba before making their way back to Nicaragua.[9] Cuba's sympathy for the Sandinistas and hatred of the Somoza dynasty was never in doubt, but it was not until the insurrection against Somoza was far advanced that Cuba again began providing the FSLN with more than moral support.

The Nicaraguan Insurrection and Cuban Solidarity

Cuba's aid to the anti-Somoza opposition during the last twelve months of the Somoza dynasty was so modest that it would be a serious distortion not to place it within the wider context of international involvement in the Nicaraguan revolution. Cuban aid was real enough, but Cuba was not the principal external actor on either side of the conflict.

As opposition to Somoza intensified in 1977 and 1978, the Cuban policy formulated at the turn of the decade remained unchanged. Except for providing statements of support and a refuge for exiles, Cuban assistance to the FSLN was virtually nil. Even the political strife following the assassination of *La Prensa* editor Pedro Joaquín Chamorro did not prompt an increase in Cuban involvement. Judging from Cuban press accounts at the time, until September 1978 Cuban officials did not believe a revolutionary situation existed in Nicaragua. Most of the FSLN's material support during this period came from Costa Rica, which allowed the FSLN to maintain camps and seek sanctuary across the Nicaraguan border. The great bulk of the FSLN's armaments were bought in the international arms market.[10]

The September 1978 insurrection in five Nicaraguan cities, which the National Guard suppressed by unleashing its full firepower against its own citizenry, prompted a new flurry of international interest and involvement. The insurrection demonstrated the depth of anti-Somoza sentiment in Nicaragua and the fragility of the dynasty's hold on power. As the dimensions of the political crisis became clear, the cast of external actors grew rapidly. The United States, the most influential actor in Nicaragua for almost half a century, initiated the ill-fated mediation in search of a moderate political solution.

For Somoza's opponents, both domestic and foreign, the lesson drawn from the September insurrection was that the National Guard could be defeated militarily only if the FSLN were better armed and organized. In the months between September 1978 and July 1979, Costa Rica, Venezuela, Panama, and Cuba initiated partially coordinated policies of increased material assistance to the FSLN. Bolivia, Ecuador, Peru, and Mexico added their diplomatic support for the insurgents. On the other side of the battlements, Israel, Argentina, Spain, Brazil, Honduras, Guatemala, and El Salvador came to Somoza's aid to replenish the depleted military stocks of the National Guard.[11]

The Cuban role in all this was relatively small, at least until the final month or two of the war. After September 1978, Cuba increased its training of FSLN combatants, provided some arms shipments to the Sandinistas, and helped them establish contact with other international arms sources. The Cubans also encouraged other Central American communist parties to provide whatever assistance they could to the Nicaraguan revolutionaries. Perhaps the most significant Cuban contribution was to help mediate the differences between the FSLN's three factions. As a result of this effort, the FSLN was able to conclude a pact in March 1979 that provided for the reunification of the movement under a new National Directorate and set the stage for the "final offensive" that deposed the dynasty.[12]

Yet, Cuba contributed less than some of the other Latin American nations providing direct assistance to the FSLN. This limited involvement was based on several considerations. First and foremost, Cuba wished to provide no pretext for direct U.S. intervention. On three separate occasions in 1979, FSLN representatives asked the Cubans for greater assistance. Each time Cuba refused, Castro explaining, "The best help we could give you is not to help you at all."[13] Nor did the Cubans want to rekindle fears of Cuban intervention among other Latin American governments, many of whom supported the anti-Somoza opposition but were nervous about the radicalism of the FSLN. Venezuelan President Carlos Andrés Pérez, for example, traveled to Cuba in June of 1979 seeking assurances that Cuba would not intervene massively in Nicaragua. Ultimately, the Cubans reasoned that as Venezuela, Panama, and Costa Rica were already providing substantial assistance to the FSLN, there was no need for a large-scale Cuban effort.[14] Thus Cuba maintained a "low key approach."[15]

Although Cuba's contribution to the Nicaraguan revolutionaries was by no means the largest, nevertheless it was Cuba that U.S. Secretary of State Vance singled out for criticism at the June OAS meeting on Nicaragua.[16] This emphasis on Cuba's involvement was a product of bureaucratic politics in the United States. As Somoza's position deteriorated in early June, the White House's Standing Consultative Committee (the National Security Council's crisis management group) took up the issue of Nicaragua. There was general agreement that the United States ought to actively seek, under OAS auspices, a collective inter-American solution to the Nicaraguan crisis; there was no agreement on how to go about it. National Security Adviser Zbigniew Brzezinski advocated emphasizing the Cuban involvement, which could then, in turn, be used as justification for an inter-American peacekeeping force. Secretary of State Vance and the State Department's Latin American experts strenuously opposed such a strategy as guaranteed to inflame Latin American sensitivities about gunboat diplomacy, but when the issue was presented to the president, Brzezinski's view prevailed.[17]

The proposal for a peacekeeping force proved to be a diplomatic blunder of unprecedented proportions. Not only was it severely criticized and soundly rejected by the OAS, it nearly scuttled U.S. attempts to elicit OAS authorization for further mediation efforts. The charges of major Cuban involvement were not taken seriously by most Latin American governments, who knew full well that Panama, Venezuela, and Costa Rica (at a minimum) were as deeply involved as Cuba. The most serious charge leveled against Cuba at the OAS meeting was that Cuban military advisers were training FSLN guerrillas on the Costa Rican border, but when several days of searching turned up no confirmation of the reports, the White House was forced to admit that it had "no direct evidence" of Cuban advisers.[18]

Cuba and the New Nicaragua

On July 17, 1979, the Somoza dynasty came to an end, the victim not of external intervention but of its own greed, corruption, and brutality. The legacy of *somocismo* was a nation bankrupt and an economy in ruins.

Cuba greeted the victory of the FSLN and installation of the Government of National Reconstruction with great fanfare and immediately pledged to help in the massive task of rebuilding Nicaragua's shattered economy. On July 25 a Cuban plane arrived in Managua with 90 tons of food and a Cuban medical team of sixty people.[19] It departed for Cuba with a high-level Nicaraguan delegation, including two members of the ruling junta (Moisés Hassan and Alfonso Robelo) and twenty-six FSLN commanders. The Nicaraguans were the guests of honor at Cuba's national celebration on July 26, at which Castro called upon all nations to aid Nicaragua in its time of need. Castro even challenged the United States to a peaceful competition to see which nation could give more to Nicaragua; Cuba, he promised, would begin sending food, teachers, and medical personnel immediately.[20]

The Nicaraguans requested Cuban aid in the fields of health and education because, as Robelo put it, "That is where the Cuban revolution has shown the greatest gains."[21] More than 100 Cuban doctors and nurses arrived in Nicaragua in the final months of 1979 and were dispatched to outlying towns and villages to establish emergency clinics. Two decades of the Somoza dynasty's anti-Cuban propaganda made real live Cubans something of a public curiosity.[22] By 1982, some 500 Cuban medical personnel were in Nicaragua helping to staff the growing health care system.[23]

In late August 1979 Cuba and Nicaragua signed an educational exchange agreement in which Cuba pledged to provide 1,000 elementary school teachers and 40 university professors to teach in Nicaragua. The agreement also included 700 scholarships for Nicaraguan students to study in Cuba.[24] The Nicaraguan literacy crusade of 1980 was modeled in part on the Cuban literacy campaign of 1961: Cubans helped the Nicaraguans plan the campaign, Cuban volunteers went into the countryside to help carry it out.[25] In the wake of the crusade, Cuban educational aid expanded rather than contracted. By 1982, there were 2,200 Cuban teachers serving in Nicaragua.[26]

Cuban technical and economic assistance went beyond the fields of health and education. Cuban construction workers helped to complete the first all-weather road between Nicaragua's Pacific and Atlantic coasts in 1981 and worked on a variety of public construction projects throughout the country. Cuban advisers assisted the Sandinistas in the task of building a new administrative bureaucracy to replace the *somocista* apparatus destroyed by the revolution.[27] In April 1982 Cuba and Nicaragua signed the most extensive economic cooperative agreement thus far. The Cubans pledged to provide 3,800 technicians, doctors, and teachers as well as $130 million worth of financial assistance in the form of agricultural and industrial machinery, food, medicine, and construction equipment.[28]

Cuba and Nicaraguan Domestic Politics

As the multiclass coalition that made the Nicaraguan revolution began to break down in 1980 and 1981, the extent of Cuban influence in Nicaragua came to be a key issue between the FSLN and its domestic opponents. The first open split in the anti-Somoza coalition came in April 1980 when Alfonso Robelo resigned from the junta of government over the composition of the newly created Council of State. Robelo led his Nicaraguan Democratic Movement into opposition. Robelo's complaint, shared by most of the private sector, was that the Sandinistas held an effective monopoly of political power and refused to give it up. The businessmen's deeper fear was that the FSLN would ultimately use its control of the state to do away with the private sector entirely, taking Nicaragua down the road of Cuban-style socialism. The Sandinistas' close friendship with Cuba naturally exacerbated those fears.

Within the nine-member National Directorate of the FSLN, there were, in fact, some *comandantes* who favored the Cuban model of development. During 1980 and 1981, however, they remained a minority, consistently outvoted by a more moderate and pragmatic group that favored maintaining political pluralism, a mixed economy, and a foreign policy of nonalignment.

Ironically, the pragmatists found an ally in Fidel Castro, who advised the Nicaraguans to avoid alienating the private sector or angering the United States if at all possible.[29] Castro warned the Nicaraguans that the cost of eliminating the private sector and of severing economic ties with the West would be immense—and that the Soviet Union might not be willing to take up the burden of "another Cuba."

Fidel Castro's efforts to moderate the more radical Sandinista leaders did not mollify the private-sector opposition, which continued to see Nicaragua's close friendship with Cuba as contrary to the principle of nonalignment and Cuban influence as dangerous to its own vision of Nicaragua's future.

The Cuban presence produced problems for the Sandinistas in other sectors as well. When former FSLN commander Edén Pastora went public with his opposition to the direction of the revolution in a press conference in Costa Rica, much of the press conference was devoted to the FSLN's relationship with Cuba. Pastora accused the National Directorate of selling out the nationalist character of the revolution by slavishly imitating everything Cuban. He called upon his former colleagues in the army to rise up against the National Directorate, promising that he himself would return to lead an armed struggle against the FSLN leadership if it did not mend its ways.[30]

On the Atlantic Coast, the presence of Cuban doctors and teachers exacerbated the tensions between the government in Managua and the people on the coast. In 1980 the first serious antigovernment disturbance in Bluefields was provoked by Cuban advisers' raising a Cuban flag outside their compound. The subsequent rioting lasted several days.[31]

Cuba, Nicaragua, and the United States

By far the most serious consequences of Cuba's relationship with Nicaragua were international rather than domestic. Seeking to avoid a repetition of the U.S. experience with Cuba in the early 1960s, when Washington's hostility drove Cuba into the arms of the Soviet Union, the Carter administration tried to maintain cordial relations with Nicaragua's revolutionary government. Through late 1979 and 1980, the United States provided economic assistance to the Sandinistas and refused to be provoked by some of the FSLN's more virulent anti-imperialist rhetoric.[32] In effect, the Carter administration chose a policy close to those of Mexico, Venezuela, and the social democratic parties of Western Europe—to compete with Cuba and the socialist bloc for influence in Nicaragua, hoping that access to Western financial aid would prove more attractive than access to Eastern arms. Although U.S. relations with Cuba deteriorated substantially during this period, the Carter administration did not allow that growing animosity to spill over and poison U.S. relations with Nicaragua, despite the Sandinistas' friendship with Cuba.

The Reagan administration began with a somewhat different agenda. The inauguration coincided with the Salvadoran guerrillas' unsuccessful "final offensive" of January 1981. In the aftermath of that offensive, the new administration decided to make El Salvador a "test case" of its resolve to stand firm against Soviet expansion.[33] By "drawing the line" in El Salvador, the administration hoped to test the willingness of Washington's European allies to take a hard line against the Soviet Union, alert the U.S. public to the dangers of communist expansion, and create a confrontation by proxy with the Soviet Union in an arena Washington felt confident was in its favor.

U.S. relations with Nicaragua were immediately and inevitably swept up in this new conceptualization of the Salvadoran insurgency as a battle in the new cold war. In February, the State Department released its White Paper, "Communist Interference in El Salvador," which charged that the war there had been transformed from a domestic conflict into armed external aggression by international communism. At the center of these charges were Cuba and Nicaragua, both accused of serving as arms conduits for the Salvadoran guerrillas.[34]

Although the White Paper was subjected to withering criticism in the press, there was little doubt that Cuba had in fact been providing arms to the Salvadoran left and that some of these arms had been shipped through Nicaragua.[35] Shortly before leaving office, the Carter administration had suspended disbursements of economic aid to Nicaragua, as required by law, because of evidence to that effect. In

public, the Nicaraguans vehemently denied they were allowing their country to be used as an arms conduit, but U.S. intelligence estimates indicated that the flow of arms through Nicaragua dropped off sharply after U.S. protests in February and March.[36]

Washington, however, did not react to these developments by trying to repair relations with Nicaragua. On the contrary, it refused to resume economic aid, suspended wheat sales, and began threatening to "go to the source" of the Salvadoran war by taking direct military action against Nicaragua and Cuba.[37]

Rhetorically, the administration's attitude toward Nicaragua was reminiscent of U.S. foreign policy during the 1950s under Secretary of State John Foster Dulles. During those years, any nation adopting a nonaligned foreign policy or establishing normal relations with the Soviet Union was regarded as an enemy of the United States. Although there were some in the Reagan administration who were convinced that Nicaragua had "gone communist" already, the administration did not move to break completely with the Nicaraguans. In part this was due to the influence of U.S. Ambassador Lawrence Pezzullo, who argued that Nicaragua was not yet "lost." Of equal importance was the administration's strategy for El Salvador. In order to avoid the growth of domestic opposition, the administration sought to minimize its direct involvement in El Salvador, concentrating instead on cutting off the guerrillas' logistical support.[38] By breaking totally with Nicaragua, Washington would forfeit whatever leverage it had in Managua, leaving the Sandinistas free to continue their cooperation with the Salvadoran left.

In short, the Reagan administration continued its predecessor's policy of competing with Cuba for influence in Nicaragua. But whereas the Carter administration had fought the competition with the inducement of economic aid, the Reagan administration fought it with threats of hostile actions, both military and economic.

In August 1981 Washington opened a dialogue with Nicaragua aimed at terminating once and for all any Nicaraguan involvement in the Salvadoran insurgency. Assistant Secretary of State Thomas O. Enders traveled to Managua, offering a resumption of U.S. economic aid, a promise of nonintervention, and a crackdown on *somocista* exiles training in the United States. Discussions continued for a few weeks but broke down in October.[39]

The failure of the dialogue coincided with growing concern in Washington that the war in El Salvador was being lost. The guerrillas had emerged from several months of retraining with a much more effective military strategy, and U.S. military analysts began saying that the war was stalemated at best—a poor long-term prognosis for the survival of the government.[40]

Such bleak predictions led the administration to launch a new public campaign of tough rhetoric about Central America. Secretary of State Alexander Haig announced that a variety of options for direct military action in the region were under review.[41] A number of administration spokesmen charged that arms flows to the Salvadoran left from Cuba and Nicaragua were on the rise again, and for the first time, the administration began to criticize Nicaragua's internal military buildup.[42] "The hour is growing late," warned presidential adviser Edwin Meese in an interview about Nicaragua.[43]

This high public profile by the administration coincided with a full review of Central American policy. Secretary of State Haig was the principal advocate of direct military action, not in El Salvador proper, but against the alleged Cuban-Nicaraguan arms link. The lesson of Vietnam, according to Haig, was to avoid fighting on the ground and to hit instead at the logistical support of the insurgents. The Department of Defense, however, was adamantly opposed to any direct U.S. military involvement. Both the Joint Chiefs of Staff and Defense Secretary Caspar Weinberger were skeptical about the ability of the United States to seal El Salvador's porous borders and were reluctant to divert substantial U.S. forces to the Caribbean basin to enforce a blockade of Cuba or Nicaragua. Finally, the Defense Department feared that the strength of public and congressional opposition to U.S. military involvement in Central America might endanger the Pentagon's first priority—the massive strategic arms buildup planned by the Reagan administration.[44]

The White House also opposed Haig's call for military action on political grounds. The growth of domestic opposition to the administration's policy in Central America made White House aides wary of risking the president's popularity on a military adventure in the region.[45]

At a series of National Security Council meetings held in mid-November 1981, Reagan adopted a series of new policy initiatives aimed at containing the crisis in Central America. The new plan called for an increase in U.S. military assistance to El Salvador, increased economic aid to selected nations in the region (the Caribbean Basin Initiative), and a public relations offensive in the United States to build support for U.S. policy. The bulk of the plan, however, dealt with sanctions against Nicaragua and Cuba designed to raise the cost of their growing friendship and their support of the Salvadoran guerrillas. Efforts to tighten the U.S. economic embargo against Cuba were planned, along with increased diplomatic and economic pressures against Nicaragua. U.S. military maneuvers in the Caribbean were stepped up in an effort to intimidate the two nations, and contingency plans were developed for a U.S. response to "unacceptable" military action by Cuba—e.g., sending troops to Central America, presumably to Nicaragua. Finally, the president approved a multifaceted covert action program targeted against Nicaragua and to be implemented by the CIA.[46]

In mid-February 1982, the administration launched a major public relations effort to convince its domestic opponents that Nicaragua had become a totalitarian state, that its military buildup was a threat to the entire Central American region, and that it was cooperating with Cuba to destabilize the government of El Salvador. In interviews with the press and in congressional testimony, administration officials accused the Sandinistas of being "more repressive than Somoza" and of committing "genocide" against the Miskito Indian minority on Nicaragua's Atlantic Coast.[47] They alleged that the insurgency in El Salvador was being "run from Managua" and accused the Sandinistas of hosting 1,500 to 2,000 Cuban military advisers.[48]

This flurry of activity reached a crescendo in early March. On the ninth, the CIA and the Defense Intelligence Agency gave an extraordinary press briefing on Cuban-Nicaraguan military ties. Using aerial photographs in a setting reminiscent of the Cuban missile crisis, the administration demonstrated that Nicaragua's new army was considerably larger than it had been under Somoza and that its new facilities were designed with Cuban assistance. The evidence, however, did not bear out the administration's claim that Cuba and Nicaragua were conspiring to aid the Salvadoran guerrillas.[49]

The Nicaraguans replied to the U.S. charges by pointing out that they had never denied an intention to increase their defense capability—that doing so was only prudent, given the reports that the United States was contemplating military action against them. Nor did the Nicaraguans deny that they were receiving military aid from Cuba, although several high Nicaraguan officials claimed that they had, at most, a dozen Cuban military advisers.[50]

The day after the aerial photography briefing, administration analysts briefed a group of high-ranking national security officials from prior administrations. This group was shown the electronic intelligence concerning Cuban-Nicaraguan aid to the Salvadoran guerrillas. The former officials pronounced the evidence compelling, but the administration continued to insist that this evidence was too sensitive to be made public.[51]

On March 13 a second press briefing backfired, bringing the administration's public relations campaign to an abrupt and premature end. A young Nicaraguan captured in El Salvador was brought before the press in Washington with the expectation that he would admit to having been trained in Cuba and Ethiopia as a guerrilla commander and dispatched to El Salvador by the Nicaraguan army. Instead, to the horror of onlooking State Department officials, he denied it all, claiming he had been tortured into his earlier confessions.[52]

As the March 28 Constituency Assembly elections in El Salvador approached, the Reagan administration found itself having little success at convincing skeptics that Nicaragua and Cuba were, indeed, at the source of the war in El Salvador. The large turnout recorded in the Salvadoran vote changed the terms of the domestic debate in the United States, giving the administration new ammunition in its battle with congressional critics. As administration officials found they could have more success extolling El Salvador's new-found democracy than they had had waving a red flag over Cuban-Nicaraguan interference, the public attacks on Nicaragua began to recede.

This change in tone was also due to the Reagan administration's decision to cooperate, superficially, with Mexico's efforts to find peaceful solutions to the Central American crisis.

In late February Mexican President José López Portillo launched a major initiative aimed at bringing about negotiated solutions for three "knots" of tension in Central America. He offered Mexico's good offices as a mediator to begin talks between the Salvadoran government and the guerrillas, between the United States and Cuba, and between the United States and Nicaragua. At first, the United States ignored the Mexican initiative, but López Portillo's proposal elicited considerable support both in Europe and among the administration's congressional critics. Cuba, Nicaragua, and the Salvadoran left accepted the proposal almost immediately, and the Reagan administration was put in the unenviable position of appearing to prefer war to a negotiated peace. Nearly a month later, when the administration's public relations campaign had come to its untimely end, the United States cautiously accepted Mexico's offer to help initiate talks with Cuba and Nicaragua.[53]

The administration did not, however, expect that much would come of the talks. It maintained its policy with regard to both Nicaragua and Cuba, insisting that any improvement in their relations with the United States would have to be preceded by an end to their arms shipments to El Salvador. As both Cuba and Nicaragua denied that they were making such shipments, there seemed to be little to discuss.

Several contacts between U.S. and Cuban officials produced no progress whatsoever, and the administration insisted on keeping talks with Nicaragua at the level of ambassadorial exchanges that did little more than restate the respective positions of the two nations. Once the results of the Salvadoran elections had reduced the domestic pressure on the administration's Central American policy, Washington evinced little interest in pursuing serious discussions on any front.[54]

By mid-1982, Central America had disappeared from public attention in the United States, supplanted in the headlines by other world crises. Within the region itself, however, the conflicts were no less acute. Border tensions between Nicaragua and Honduras escalated in tandem with a rising tide of exile forays into Nicaragua from Honduran sanctuaries. At the same time, Honduran troops intervened in the Salvadoran civil war more directly and openly than ever before. These developments, along with a gradually deepening war in Guatemala, threatened to engulf the entire region in armed conflict—potentially a conflict in which neither right nor left paid much heed to international boundaries.

The danger of a regionalized war also carried with it the seeds of potential confrontation between the superpowers. Nicaragua's close and growing friendship with Cuba, particularly their military cooperation, raised the possibility that Cuba might come directly to Nicaragua's aid in the event of a war between Nicaragua and Honduras. Throughout early 1982 the Reagan administration warned that Nicaragua was intent upon acquiring MiG fighter aircraft, probably from Cuba. Some officials advocated, within administration councils, that such a development should be met by the United States with air strikes against Nicaraguan airfields.[55] Washington also seemed prepared to take military action to prevent the deployment of Cuban troops to Nicaragua. As this would require some sort of blockade of Cuba, it would violate the U.S.-Soviet agreement that ended the Cuban missile crisis of 1962 and would thereby provoke a confrontation between the United States and the USSR.

Conclusion

For the Reagan administration, the Nicaraguan revolution and the Sandinistas' subsequent friendship with Cuba raised anew the specter of Soviet subversion in the Western Hemisphere. With almost all Third World conflicts viewed through the prism of East-West rivalry, Washington became convinced that Soviet proxies in Havana, acting through Cuban puppets in Managua, were intent upon spreading revolution throughout Central America. Nicaragua's friendship with Cuba was thus seen as prima facie evidence that the Nicaraguans endangered vital U.S. interests.

This apocalyptic vision was reinforced by the fact that both Cuba and Nicaragua did, indeed, support the Salvadoran guerrillas politically and to some extent materially. It was strengthened by the fact of Nicaragua's military buildup, undertaken with Cuban assistance and Soviet-bloc arms. The possibility that the Nicaraguans were arming themselves out of fear that the United States would attack them was not seen as credible in Washington. Nor were Nicaragua's denials that it was involved in arming the Salvadoran left.

Ironically, Washington's deep fear of "another Cuba" in Latin America made normal relations between the United States and Nicaragua virtually impossible once the Sandinistas began to develop a close relationship with Cuba. As hostility between Nicaragua and the United States escalated, the Sandinistas were pushed even further into the arms of Cuba and the Soviet Union for lack of any alternative. Although the Cubans warned the Sandinistas of the costs and dangers of following the Cuban path of development, the hostility of Washington seemed destined to make Nicaragua another Cuba after all.

Notes

1. Richard Millett, *Guardians of the Dynasty* (Maryknoll, N.Y.: Orbis, 1977), p. 213.

2. Ibid., p. 225; U.S. Congress, House, *Foreign Assistance and Related Agencies Appropriations for 1978: Hearings, Part 3* (Washington, D.C.: Government Printing Office, 1977), p. 581.

3. Millett, *Dynasty,* p. 225; Hugh Thomas, *Cuba: The Pursuit of Freedom* (New York: Harper & Row, 1971), p. 1303.

4. Millett, *Dynasty,* p. 225.

5. Ibid., pp. 225–226; Thomas, *Cuba,* pp. 1355ff.; "Central American Fixer," *NACLA's Latin American and Empire Report,* Vol. 10, no. 2 (February 1976):13–16.

6. Ibid.

7. Millett, *Dynasty,* p. 258.

8. *Hearings, Part 3,* p. 582.

9. Millett, *Dynasty,* pp. 233, 242–243.

10. *Newsweek,* July 9, 1979.

11. *New York Times,* November 12, 1978; *Washington Post,* May 24, June 8, and July 24, 1979.

12. This was the gist of the widely disseminated CIA report of May 2, 1979, on Cuban aid to Central American guerrillas.

13. Edén Pastora ("Comandante Cero"), as quoted in *Newsweek,* July 9, 1979; *Washington Post,* July 24, 1979.

14. *Washington Post,* June 26, 1979.

15. This phrase is from the CIA report cited in note 12 above.

16. *Washington Post,* June 23, 1979.

17. *New York Times,* June 22, 1979; *International Bulletin,* July 2, 1979.
18. *New York Times,* June 23, 1979.
19. *Washington Post,* July 27, 1979.
20. *Granma Resumen Semanal* (Havana, Cuba), August 5, 1979.
21. *New York Times,* July 29, 1979.
22. *Washington Post,* August 11, 1979; Richard C. Leonard, "Para Nicaragua todo nuestro apoyo," *Bohemia* (Havana, Cuba), August 10, 1979, pp. 56–59.
23. *New York Times,* March 10, 1982.
24. *Washington Post,* September 1, 1979.
25. The best description of the literacy crusade is Valerie Miller's "The Nicaraguan Literacy Crusade," in Thomas W. Walker, ed., *Nicaragua in Revolution* (New York: Praeger Publishers, 1981), pp. 259–272.
26. *New York Times,* March 10, 1982.
27. Ibid.
28. *Washington Post,* April 7, 1982.
29. Ibid., November 9, 1980.
30. Ibid., April 16, 1982.
31. Margaret D. Wilde, "The Sandinistas and the Costeños," *Caribbean Review,* Vol. 10, no. 4 (Fall 1981):8–11.
32. William M. LeoGrande, "The United States and the Nicaraguan Revolution," in Walker, *Nicaragua,* pp. 63–78.
33. The policy of making El Salvador a "test case" was announced initially in not-for-attribution press briefings. See *New York Times* and *Washington Post,* February 14, 1981.
34. U.S. Department of State, *Communist Interference in El Salvador,* Special Report Number 80, February 23, 1981.
35. In April 1982 a senior Cuban official met with a group of U.S. foreign policy specialists in Cuba and admitted that Cuba had provided "material assistance" to the Salvadoran guerrillas prior to January 1981. Seweryn Bialer and Alfred Stepan, "Cuba, the U.S., and the Central American Mess," *New York Review of Books,* May 27, 1982, pp. 17–21.
36. *Washington Post,* February 24, 1982.
37. The phrase "going to the source" was first used by Haig in late February. See *Washington Post,* February 29, 1982.
38. U.S. strategy is described in length in the *Washington Post,* March 4, 1982.
39. The course of U.S.-Nicaraguan relations in 1981 is outlined in the *New York Times,* December 3, 1981.
40. Ibid., November 5, 1981.
41. Ibid.
42. *Newsweek,* March 22, 1982.
43. *New York Times,* November 23, 1981.
44. *Washington Post,* March 4, 1982.
45. Ibid.
46. Ibid.

47. See the remarks by U.N. Ambassador Jeane Kirkpatrick, CIA Director William Casey, and former Secretary of State Haig as reported in the *New York Times* and the *Washington Post,* February 21 and March 1, 2, and 5, 1982.

48. *Washington Post,* March 1, 1982.

49. The text of the aerial photography briefing is in the *New York Times,* March 10, 1982.

50. *Boston Globe,* March 11, 1982.

51. *New York Times,* March 10, 1982.

52. *Washington Post,* March 13, 1982.

53. Ibid., February 22, 1982.

54. Ibid., April 4 and May 1, 1982.

55. Ibid., March 4, 1982.

4
Cuba and Panama: Signaling One Way, Going Another

Steve C. Ropp

As with any other nation-state, Panama's foreign policy is shaped by a large number of factors. Geographical location dictates a concern with regional developments in Central America and the Caribbean and also a sensitivity to the foreign policy positions taken by the "Colossus of the North." National attributes such as size and social organization are important features both defining and limiting the capacity to act in the world arena. The nature of the political regime in power at any given time and the personal characteristics of leaders also contribute to the mix of policy choices. Finally, as foreign-policy making is an interactive process, it responds to the positions taken by other nations and the structure of the international system at any given time.[1]

Panama is a small country, approximately the size of West Virginia, with a population of 1.8 million. Its economy has historically been tied to activities in the transit area that surrounds the canal. Transit services were provided first to the Spanish Empire and later to business interests operating within the expanding capitalist world. This in turn means that the Panamanian economy has historically remained heavily dependent on major capitalist powers, particularly the United States. Any analysis of specific aspects of Panamanian foreign policy must begin with a realization of the major constraints that these broad structural features impose on national behavior.

After the overthrow of Fulgencio Batista in 1959, Fidel Castro led Cuba into the communist orbit, where it has since remained. When Castro came to power, Panamanian-Cuban relations were not good, but they improved rapidly after the 1968 coup that brought General

Omar Torrijos to power. From 1968 until Torrijos's death in a plane accident in 1981, there was a good deal of revolutionary symbolism in Panamanian politics. The political process was referred to as a "revolution," and Torrijos continued to wear battle fatigues, as did Castro. It was such similarities of style and sometimes substance that led conservatives like Senator Jesse Helms to conclude that General Torrijos was not just another cigar-chomping Latin American dictator. This dictator smoked fine Havanas with his name prominently displayed on the band.

At the same time, a number of observers have noted that the rhetoric of General Torrijos's "revolution" may have vastly exceeded the reality. An old Panamanian joke illustrates the point. Omar Torrijos was traveling in an automobile with Leonid Brezhnev and Richard Nixon. When the three leaders came to a fork in the road, Brezhnev recommended that they proceed to the left while Nixon suggested that they go to the right. Torrijos winked slyly and said, "Signal a left turn and then go right."

Panamanian Policies and Cuba: 1959–1981

Panama was one of the first nations to feel the impact of Fidel Castro's triumph when two small invasionary forces sent from Cuba landed on Panama's littoral. Backing for one expedition came from Roberto Arias, who argued that the existing government of Ernesto de la Guardia was led by "communists." Backing for the other expedition came from disparate Panamanian leftists and student elements who believed they had a green light from Fidel Castro. Castro asserted that he had nothing to do with the invasion and that the Arias clan was using Cuban revolution for its own ends. He further indicated that the Panamanian regime was not a dictatorship such as existed in Nicaragua.[2]

After the aborted invasions of May 1959, relations between the two countries rapidly deteriorated. The Cuban consul in Panama was accused of attempting to subvert the government through a propaganda campaign. Diplomatic relations were severed in December 1961, after Castro delivered a speech in which he referred to Panama as a "government of traitors and accomplices of the imperialist Yankees."[3] Throughout the early 1960s, the break between the two nations was complete. Panama asserted at the 1962 Organization of American States (OAS) conference at Punta del Este that it would leave the organization if Cuba was allowed to retain membership. The Panamanian government did not object when Cuban exiles were trained for the Bay of Pigs invasion at Fort Sherman in the Canal Zone. And in 1964, when the OAS adopted economic sanctions against Cuba, Panama was fully supportive of the measure.[4]

Panama broke relations with Cuba in 1961 and did not reestablish them until 1974. The renewal of relations came as the result of a number of complementary interests that had developed by the early 1970s. Panama for its part wished to negotiate with the United States for new canal treaties and sought to internationalize the issue in late 1971 as a way of supplementing lagging bilateral talks. The Panamanian strategy called for marshaling support from two types of international allies. First, the heads of democratically elected governments in the region, such as Carlos Andrés Pérez of Venezuela, Daniel Oduber of Costa Rica, and Alfonso López Michelson of Colombia lent an aura of respectability to the effort within U.S. policymaking circles. Second, Panama cultivated the backing of a broader range of Third World leaders, such as Fidel Castro, who would take up the cause in international forums like the United Nations. The first hint of reliance on these broad international support bases came in 1972 at a meeting of the United Nations Security Council in Ethiopia. Panama's ambassador, Aquilino Boyd, publicly drew parallels between African colonialism and the situation in the U.S.-controlled Canal Zone. When the Security Council met one year later in Panama, Cuban Foreign Minister Raúl Roa backed the Panamanian position on the need for new treaties.[5]

Cuba, on the other hand, was increasingly concerned with ending its diplomatic and economic isolation within the Western Hemisphere and was increasingly willing to deal with regional governments that were partially sympathetic to the revolution. In return for support on the canal treaty issue, Torrijos moved quickly in the direction of rapprochement. During the mid-1970s, Panama contributed more than rhetoric toward the mitigation of Cuban economic isolation. Although direct trade between the two countries was not substantial, Cuba used the Colón Free Zone to purchase merchandise that would probably not have been directly available. In 1975 Cuba obtained $7 million worth of insecticides, fungicides, and animal disinfectants through the zone. Business became so brisk that a branch office of the National Bank of Cuba was established in Panama to handle the transactions.[6]

By 1976, relations between the two governments had improved to such an extent that General Torrijos was invited to visit Cuba. There he received the José Martí National Order, the highest award given by the Cuban government. Castro not only praised Torrijos for encouraging removal of the U.S. blockade but also went on to suggest that Cuba and Panama were ineluctably tied by their common historical experience with U.S. imperialism:

> We are brothers in our history, filled with acts of aggression, aggression on the part of the imperialists. The imperialists did the same things in Panama as they did here. They have wanted to take over Cuba ever since the last century, and they have wanted to take over Panama ever since then too. They forced the Platt Amendment and a base on us, and they forced a treaty on Panama at about the same time, on us in 1902 and on Panama in 1903.[7]

General Torrijos seemed to share this perspective, saying upon departure:

> Flying over Cuba on the way back to my country to take up the struggle and daily intercourse with the people and to lead a nation that loves you [Castro] very much, I leave impressed with my trip because it gave me the opportunity to see for myself that a new Cuban man is in the making. . . . I'm proud of the fact that our two peoples are on the same revolutionary wavelength.[8]

Were Panama and Cuba operating on the same "revolutionary wavelength" during the Torrijos years? To answer this question, it is necessary to look at the origins of the military coup that brought General Torrijos to power. At one level, the coup reflected divisions within the commercial elite that had dominated Panamanian politics since the republic was established in 1903. These divisions allowed the National Guard, which had been growing in power and influence since the early 1950s, to assume a central role in politics. But at a second level, the coup also reflected the attempt of certain rural and urban "middle-class" groups to enter the political arena. Through reformist appeals to marginal lower-class elements in the interior and the transit zone, General Torrijos and his political allies sought to counterbalance the traditional power of the commercial elite allied with the United States.

Clearly, the new regime established under Torrijos was not revolutionary if this term is taken to mean a total reordering of the class structure. However, although the economic power base of the commercial elite was not seriously compromised, that elite no longer held political power. The government implemented a number of reform programs, such as the establishment of agricultural cooperatives and recognition of the rights of urban organized labor. Many of these reforms took on the structural and ideological trappings of the Cuban revolution. For example, an organization called the Dirección de Desarrollo de Comunidad (DIGEDECOM) was established. DIGEDECOM worked through *juntas comunales* and *juntas locales* in each of Panama's 505 subdistricts in mobilization activities similar to those found in Cuba.

Just as important as internal considerations is the extent to which Panama and Cuba operated on the same revolutionary wavelength with regard to their foreign policies. An example of the degree of convergence during the Torrijos years is the behavior of the two governments in relation to the overthrow of General Anastasio Somoza Debayle and his subsequent replacement by a Sandinista junta in July 1979. Two questions can be posed. What were the historical reasons for the hostility exhibited toward Somoza by both Omar Torrijos and Fidel Castro? To what extent did the motivations of these two leaders converge or diverge?

Playing the Nicaraguan Card

Certainly, there can be little doubt as to why Fidel Castro was hostile toward the Somoza regime and vice versa. When Castro came to power in 1959, he made no secret of his dislike for President Luis Somoza. The existence of a new revolutionary government in the Caribbean created considerable internal problems for the Somoza dynasty. Nicaragua's participation in preparations for the Bay of Pigs invasion was extensive, and both troop movements and air strikes were coordinated from Nicaraguan bases.[9] Luis Somoza made a special point of visiting Puerto Cabezas on the Nicaraguan coast to say good-bye to the departing brigade of Cuban exiles. As the ships left the dock, he called to the exiles, "Bring me a couple of hairs from Castro's beard."[10]

The increasing hostility of both Castro and Torrijos toward the Somoza regime during the 1970s was the product of perceptions that the Nicaraguan dictator was nurturing close relationships with a network of powerful groups in the United States that viewed both leaders as threats. The most important element in this network was the Nixon administration itself. Under the guise of implementing a tough policy on the international drug trade, Nixon and the White House "plumbers" apparently contemplated the assassination of Torrijos.[11] A key individual in these discussions was E. Howard Hunt, who served as a link between the "plumbers" and anti-Castro Cubans in Miami. Certain Cuban exiles viewed the Panamanian dictator as a particularly dangerous ally of Castro.

A second major group in this anti–Torrijos/Castro axis was Somoza's acquaintances in Congress. The central figure was Congressman John Murphy of the House Panama Canal Subcommittee. Murphy was a long-time friend of Somoza's and had supported him in his effort throughout the early 1960s and 1970s to contain radical tendencies in the Caribbean. These containment policies had been extended to include the Torrijos regime by the early 1970s.

Issues that brought Somoza and Torrijos into direct conflict included Somoza's apparent effort to convince U.S. financiers such as Howard Hughes and Daniel Ludwig to bankroll construction of a new sea-level canal through Nicaragua. After the extremely thorough U.S. government study of alternative routes for a new canal was released in 1970, there was little real hope that a Nicaraguan route would be selected.[12] However, the mere possibility of a Nicaraguan route was used by conservatives in Congress to argue against a new Panama Canal treaty. Until the treaties were ratified in 1978, conservatives maintained that the political safety of the Nicaraguan route stood in sharp contrast to U.S. political vulnerability in Panama while Torrijos remained in power. Congressman Murphy proved to be particularly adept at linking the treaty negotiations to the issue of alternative and presumably safer routes for a new canal. Thus, a network of anti-Castro Cuban exiles, U.S. businessmen with ties to the Nixon administration, and Somoza supporters in Congress worked to undermine the Torrijos regime. It is little wonder that Torrijos viewed Somoza with alarm and Castro (a potential ally in this regard) with favor.

There is considerable evidence to indicate that Cuban-Panamanian cooperation in supporting the Sandinista guerrillas was quite close. A CIA report that was leaked to the *Chicago Tribune* in September 1978 indicated that eight crates of arms had been flown from Cuba to Panama by the Panamanian Air Force. The following month, a similar shipment passed through Costa Rica on its way to the Sandinistas.[13] Cooperation between Panama and Cuba intensified in January 1979, when the two countries agreed that FSLN guerrillas who sought exile in Panama would be transported to Cuba for additional training before returning to Nicaragua.[14] Some of the arms captured at the border in March by the Nicaraguan National Guard allegedly came from Cuba by way of a Panamanian Firestone Rubber truck. Arms found hidden in the truck included Belgian FAL 7.62 rifles, which Nicaragua claimed had been sold only to Cuba. There were also reports in May that a Cuban Ilyushin 62 landed at a Panamanian military airport and 200 men disembarked.[15]

Panama had also been cooperating extensively with several other Latin American countries to the same end. In January 1979 Torrijos flew to Caracas, where he arranged for a joint military exercise with Venezuela. Under the terms of his agreement with Carlos Andrés Pérez, 1,000 Venezuelan soldiers were to conduct maneuvers in Panama. Clearly designed to pressure Somoza, the joint exercise was never held.[16]

Many of Panama's anti-Somoza activities were conducted independently of any other government. For example, Panama attempted in March to smuggle a number of .30 caliber M-1 carbines into Nicaragua. The carbines had been purchased by the Panamanian consul in Miami (a former military intelligence officer) from U.S. firearms manufacturers. The arms were then flown from Miami by commercial aircraft to the Panamanian Hunting and Fishing Club. The principal stockholder in the club was Colonel Manuel Antonio Noriega, head of military intelligence.[17]

Torrijos would have probably preferred to be more openly supportive of the Sandinistas but had to be concerned with a negative reaction from the United States. The new canal treaties had been ratified by this time, but equally crucial implementing legislation had not yet passed Congress. Somoza's allies in the House of Representatives still had the option to play on feelings that the House had not been given an adequate role in the ratification process and could therefore sabotage this legislation. Facing these facts, the U.S. executive branch felt that any overt Panamanian intervention in Nicaragua would have a disastrous effect on congressional action and warned Torrijos of this possibility.

Given these constraints on overt support for the Sandinistas, Torrijos formed a clandestine paramilitary unit called the Victoriano Lorenzo Brigade.[18] The brigade's leader was Hugo Spadafora, who had served in the Panamanian government as vice-minister of health. Spadafora was chosen because of his previous experience serving with the guerrilla forces of Amilcar Cabral as a volunteer medical doctor in Guinea-Bissau during the mid-1960s.

Spadafora sought to organize the brigade in such a way as to prevent a violent conservative reaction both in the United States and at home. On September 27, 1978, 320 Panamanians met at the Don Bosco Church in Panama City. There they expressed their revolutionary solidarity with the Sandinistas, commended their future guerrilla efforts to God, and said good-bye to their families. Immediately after the brigade was assembled, Spadafora left for Nicaragua with eight other Panamanians to contact Edén Pastora, who led the Sandinista guerrillas in the southern area along the Costa Rican border.

The remaining brigade members were transported by bus to Veraguas Province. From there, they moved to the island of Coiba (a government penal colony), where guerrilla training began. After three weeks of rigorous physical training, only 75 of the volunteers remained. An initial contingent of 65 was sent to Nicaragua after completion of training, and the brigade had expanded to some 200 men by the time of Somoza's overthrow in July 1979. There is a certain amount of evidence to suggest that "retired" members of the Panamanian National Guard accompanied the brigade to Nicaragua. They probably served in a training capacity and also handled the heavy weapons.

The ideology of members of the Victoriano Lorenzo Brigade is suggested by its name. Lorenzo was an Indian "general" and Liberal who was put to death by the Colombian garrison commander in 1902. The Torrijos government used Lorenzo as a symbol of both revolutionary nationalism and anti-aristocratic sentiment. The following account of discussions among brigade members while on Coiba may be indicative of the views that guided their action: "We talked about who Sandino was, about the significance of the Sandinista struggle. We talked about a united Latin America, the dream of Bolivar, and about the Panama Battalion commanded by Tomás Herrera. Also, we talked about social and economic differences in Latin America."[19]

There were, thus, a number of reasons why Panama gave support to the Sandinistas that had little to do with Cuban influence. Many Panamanians had a strong historical sense of the role General Augusto Sandino had played in the struggle against U.S. domination. It is said that, upon learning of a new victory by Sandino, some used to sing:

> Ya llegó Sandino
> Con su batallón
> Matando marines
> Sin compasión.[20]

The evidence suggests that the Panamanian government played a direct role in the formation of the Victoriano Lorenzo Brigade. Its leader was a former government official, and guerrilla training on the island of Coiba could not have taken place without the full support of the regime. In addition, the government gave wholehearted backing to the Panamanian Committee for Solidarity with Nicaragua. This committee probably had access to state funds for its activities in support of the Sandinistas.

It could be argued that Torrijos's "radical" foreign policy with regard to Nicaragua was premised partially on the belief that a substitute issue had to be found for the struggle to gain control over the Panama Canal Zone. In 1974, the economy had begun to experience serious problems that made it increasingly difficult for the state to subsidize the more progressive aspects of domestic policy. With growing public unrest and with groups on the left no longer appeased by the effort to recover the zone, playing the Nicaraguan card may have appeared to be an attractive option, particularly after the U.S. Senate voted on the treaties.

Support for the Sandinista cause certainly preceded signing of the new canal treaties. Yet it seems likely that government leaders felt that both the pre- and post-treaty domestic political situations required a foreign policy issue that could rally support of the nonofficial left. While the government controlled a stablc of house "communists," there was considerable dissatisfaction on the left that was difficult to contain. Strong government support for the Sandinistas would mute the voice of the nonofficial left in the internal debate over the new treaties and the economy.

Indeed, support for the Sandinistas was probably the only issue on which all segments of the Panamanian left agreed. Even the Communist party, which was much out of favor with other leftist elements because of its strict adherence to the government line, took a parallel position on this issue. Furthermore, Torrijos could brand his political enemies as dangerous *somocistas* during the delicate process that took place in the late 1970s of removing the National Guard from politics and replacing the military with a new "civilian" regime. The Panamanian government "discovered" a number of plots linking the supporters of opposition leader Arnulfo Arias to Somoza.[21] Given the ties between Somoza and the anti-Torrijos forces, the charges of conspiracy cannot be taken lightly.

In sum, there are a number of reasons for Panamanian participation in the overthrow of Somoza that had little to do with the Cuban connection. There was a strong pro-Sandino historical legacy in Panama and personal enmity between the two national leaders, particularly with regard to Somoza's efforts to undermine Torrijos on the canal issue. These factors, coupled with domestic political necessities, led the government to take a strong forward position in support of the Sandinistas.

With regard to policy toward post-Somoza Nicaragua, it is difficult to determine whether Panama under Torrijos played a "pro-Cuban" or "pro-U.S." role. Panama's ties since 1978 had been to the moderate Tercerista faction of the Sandinistas led by Edén Pastora. The most significant Panamanian role after the Sandinista victory was in the training of the police force. Many of the instructors at the new Augusto Sandino Training Center were members of Torrijos's National Guard. Panamanian instructors were present when the first class of 100 cadets graduated in September 1979.[22]

How do we interpret this military aid to the Sandinistas? Was Torrijos, as had been true so often in the past, "*jugando dos cartas al mismo tiempo*"? While appearing radical, Panamanian instructors were offering training in the use of U.S. weapons and relying on U.S. techniques. From such a perspective, it is important to note that

Panama opposed the effort made at the Nonaligned Movement conference in 1979 to eliminate the Central American Defense Council (CONDECA) and the Inter-American Reciprocal Defense Treaty (TIAR).[23]

Global Policies

Panama's global policies during the Torrijos years converged with Cuba's on certain issues but diverged on others. At the global level, the most obvious difference was the position Panama took with regard to the Nonaligned Movement. Speaking at the 1979 gathering of nonaligned nations in Havana, President Aristides Royo argued that the principles of the first meeting in Belgrade should be upheld and that movement members should be discouraged from aligning themselves with any great power.

> Let us then consider the Nonaligned Movement as a collective effort of the three Third World regions, with the cooperation of its European members, to solve their social and economic problems and coordinate their political action in order to establish an international relations system that will favor positive solutions to the challenges of today's world. From this point of view, my government believes that the nonaligned policy emphatically rejects the policy of blocs, military alliances and any system tending to divide the world in spheres of domination or influence.[24]

Panama did not open diplomatic relations with either the Soviet Union or the People's Republic of China. In Eastern Europe, Panama recognized Czechoslovakia, Hungary, Romania, Poland, and Albania but not East Germany and Bulgaria. There was, however, considerable movement toward establishing formal and informal relations with a wide range of groups in the Third World. President Royo met with Yasir Arafat while in Havana in 1979, although Panama did not go so far as to recognize the Palestine Liberation Organization.[25]

One of the major reasons for Panama's effort to improve relations with a variety of Third World countries was to encourage signing of the Protocol of Neutrality attached to the new canal treaties. The Panamanian government felt that if a large number of countries could be encouraged to sign, arbitrary and/or unilateral interpretation of the protocol by the United States would be less likely. Panama offered specific policy concessions to Third World countries in exchange for adherence to the protocol. For example, when Vietnamese Premier Pham Van Dong (whose government was the first to sign the protocol) visited Panama in 1979, President Royo announced that the People's

Republic of Kampuchea should be recognized as the legitimate government of Cambodia.[26]

Panama's aggressive attempt to play a larger global and regional role during the 1970s can be attributed primarily to the character and instincts of General Omar Torrijos. However, it should also be recognized that this activist thrust was partly the product of a new tendency on the part of Panamanians to see themselves as capable of playing an independent leadership role in the Third World. With ratification of the canal treaties in 1978, Panama felt that it had gained an important victory in its struggle with one of the world's superpowers. The status of international neutrality implicit in the new treaties led Panama to feel that it could stand apart from the two great world power blocs.[27]

Policy After Torrijos

Panamanian and Cuban foreign policies during the Torrijos years frequently converged in their anti-imperialist instincts and sometimes in their actions. However, it would be a mistake to view Torrijos's foreign policy as merely the reflection of some Cuban grand design. Differences in perspective appeared both at the global level and with regard to political developments within the Caribbean basin.

There are good reasons why the Panamanian government often signaled left and turned right or, more accurately, attempted to turn left and right at the same time. Panama in effect had two foreign policies. The one most compatible with that of Cuba reflected the "populist" nature of the Panamanian civil-military regime and the attempt after 1978 to institutionalize a civilian component of that regime. On the other hand, the Panamanian economy remained closely tied to the United States, through both the presence of the canal and rapidly expanding U.S. business interests. Of particular importance in this regard was growth in the number of U.S. banks that serviced the transactions of multinational corporations and governments throughout Latin America.

The leftist/populist foreign policy of the Torrijos regime was most clearly expressed through support for the Sandinistas and through attempts to establish relations with a large number of left-leaning Third World governments. The more conservative economic dimension was less visible but nonetheless quite real. Torrijos maintained good relations with the international business and banking community, relations that largely explain his success in negotiating with the U.S. government over new canal treaties.

Analysis of Panamanian foreign policy during the Torrijos years suggests that there are a number of "constants" that virtually dictate a continuation of the two tendencies mentioned above under any successor regime. Barring any radical change in the political system, Panama will continue to maintain close ties to the United States and the multinational corporations. At the same time, concern over the possibility of U.S. military intervention in the wake of ratification of the 1978 canal treaties suggests a continued effort by Panama to strengthen its ties with Third World countries.

Although the idea may be somewhat offensive to academic sensibilities, there does not appear to be any inherent incompatibility between these two long-term tendencies in Panamanian foreign policy. In fact, they can be viewed as mutually supportive, with the "leftist" tendency lending domestic support to the "rightist" tendency, designed to keep the national economy solvent. What is really at issue, then, is not the continuation of such a foreign policy but rather the "mix" within it. Conditions of global economic dislocation appear to have been partially responsible for reinforcing the "rightist" tendency during the latter Torrijos years, and this trend is likely to continue.

The mix during the post-Torrijos years will also be affected by changes in national leadership. It seems clear that the National Guard intends to retain the perquisites with regard to foreign-policy making that were established by Torrijos. This means that there will continue to be more concern than before 1968 for regional and geostrategic aspects of foreign policy.[28] Generational change within the Guard may play an important role in foreign-policy making because the lines between different generations are quite distinctly drawn. General Torrijos was part of a semiprofessional generation of military officers who came up through the ranks or were trained in Central American academies. By the late 1980s, this generation will have been partially replaced by a more professional generation of officers trained in the academies of the larger Latin American countries.

After Torrijos's death, the Partido Revolucionario Democratico (PRD) that he had established to institutionalize his political power remained intact. Within the National Guard, General Rubén Darío Paredes emerged as one of the two strongest figures and is a likely candidate for the presidency in the 1984 elections.[29] However, personalist parties such as the PRD are frequently short-lived. Moreover, it is not yet clear that Paredes has the skill and breadth within his political base to remain in power.

Panama's global and regional policies have not been radically altered in the wake of Torrijos's death. And Panama has continued to champion a variety of Third World causes within international forums such as the United Nations. For example, strong support was given to Argentina during the Falkland/Malvinas Islands conflict, reflecting Panama's long-standing concern with issues of decolonization. President Royo wrote Ronald Reagan requesting written assurance that U.S. military installations in the Canal Area would not be used to support British activities.[30] At the same time, Panama continued to support the global and regional positions of the United States in cases in which costs in terms of her Third World image were not exorbitant.

The basic duality in Panama's foreign policy will probably continue to be reflected in its effort to serve as a mediator in the struggle between the United States and its perceived adversaries within the Caribbean basin (primarily Cuba, Nicaragua, and the Salvadoran guerrillas). Future Panama-Cuba relations will depend as much on the regional policies Cuba chooses to pursue as on Panama's inclinations. Although the Panamanian regime has continued its drift to the right since Torrijos's death, lines of communication with Cuba have been kept open. There is evidence that it was through the good offices of the Panamanian government that Nicaraguan Sandinista leader Edén Pastora was allowed to leave Cuba after his self-imposed exile from Nicaragua in the spring of 1982.

The trajectories of Panamanian and Cuban foreign policies converged and diverged during the Torrijos years and will continue to do so depending on the nature of the specific issue involved, changes in regime orientation, and the inclinations of key leaders. Panama may continue to signal left and turn right with a mix of policy reflecting both "constants" such as the nature of a multinational-based economy and the need to maintain Third World support for the neutrality of the canal, as well as shifting issues such as current economic difficulties. However, Panama's position within the spectrum of world nations suggests that the country may also prove equally adept at signaling right and turning left. Such maneuvers will on certain occasions lead to Panamanian-Cuban policy convergences, on other occasions, to divergences. Nothing more than that can be seriously claimed.

Notes

1. Maurice A. East, Stephen A. Salmore, and Charles F. Hermann, eds., *Why Nations Act: Theoretical Perspectives for Comparative Foreign Policy Studies* (Beverly Hills, Calif.: Sage, 1978).

2. Walter LaFeber, *The Panama Canal: The Crisis in Historical Perspective* (New York: Oxford University Press, 1978), pp. 126–127. Also, Rómulo

Escobar Betancourt, *Torrijos: Colonía americana, No!* (Bogotá: Carlos Valencia Editores, 1981), pp. 216–217.

3. Sheldon B. Liss, *The Canal: Aspects of United States–Panamanian Relations* (Notre Dame, Ind., and London: University of Notre Dame Press, 1967), p. 105.

4. LaFeber, *Panama Canal,* pp. 133–134.

5. Steve C. Ropp, *Panamanian Politics: From Guarded Nation to National Guard* (New York: Praeger Publishers, 1982), pp. 103–104.

6. U.S. Central Intelligence Agency, *Communist Aid to Less Developed Countries of the Free World: 1977* (Washington, D.C.: Central Intelligence Agency, National Foreign Assessment Center, November 1978), p. 28; and Republic of Panama, Contraloría General de la República, *Estadística panameña: Anuario de comercio exterior, 1975* (Panama City, 1975), p. 746.

7. *Granma* (Havana), January 25, 1976.

8. Ibid.

9. Richard Millett, *Guardians of the Dynasty* (Maryknoll, N.Y.: Orbis, 1977), p. 225.

10. Haynes Johnson, *The Bay of Pigs* (New York: Dell, 1964), p. 85.

11. Much of the information used in this account is drawn from Jonathan Marshall, "The White House Death Squad," *Inquiry,* March 5, 1979.

12. The Nicaraguan canal would have cost $11 billion to construct as opposed to approximately $3 billion for either of the two Panamanian routes. In addition, Nicaragua is more susceptible to volcanic activity and earthquakes. U.S. Congress, Senate, Committee on Foreign Relations, *Panama Canal Treaties: Part 2,* 95th Congress, 1st Session (Washington, D.C., 1977).

13. *Congressional Record,* July 26, 1979.

14. Ibid.

15. Ibid.

16. *Crítica* (Panama), January 18, 1979.

17. *Congressional Record,* July 26, 1979.

18. Rafael E. Candenedo, "En suelo patrio se entrenaron para volarle la cabeza a Somoza," *Más Para Todos,* Vol. 3, no. 2 (December 27, 1978).

19. Ibid.

20. *Tarea,* no. 42 (April-August 1978):64. Another source of historical solidarity was the military support Panamanian Liberal Belisario Porras had received from Nicaragua in 1902 during the War of 1000 Days. See Hugo Spadafora, *Experiencias y pensamiento de un médico guerrillero* (Panamá: Centro de Impresión Educativa, 1979), p. 219.

21. See, for example, "Panameñistas buscan plata de Tacho Somoza," *Crítica,* January 24, 1979.

22. *Foreign Broadcast Information Service,* September 24, 1979.

23. Ibid., September 10, 1979.

24. *Matutino* (Panama), September 6, 1979.

25. *Foreign Broadcast Information Service,* September 7, 1979.

26. Ibid., September 17, 1979.

27. "Panamá: Misión de liderazgo en el Tercer Mundo," *La Estrella de Panamá,* January 21, 1979.

28. Ropp, *Panamanian Politics,* p. 125.

29. The other is Manuel Antonio Noriega, long-time head of military intelligence.

30. *Matutino,* May 26, 1982, pp. 1-A and 8-A.

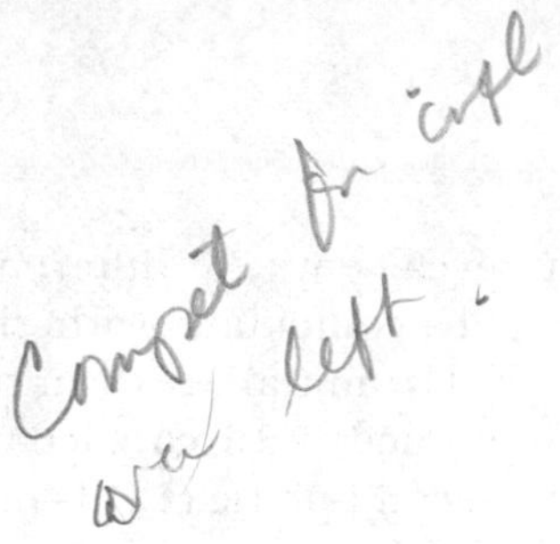

5
Cuba and Mexico: A Special Relationship?

Henry S. Gill

In the twenty-three years since the beginning of the Cuban revolution, Mexico has been the only Latin American country to maintain unbroken ties with the Castro government. This unique relationship survived four Mexican presidential administrations (Adolfo López Mateos, 1958–1964; Gustavo Díaz Ordaz, 1964–1970; Luís Echeverría, 1970–1976; and José López Portillo, 1976–1982). This is so despite obvious differences in the two countries' social circumstances, political systems, and ideological orientations and in the face of pressures, particularly from the United States, which has never ended its hostility to the revolutionary government in Havana.

Cuban-Mexican relations have not always encountered smooth sailing; nevertheless they appeared almost enthusiastic in the early 1980s. This development has taken place against the backdrop of instability and tension in Central America, where both countries have a clear stake in the outcome of political events. The positions they support in that crisis-ridden area place them at odds with U.S. policy; Washington has increasingly viewed political change in the Caribbean basin, which it regards as a global tension point, through ideological and strategic lenses. These circumstances give added significance to Cuban-Mexican friendship and constitute an essential dimension of an understanding of the bilateral relationship.

The Evolution of Bilateral Relations: 1959–1982.

The history of revolutionary Cuba's relations with Mexico can be conveniently divided into two main phases, each spanning two Mexican presidential terms, that reveal entirely different trends. In the first phase (1959–1970), roughly coinciding with the administrations of López Mateos and Díaz Ordaz, initial Mexican support for the Cuban revolution was gradually eroded until contact was finally reduced to the barest minimum. The second phase (1971–present) marks a period of progressively intensified relations, starting with Echeverría's term of office and reaching an unprecedented level of cooperation in the course of López Portillo's administration.

The Early Period (1959–1970)

The appearance of the Cuban question on the inter-American agenda at the seventh meeting of Organization of American States (OAS) foreign ministers in 1960 forced the Mexican government to formulate a position regarding the Cuban revolutionary regime. The fact that the Cuban revolutionaries had launched the anti-Batista offensive from their exile base in Mexico had heightened Mexican interest in the fortunes of Castro's movement. Mexico was sympathetic to Castro's triumph, for it was equated with Mexico's own revolutionary experience—especially because it was not imagined that circumstances would force Cuba to depart from the bourgeois-democratic revolutionary model.[1] Thus, the López Mateos government, drawing on traditional Mexican doctrine, invoked Cuba's right to self-determination in an effort to shield the Castro government from hemispheric rejection. The mild resolution adopted at the San José conference made no mention of Cuba while condemning extrahemispheric involvement in hemispheric affairs.

With the radicalization of the Cuban revolution and Castro's open adherence to Marxism-Leninism in December 1961, Mexico's position began to change. The economy was experiencing a most difficult period in 1961. U.S. investors also began to pressure Mexico and, together with Mexican business interests opposed to the pro-Cuban policy, aggravated a flight of capital already under way. This situation made the Mexican government far less enthusiastic and predictable in its support for Cuba. At the Seventh OAS Meeting of Consultation in 1962, Mexico advanced the thesis that Marxism-Leninism is incompatible with the inter-American system. Although this position was accepted by the conference and gave rise to Cuba's expulsion from the OAS, Mexico nevertheless voted against such a move, arguing its case on procedural grounds.[2] At the crucial Ninth Meeting of Consultation, held in Washington in 1964, Mexico opposed the decision to break all ties with Cuba and refused to comply with it—the only OAS member to do so.

But even as Mexico was unwilling to be a party to Cuba's condemnation at the multilateral level, the Mexican government took certain decisions that led to the cooling of bilateral relations. For instance, the number of Mexican airline flights to Havana was reduced, and two-way travel to Havana was obstructed. The Mexican government also eventually ceased making declarations supportive of or sympathetic to the Cuban revolution.[3] This incompatibility in Mexico's position is explained by the continuing need of that country to cater to two conflicting diplomatic imperatives—the need to support the principles of self-determination and nonintervention on the one hand and the need to avoid angering the United States on the other.

Adherence to the principles of self-determination and nonintervention (and, one might add, respect for sovereignty) is a policy deeply rooted in Mexico's historical experience. U.S. interventionism in the first half of the nineteenth century deprived Mexico of approximately 2 million square kilometers of territory, today embracing Texas, California, Arizona, New Mexico, Nevada, Utah, and parts of Colorado and Wyoming. During the Mexican revolution, the United States used diplomatic and military means to influence its outcome. Mexico also lived through the bitter experience of U.S. occupation of Veracruz in 1914 and Pershing's 1916–1917 military incursion into Mexican territory. The Lázaro Cárdenas administration faced severe pressure from Washington over its decision to nationalize the petroleum industry. Such experiences have forged a strong sense of Mexican nationalism, as well as a consistent diplomatic line in support of self-determination and nonintervention, and have dictated Mexico's effort to pursue an independent foreign policy. Thus Mexico's foreign policy has traditionally been far more radical than its domestic policies.

The other side of the coin, however, derives from Mexico's excessive dependence on the United States as its major trading partner, chief source of finance and investment, principal market for tourism, and exclusive outlet for migration. The asymmetry in this relationship makes Mexico vulnerable to U.S. pressures and therefore sensitive to Washington's foreign policy concerns. By contrast, Cuba's economic importance to Mexico has been negligible. Faced with these circumstances, the Mexican government was forced to accommodate political preferences to economic realities. By maintaining diplomatic relations with revolutionary Cuba at a fairly low level of interaction, López Mateos could cater to demands for an independent stance and yet avoid the impression of flaunting Mexican defiance before the U.S. government. Not surprisingly, Mexico justified its position on the ground that it was acting not in defense of Cuba or of its revolutionary government but rather in defense of the principle of nonintervention.

This compromise posture nevertheless appeared sufficient to merit the Cuban government's gratitude.

Despite the cooling of bilateral relations, the Cuban leadership continued to refer to Mexico in cordial and respectful terms.[4] In fact, Castro himself attended Mexican Embassy receptions in Havana on more than one occasion. It is clear that the relationship meant more to Cuba than to Mexico in the 1960s as the latter was Cuba's only formal link with Latin America in both a diplomatic and communications sense. For the Cubans, Mexico stood as a symbol of resistance to U.S. hemispheric domination and a precedent to be followed by other Latin American states in the breaching of the diplomatic sanctions policy. Cuba's hope, too, was that trade would be expanded, thereby breaching the trade sanctions as well. For these reasons, the Cuban leadership, no doubt also aware of the internal and external pressures faced by Mexico, continued to act with a high degree of restraint even as bilateral relations deteriorated after 1967. In December of that year, the relatively conservative Díaz Ordaz government angered the Cubans by a surprise decision to suspend the shipment to Cuba of 200 tons of bananas and half a million pineapple suckers. Serious misunderstandings also arose from Cuba's refusal to extradite air pirates after a spate of Mexican airline hijackings from the latter half of 1968, culminating in Mexico's August 1970 decision to cancel the airline agreement in force since 1954.

The payoff to Mexico for not severing bilateral ties with Havana became obvious when Cuba maintained its neutrality in the face of Mexico's internal troubles in 1968. A widespread student protest movement in early October was put down brutally by the army. This spawned a guerrilla campaign and acts of terrorism involving the left, which threatened Mexico's traditional stability. Significantly, there was not a single accusation fired from Mexico throughout this unsettled period about Cuban support for these groups, even though official relations were at a very low ebb.

Another advantage of the relationship to Mexico derives from the independent image that its refusal to break with Cuba secured for that country. This is not to say that Mexico was for the first time in its history adopting a position that was at variance with the policies of its northern neighbor on an important issue. Mexico had been the first country in the Western Hemisphere to recognize the Soviet revolutionary regime, with which it established diplomatic relations in 1924. Mexico also opposed U.S. intervention in Guatemala in 1954 and in the Dominican Republic in 1965. But its refusal to sever ties with Cuba, more so than any other case, established Mexico's independent image, an attribute that has given the country a certain prestige internationally. This prestige has in fact made it difficult for Mexico to reverse its policy.

The Second Period (1971–Present)

Cuban-Mexican relations gradually began to thaw only after Echeverría came to power at the end of 1970. He inherited an economy whose serious deficit and debt problems were aggravated by the U.S. government's decision earlier that year to impose a 10 percent surtax on imports. With 70 percent of its exports going to the U.S. market, the Mexican economy was severely hit by this policy, making manifest the consequences of excessive economic dependence.

The Echeverría government, appearing to view this setback within the broader context of the North-South *problematique,* shaped a response that changed the pattern of Mexico's traditionally quiet diplomacy, dominated by relations with the United States. Echeverría undertook a Third World diplomatic offensive aimed at forging a united stand to pressure developed countries into making more concessions to the developing world. The scale of this diplomatic activity can be gauged from the fact that, by the end of his six-year term, Echeverría had traveled to 36 nations (mainly in the Third World), held meetings with 64 heads of government, and exchanged diplomats with 67 additional countries, thereby raising to 129 the number of countries with which Mexico had relations.[5] This activity must also be viewed as consistent with an effort to demonstrate Mexico's political independence and in keeping with Echeverría's highly personal ambitions to be regarded as a Third World leader. Herein lay the significance of Mexico's rapprochement with Cuba, because, to be accepted as a Third World leader, Echeverría needed Castro's blessing. Moreover, a strengthening of ties with Cuba would be the clearest expression of Mexico's independent line. The new attitude to Cuba was demonstrated at both the multilateral and bilateral levels.

A necessary plank of Echeverría's Third World policy was the building of Latin American solidarity. Mexico sought to do this by arguing the case for ideological pluralism, the corollary of which was Cuba's reacceptance among Latin American states. This was one of the major reasons for the Mexican president's July 1974 Latin American tour, which took him to Costa Rica, Ecuador, Peru, Argentina, Brazil, Venezuela, and Jamaica.[6] The international political climate was conducive to such an effort. The process of international détente had already begun, and individual Latin American countries were unilaterally reopening relations with Havana, starting with Allende's Chile in 1970 and followed by the Peruvian military regime and subsequently by four Commonwealth Caribbean countries in 1972.

Thus, as the anti-Castro mood in Latin America gradually subsided, Mexico successfully proposed a review of OAS diplomatic and commercial sanctions against Cuba at the fifth OAS General Assembly in May 1975. This proposal eventually resulted in the "Freedom of Action Resolution," adopted in San José in mid-1975, giving OAS approval to individual Latin American countries to reopen ties with Havana. Another major milestone in Cuba's gradual reacceptance was the signing of the Charter of the Latin American Economic System (SELA) on October 17, 1975. This idea, first mentioned by the Mexican leader in a July 15, 1974, speech in Lima, won Latin American approval, with strong support from Venezuela. SELA represented a major step in the building of regional solidarity on the basis of ideological pluralism by including Cuba and excluding the United States.

At the bilateral level relations moved apace, starting with a new aviation agreement in July 1971. Greater impetus was injected into bilateral cooperation with the signing of a financial payments agreement, allowing for the reintroduction of a direct payments system in place of using Canada as an intermediary, which had been the practice for the previous twelve years. The signing of a hijacking agreement in June 1973 eliminated this source of bilateral conflict. In July Mexico's secretary of national patrimony visited Cuba (the highest Mexican dignitary to have done so since 1959) to try to resolve obstacles to bilateral trade, this being subject to sharp annual fluctuations and heavily weighted in Mexico's favor. High-level interchange continued with the visit to Havana of Foreign Minister Emilio Rabasa in March 1974, and in September a wide-ranging agreement on scientific and technical cooperation, and another on cultural and educational cooperation, were signed.

The climax of these bilateral developments was the visit of Echeverría himself to Cuba in August 1975, an event that served to consolidate the deepening friendship. On that occasion, Castro proclaimed SELA, due to be inaugurated the following month, as "one of the great historic ideas" of the Mexican president, and Echeverría eulogized Cuba as "the Latin American country with the most advanced level of social and economic development at the present time."[7] In the course of this visit agreements were signed in the areas of economic and technical cooperation in the sugar industry, cooperation in the field of tourism, exchange and cooperation between the Mexican Radio and Television Corporation and the Cuban Radio Broadcasting Institute, and the supply to Mexico of Cuban nickel.[8]

Cuban-Mexican friendship became further intensified and acquired new meaning during López Portillo's term of office. The discovery of vast petroleum deposits in Chiapas and Tabasco in 1975 enhanced Mexico's international position, giving Mexican diplomacy a solid resource base. Between 1970 and 1974 Mexico had been a net petroleum importer. When López Portillo took office in 1976, the state petroleum company (PEMEX) was producing a mere 327,285 barrels per day, of which 34,470 barrels were exported. Proven reserves stood at 6.3 billion barrels. By September 1981, output had reached 2.6 million barrels daily, about half of which was sold abroad, proven deposits exceeded 70 billion barrels, and potential reserves were estimated at 300 billion barrels. Between 1976 and 1980, petroleum export revenue rose from $311 million to $10.4 billion.[9] Mexican oil therefore provided López Portillo with options that his predecessors never had.

The key Mexican priority was the mending of relations with the Carter administration after the deterioration that had set in by the end of Echeverría's term. U.S. interest in increasing its purchases of Mexican oil in place of supplies from less secure sources at first facilitated this process. A mechanism for consultation was established to hold discussions on trade, energy, and migration issues. However, relations became troubled once more over natural gas pricing disagreements and Mexican insistence on limiting petroleum sales, which resulted in a November 1980 decision not to sell more than 50 percent of its petroleum exports to any one country—a policy aimed at reducing its dependence on a single market. This decision was taken at a time of serious disagreements with the United States over other issues, such as the sale of agricultural products, the cutting off or diminution of quotas for Mexican goods, the persecution of undocumented workers, and a tuna controversy resulting in an embargo against Mexican tuna production.[10]

Meanwhile, the slow moves towards rapprochement that had been started between Washington and Havana in the first half of the 1970s collapsed altogether in the wake of Cuban military involvement in Africa, starting in Angola. Whatever chances for rapprochement were left after Cuba became involved in the Ethiopian war undoubtedly evaporated with the Cuban refugee crisis in 1980, as U.S. propaganda exploited Cuba's internal difficulties and its worsening relations with such Latin American states as Colombia, Costa Rica, Ecuador, Peru, and Venezuela.

Cuban-Mexican friendship, however, continued to grow on the basis of increased cooperation and high-level exchanges as both countries faced increasing difficulties with Washington. In May 1979 Fidel Castro was given an effusive reception when he visited Mexico for the first time since his *Granma* departure. He congratulated López Portillo on the latter's earlier statement that it was not his intention to regard Mexican petroleum development as a function of U.S. petroleum needs, and in offering Cuba's support for Mexico's "just and patriotic struggle" Fidel spoke of "the imperishable friendship between our peoples."[11] In July of the following year the Mexican president announced his intention of visiting Havana at a time of heightening Cuban-U.S. tension over Cuban refugees who had entered the Peruvian embassy. In the course of this visit, which was interpreted as a gesture of support for Cuba, López Portillo stated that "Martí's causes are those of Cuba and Mexico together. We will in no way allow anything to be done to Cuba because we would feel that it is being done to ourselves."[12] The communiqué signed at the end of this visit expressed Mexico's support for Cuba's main demands against Washington: the lifting of the nineteen-year-old embargo, the closure of the U.S. naval base at Guantánamo, and the cessation of overflights by U.S. surveillance planes.[13]

The Reagan administration offered a different kind of challenge to Cuban-Mexican friendship. Reagan appeared eager to improve relations with Mexico. In regard to Cuba, however, he adopted a threatening stance in keeping with his administration's determination to launch a global offensive against international communism. Mexico's support for Cuba was obviously a disturbing factor, especially in the light of events taking place in Central America. Reagan seized the opportunity to place a wedge in the relationship by indicating his refusal to attend the important Cancún summit conference, which Mexico was organizing to tackle international economic problems, if the Cuban leader was present. This placed the Mexican government in an embarrassing position, as such a conference was unthinkable without the highest level of U.S. participation. Cuban-Mexican friendship survived this test, however, when the Cuban leader consented to absent himself after discussions with López Portillo on the Mexican island of Cozumel in August 1981.

Relations between Havana and Mexico in the early 1980s were more closely knit than ever owing to a number of ongoing joint activities. By the end of 1980 both countries had, for example, completed work on 294 specific projects in accordance with a scientific and technical cooperation agreement that came into force in 1974.[14] Collaboration on a further 142 projects was under way by early 1981.[15] The agreement embraces eleven sectors of cooperation: agriculture, industry, construction, fisheries, support services, transport, communications, basic research, labor, health, and urban administration. Important agreements have also been signed on the transfer of technology and on oil cooperation, including offshore prospecting and the boosting of Cuban refinery capacity. Bilateral trade has increased dramatically as compared with the 1975–1978 years, when totals varied between $23 million and $39 million, with a consistently huge Mexican surplus. By the end of 1981, huge Mexican sugar purchases had brought trade to a total figure of $215 million, with Mexican imports amounting to $190 million,[16] thus reversing the trade balance in Cuba's favor.

The Subregional Dimension

An examination of the respective roles played by Cuba and Mexico in Central America in particular, and the Caribbean basin more generally, will offer additional insights into the subtleties and nuances of this bilateral relationship. Whereas revolutionary Cuba has always supported movements for political and social change in Central America, Mexico appeared indifferent to the political destiny of that area until the late 1970s.[17] By that time popular opposition groups with strong links to the people, disciplined organizations, and substantial military capabilities emerged as forceful challengers to traditional oligarchical rule in those countries. This has led to the collapse of long-standing Somoza rule in Nicaragua with the triumph of the Sandinista National Liberation Front (FSLN) in July 1979, an ongoing civil war in El Salvador, and intense guerrilla campaigns in Guatemala and Honduras.

Cuba's support for political change in Central America has been motivated by ideological and security considerations. From the ideological standpoint, a permanent mutual hostility existed between the Castro government and the right-wing rulers in Central America. These regimes, which have been supported by the United States, have in the past also actively supported U.S. efforts to destroy the Cuban revolution. Thus, from a security standpoint, the Cubans regard the replacing of traditional ruling elites in Central America by more nationally oriented and socially responsive movements as enhancing Cuban national security, as the Castro government considers that any weakening of U.S. power serves to strengthen Cuban security.

Cuban policy has been aimed, therefore, at encouraging disparate leftist factions in Central America to forge united opposition fronts as a way of combating right-wing dictatorial rule from a position of unity and strength. In the case of the Nicaraguan struggle, for example, Cuban efforts were instrumental in the decision of three Sandinista groups to form a common front. A similar situation has come about in El Salvador. Cuba has also given political as well as propaganda support and provided training to a number of left-wing opposition groups elsewhere in Central America. The Sandinista victory represented, therefore, a major breakthrough for Havana's Central American objectives. A Cuban Communist party official, Jesús Montané, subsequently declared that "the revolutionary victories in Nicaragua and Grenada are the most important events in Latin America since 1959."[18]

Despite Mexico's strict adherence to a policy of nonintervention, in May 1979 López Portillo broke off relations with Somoza's Nicaragua. This decision, it may be noted, was taken on the day after Fidel Castro's visit to Yucatán, where both leaders recognized the Sandinista insurgents as the legitimate representatives of the Nicaraguan people. The only precedent for Mexico's action in the recent past had been Echeverría's decision to break with Pinochet on human rights grounds, the *raison d'être* of the so-called Echeverría corollary to the nonintervention policy. Mexico then openly supported the FSLN in much the same way as did Venezuela, Panama, and Costa Rica. With Somoza's overthrow, Mexico undertook a program of assistance by committing material and financial resources, human resources, and technical assistance. It is estimated that about 400 Mexican technical experts have been assisting the Nicaraguan government in areas varying from agronomy to medicine to petroleum engineering.[19] High-level delegations have been frequently exchanged, and López Portillo became the first holder of the Orden General Augusto César Sandino, Nicaragua's highest honor, in February 1982.

Mexico's new willingness to take a political position is perhaps best illustrated by the signing in September 1981 of the Franco-Mexican declaration, in which both countries recognized the Salvadoran insurgents as "a representative political force," thereby giving official opposition status to the broadly based Democratic Revolutionary Front (FDR), whose military wing, the Farabundo Martí National Liberation Front (FMLN), has been engaging government forces. This position, which was condemned as "interventionist" by nine Latin American governments, angered Washington, whose aim has been to encourage a center-democratic solution through the electoral process without the participation of insurgency groups. Mexico was one of three Latin American countries that opposed the idea of an electoral solution when the Organization of American States debated the issue. The López Portillo government has supported the idea of a negotiated settlement in the belief that to disregard insurgency forces is unrealistic and that proper elections would not be feasible in the context of widespread violence in El Salvador.

Such positions appear to have placed Mexican policy regarding these two crucial arenas close to Cuba's position, which supports revolutionary solutions, and at odds with the Reagan administration, whose concern is to prevent other Cubas and to avert the domino effect of communist takeovers in the region. Mexico's policy, however, has been framed by concerns different from those of either Cuba or the United States.

It is a fact that Mexico has traditionally pursued a left-leaning diplomacy. It is, however, simplistic to believe that policy in regard to Central America has been motivated merely by a desire to placate domestic leftist political circles. Far more important national considerations have inspired Mexican policy. The López Portillo government was deeply concerned with the growing instability to the south of Mexico. It viewed this instability as endemic to the condition of socioeconomic deprivation and political repression that characterized most of Central America. It therefore believed that the old dictatorial order in those countries must end. Continued instability and escalation of conflict in the subregion could affect the stability of the Mexican political system itself, place its economy and social services under tremendous stress with a continuing influx of refugees, and lead to a spillover of fighting onto Mexican territory. Relations with the dictatorial regimes in Central America have, moreover, been tense and difficult, even though Mexico had included these countries in programs of economic cooperation. For these reasons, the Mexican government considered that stability could be restored only through the emergence of popular governments willing to tackle the enormous social problems in those countries.

Moreover, López Portillo believed the Central American crisis had become a spiral, with El Salvador as its epicenter, threatening to engulf all the states of the area.[20] He was therefore anxious to avoid the internationalization of the crisis. Mexican officials were less disconcerted by fears of communist expansion than by the specter of U.S. intervention in the area, first in El Salvador and perhaps eventually in neighboring Guatemala, having dismissed any notion of Mexico's being the final domino in any communist grand plan. Instead Mexico regarded its northern neighbor as representing a greater threat to national security. Having experienced privation historically at the hands of the United States, Mexico viewed with alarm the possibility of U.S. troops being deployed on its southern border close to its oil fields. Such a reality would leave Mexico boxed in by U.S. forces to the north and to the south. The Mexican government vigorously campaigned for the internal processes in Nicaragua and El Salvador to be allowed to take their course without outside intervention. For that reason, the López Portillo government had earlier voted against a U.S. attempt to send an OAS peacekeeping force into the Nicaraguan civil war.

Mexico has also actively sought to reduce regional tension by launching a peace offensive aimed at settling a number of outstanding problems. This Mexican plan was first disclosed on February 21, 1982, by López Portillo in a speech in Managua. A key portion of it was an offer of Mexican mediation between both the United States and Nicaragua, and the United States and Cuba, and of Mexican help in ending the El Salvador war. Cuba and Nicaragua have been generally supportive of the idea, but few concrete achievements can be pinpointed to date.

Mexico had therefore been walking a diplomatic tightrope, calculating perhaps that its oil resources could continue to ensure good relations with Washington while it attempted to moderate U.S. interventionist impulses, continued to support the Nicaraguan government as well as antidictatorial movements, and maintained close relations with Havana. Mexico was indeed best placed to act as honest broker in the context of regional tension, as the only country that maintains good relations with all sides.

The value to Cuba of Mexico's stance, apart from the obvious benefits of bilateral cooperation, rests primarily on the extent to which Mexico's considerable international prestige gives diplomatic currency to the idea of nonintervention, thereby making it difficult for the United States to project more power subregionally, and thus providing Cuba itself, Nicaragua, and the Salvadoran insurgents with greater political breathing space. Mexico meanwhile has been gradually positioning itself diplomatically in such a way that it has become a major political force in Central America, and it is beginning to attain that status in the wider Caribbean, despite its traditional low political profile. It has been aided in this regard by the fact that Venezuela, more generally influential in the Caribbean basin in the past, had recently found its diplomatic clout diminished. This is due to the emergence of disagreements with the Sandinista government, embittered relations with Havana, and an inaccurate assessment of the political chess game in El Salvador. Herrera Campins's Christian Democratic government, in backing El Salvador's Duarte-led civilian-military junta, supported the U.S. proposal for an electoral solution. This resulted in the rise to power of the same ultra-right elements that Venezuela abhors.

The Reagan government, still placing high value on Mexican friendship, has not been opposed to an increased Mexican political role in Central America and the Caribbean despite clear differences in positions. It has appeared unwilling, however, to concede to Mexico the level of regional recognition and equality that Mexico has desired, particularly in the context of its oil wealth. Ironically, it is precisely Mexico's new leverage that brings to Cuban-Mexican relations a new dimension, which may be regarded from another angle as favoring U.S. subregional interests.

Cuba's commitment is clearly one of support for the emergence in Central America and the Caribbean of new regimes espousing revolutionary socialist causes. Cuba's attractiveness as a model in Latin America lies in the social advances made by the Castro-led revolution. Cuba's leverage in the subregion derives less from its financial position than from its human capital. Its willingness to deploy personnel promptly and on a massive scale for assistance, and the political and propaganda support that Havana can offer, are valuable assets. These have been mobilized in the cases of both Nicaragua and Grenada, whose regimes have welcomed much-needed assistance from Cuba, thereby providing Havana with a major avenue of political influence.

Mexico does not, on the other hand, maintain an unequivocal commitment to the revolutionary left. In view of its own social problems and the fundamental market orientation of its economy, Mexican authorities are naturally concerned about the possible effects on Mexico's internal situation of the rise of the revolutionary left in Central America. The Mexican government is not altogether frightened by the emergence of revolutionary regimes to the south, as Mexico itself has a revolutionary self-image. However, its preference would be for center-left pluralist solutions similar in orientation to the Mexican PRI (Institutional Revolutionary party) and for the maintenance of a mixed-economy model. These are telling differences in the subregional objectives of the two countries.

Mexico's oil power provides it with a powerful instrument for projecting influence in the Caribbean basin. It showed itself willing to develop programs of assistance in signing the San José oil agreement with Venezuela in August 1981, by which both countries pledged to supply eleven Caribbean countries with oil requirements amounting to 160,000 barrels a day. The agreement called for immediate payment of 70 percent of the current oil market price, with the remaining 30 percent retained as a five-year loan. Softer terms were to be provided if oil-recipient countries undertook to develop energy resources.[21] Mexico, with a relatively advanced industrial sector, is also in a position to provide technical personnel in a broad range of areas. The size of the Mexican market provides an added incentive for good relations with Mexico, and its relationship with the United States makes it a useful go-between.

The López Portillo government, aware of these assets, had used its political influence to moderate revolutionary radicalism in the subregion and attempted therefore to counterbalance the influence of Havana. In this respect Mexico's policy benefited U.S. interests, as the López Portillo government provided revolutionary leaders with an alternative to exclusive reliance on Cuban sponsorship. This was indeed a conscious policy. One Mexican diplomat was, for instance, reported as reasoning that "we want the Nicaraguans to feel that they can look to us if they need something. . . . they have no reason to believe that the Cubans are their only friends."[22] Mexico's growing ties with the Bishop regime in Grenada could also be looked at in this light. In signing a wide-ranging agreement on technical cooperation when the Grenadian leader visited Mexico in late 1981, López Portillo agreed to help in oil-storage-tank construction, road building, hotel design, house construction, the purchase of nutmegs and minor spices, and the determination of the existence and extent of petroleum resources in Grenada. The seriousness with which Mexico regarded this agreement is evidenced by a statement subsequently made to this writer by Ambassador Richard Jacobs, former Grenadian representative in Havana with accreditation to Mexico, that much of his time had been spent in Mexico City dealing with various aspects of the implementation of that agreement.

Mexico's relatively recent efforts to gain influence with the revolutionary left in the subregion and counterbalance the influence of Havana have brought an altogether new dimension to Cuban-Mexican relations. Both countries are now engaged in active, although tacit, competition for influence in the subregion. This competition does not appear, however, to have affected bilateral friendship. Mexico's goal of providing an alternative to exclusive Cuban sponsorship of the revolutionary movement in the Caribbean basin may also be said to serve the interests of both Mexico and Cuba. To the extent that Mexico's involvement can help diminish the East-West interpretation of the revolutionary struggle and place that struggle in its more proper focus as deriving from domestic determinants, it serves those interests.

Conclusions

Mexico's consistent position of resisting the move to isolate Cuba and of continuing bilateral ties was maintained at the expense of severe pressures from the United States, Mexico's main economic partner, and in the face of opposition from certain domestic sectors. Mexican support for Cuba hinged on its strict adherence to the principles of self-determination and nonintervention and not on any basis of economic advantage. The benefits to Mexico lay primarily in an image of greater independence that has facilitated Mexico's Third World diplomacy. Its support for Cuba also guaranteed Havana's nonintervention in Mexican internal affairs.

Cuba, on the other hand, needed to maintain continuing Mexican support in the 1960s to avoid complete isolation from Latin America. Mexico seemed in fact the only possible starting point of any future move to reverse this isolation, and indeed Mexican policy in the 1970s was instrumental in helping to diminish the climate of hostility to Cuba among Latin American states. For these reasons, the bilateral relationship has meant more to Cuba than to Mexico. The latter could survive quite easily without Cuba, but the difficulties of the Havana regime would have been aggravated in the absence of its Mexican connection.

The relationship has become somewhat less one-sided with the reopening of Cuban ties with other Latin American countries. The ending of isolation removed Cuba's dependence on exclusive Mexican diplomatic support and cooperation. The development of important functional cooperation between the two countries in a broad range of areas allowed the relationship to be placed on a more solid footing of reciprocal benefit. At the same time, however, special benefits have also accrued to Cuba. Mexico's increased status as an important oil producer has resulted in a more active Mexican policy in the Caribbean basin, particularly in Central America, where both countries pursue parallel policies. This benefits Cuba to the extent that Mexico is now better placed not merely to resist U.S. pressures aimed at forcing Mexico to abandon its relationship with Havana, but more important, Mexico is also better placed to check new U.S. interventionist tendencies against Cuba and the revolutionary left in Central America.

Although I have taken the view that Cuba and Mexico are now actively engaged in a competition for influence among the revolutionary left in the subregion, this remains a more muted aspect of the two countries' relations and is hardly likely to affect a friendshp whose foundations are deeply rooted. The change of administration in Mexico is not likely to bring about a shift in Cuban-Mexican friendship, if one is to judge by the public statements of President Miguel de la Madrid Hurtado. The Mexican leader can be expected, however, to develop more inward-looking policies in view of the major economic difficulties Mexico has been facing, despite the country's oil abundance.

Notes

1. Olga Pellicer de Brody, "Los grupos patronales y la política exterior mexicana: Las relaciones con la revolución cubana," *Foro Internacional,* Vol. 10, no. 1 (julio-septiembre 1969):7.

2. See Mario Ojeda Gómez, "Las relaciones de México con el régimen revolucionario cubano," *Foro Internacional,* Vol. 14, no. 4 (abril-junio 1979):481.

3. Ibid., p. 482.

4. Ibid., pp. 482–484.

5. George W. Grayson, "Mexican Foreign Policy," *Current History,* Vol. 72, no. 425 (March 1977):98.

6. See Ben F. Meyer, "Mexican President on Pro-Cuba Tour," *Jamaica Gleaner,* July 28, 1974.

7. See *El Día* (Mexico City), August 19, 1975.

8. "Texto íntegro del comunicado conjunto Cuba-México," *El Día,* August 22, 1975.

9. George W. Grayson, "Oil and Politics in Mexico," *Current History,* Vol. 80, no. 469 (November 1981):379.

10. See Susan Kaufman Purcell, "Mexico-U.S. Relations: Big Initiatives Can Cause Big Problems," *Foreign Affairs* (Winter 1981/82), pp. 382–384.

11. See Castro's speech at a luncheon given by López Portillo, *El Día,* May 18, 1979.

12. Reported in *El Día,* August 1, 1980.

13. Communiqué of August 3, 1980, in *El Día,* August 4, 1980.

14. "Mexican-Cuban Trade Relations," *Comercio Exterior,* English edition (November 1980), p. 432.

15. "Las relaciones entre México y Cuba, un ejemplo de cooperación sur-sur," *El Día,* March 3, 1981.

16. Foreign Broadcast Information Service, *Latin American Daily Report,* April 29, 1982, p. M.2.

17. Olga Pellicer, "Mexico's Position," *Foreign Policy* (Summer 1981), p. 89.

18. Jesús Montané, head of the General Department of Foreign Relations of the Central Committee of the Communist Party of Cuba, at the Berlin International Scientific Conference on the Struggle of the Working Class Against Imperialism, quoted in *Granma Weekly Review,* November 2, 1980, p. 12.

19. Bruce Bagley, "Mexico in the 1980's: A New Regional Power," *Current History,* Vol. 80, no. 469 (November 1981):354.

20. López Portillo, quoted in Jenny Pearce, *Under the Eagle: U.S. Intervention in Central America and the Caribbean* (London: Latin American Bureau, Research and Action Ltd., 1982), p. 150.

21. See *Keesing's Contemporary Archives, 1981,* p. 30978.

22. See Alan Riding, "Mexico busca liderato en Centroamérica y el Caribe," *El Caribe* (Dominican Republic), August 22, 1980.

6
Cuba and Venezuela:
Liberal and Conservative Possibilities

Demetrio Boersner

Venezuela's relationship with Cuba has been close throughout the history of the two countries. Their peoples have much in common in matters of race, culture, collective psychology, humor, and sympathies and antipathies. Cubans and Venezuelans have regularly migrated from one country to the other and have intervened in various ways in each other's respective political histories. From colonial times onward, Havana and Caracas have been aware of each other's existence and activities; their *rapport* has often been good, although at other times amazingly acrimonious.[1]

Brotherhood, Conflict, and Reconciliation (1958 to 1978)

Both the Venezuelan democratic revolution against the Pérez Jiménez dictatorship in 1958 and the Cuban overthrow of Fulgencio Batista in 1959 were conditioned by an international trend toward East-West détente and increasing North-South confrontation.

From 1947 until the death of Joseph Stalin in 1953, the world scene was dominated by the cold war. Bipolarity between Washington and Moscow was almost absolute, and "third-force" advocates were in a difficult position. Stalin's demise, thermonuclear stalemate, and the Korean truce ushered in a new period of a slow but steady "institutionalization" of the cold war between the two main powers. This new situation provided a basis for the Bandung Conference of 1955 and the proclamation of "positive neutralism," which would later be rebaptized "nonalignment."

From 1948 on, the United States had taken the cold war as an excuse to back right-wing military dictatorships and the repression of democratic, nationalist, and socially reformist movements in Latin America. Growing economic inequality between the industrialized North and underdeveloped South was ignored, particularly by the Eisenhower administration during the tenure of John Foster Dulles in the State Department. In the increasingly complex international scene of the late 1950s, with ever stronger nationalism in Asia and Africa and a somewhat decreasing U.S. emphasis on anticommunist vigilance, Latin American resentment of the alliance between Washington, transnational companies, and oligarchic despotisms exploded in the form of national democratic rebellions based on alliances of the middle sectors with both urban and rural workers and the poorest strata of society.[2]

The Venezuelan and Cuban democratic revolutions of 1958 and 1959 shared these essential characteristics, but they differed in a few important aspects. In Venezuela, the armed forces joined the rebellion; in Cuba, Batista's army fell apart, to be replaced by new revolutionary armed forces. Venezuela's dependence on the export of oil obliged it (this was admitted even by the communists in 1958) to adopt a more cautious attitude vis-à-vis the United States than was the case of a sugar exporter.[3] For Venezuela in 1958, the road taken was that of democratic reformism within the limits of tolerance of both the United States and its own armed forces. Meanwhile Cuba embarked on a more radical course in 1959.

Nevertheless, during 1959, understanding between Cuba and Venezuela was excellent. The two governments, founded on politically aroused and alert antidictatorial masses, cooperated closely in trying to promote the democratization of the rest of Latin America and the establishment of a more just and equitable economic and political relationship with the northern power.[4]

In 1960 the relationship began to deteriorate. "Reform" and "revolution" took separate courses and began to fight each other. Castro's support of leftist rebellion against Betancourt, and the Venezuelan leader's conviction that a moderate policy based on friendship with U.S. liberals and rejection of Marxism was necessary, brought about enmity and, by the end of 1961, the interruption of diplomatic relations. In the cold war ensuing within the Western Hemisphere between Soviet-backed Cuba and the U.S.-led "inter-American system," Venezuela was solidly on the anti-Cuban side, even though both Rómulo Betancourt and his successor Raúl Leoni (1963–1968) took care to differentiate themselves sharply from reactionary and authoritarian governments.[5]

Between 1959 and 1968, the consolidation and defense of political democracy was the primary concern of the Venezuelan government; its foreign policy was conceived largely to serve that aim. Betancourt and Leoni constantly sought to isolate and to neutralize right-wing dictatorships and at the same time to counter Cuban support of ultra-left guerrillas.

From 1968 onward, a new international framework developed. With the United States's recognition that the Vietnam war could not be won and that bipolarity was being replaced by a multipolar reality, and the Soviet realization that it needed more Western technology and could not fight NATO and China at the same time, the world moved toward détente and greater sociopolitical diversity. Cuba admitted that revolution could and should not be exported but that every Latin American nation had a right to its own road to progress.

In this new atmosphere, President Rafael Caldera's Christian Democratic (COPEI) government was able to initiate a new phase in Venezuelan foreign policy. Instead of the defense of democracy, the promotion of independent development was placed in the forefront. In the name of the search for "international social justice," Venezuela stressed Latin American, Caribbean, and Third World unity for the North-South dialogue and South-South cooperation.[6]

In regard to the Caribbean, the Caldera government began to think in more or less systematic geopolitical terms. The chain of islands surrounding the Venezuelan territory to the north and the east (Greater and Lesser Antilles) vitally affects the country's security and defense. In friendly hands, the islands are a first line of defense; if possessed by hostile forces, they could turn into a noose to strangle the Venezuelan Republic. The Caribbean is Venezuela's vital link with the outside world: 90 percent of its foreign trade passes through that sea. In addition, the 30 million inhabitants of the West Indies constitute an important potential market for Venezuelan export goods and investment. Last but not least, the new independent states of the Caribbean are valuable allies in international organizations and links between Latin America and the Afro-Asian world.

For these reasons, Caldera and his foreign minister, Arístides Calvani, systematically sought to implant the "Venezuelan presence" in the neighboring English-speaking Caribbean islands. In order to gain the fuller confidence of the Commonwealth Caribbean, they agreed to "freeze" for twelve years the border dispute with Guyana and to that end drafted and signed the Port-of-Spain Protocol of 1970.

In line with the worldwide growth of détente and the developing countries' stress on Third World unity, the Caldera government proclaimed the need for "ideological pluralism" and took the first steps to reestablish normal relations with Cuba. The Castro government responded positively, even eagerly, to the Venezuelan overtures.[7]

Carlos Andrés Pérez and the social democratic Acción Democrática (AD) party, elected in 1973 and in government from March 1974, continued and even intensified the Third World emphasis in Venezuelan foreign policy. The nationalization of the oil industry in Venezuela during the Pérez administration placed a new instrument of foreign policy in the government's hands. The supply of government oil under preferential conditions to Latin American and Caribbean countries served to strengthen Venezuelan prestige and influence. Together with Mexico's Luis Echeverría, Pérez founded the Latin American Economic System (SELA) to further the cause of the subcontinent's economic autonomy and independent development. He mobilized wide Latin American and Third World support for Panama in its struggle to regain control over the Panama Canal. He actively aided the Sandinista overthrow of Somoza.[8] He traveled widely, and became a highly respected figure in the Socialist International and the community of developing and nonaligned countries.

The dynamism of the Carlos Andrés Pérez government was obviously made possible by the energy crisis of 1974. All of a sudden, the countries in OPEC (Organization of Petroleum Exporting Countries) (Venezuela's former petroleum minister, Juan Pablo Pérez Alfonzo, is considered, together with Saudi Arabia's Sheikh Abdallah al-Tariki, the main founding father of OPEC) tripled their income and became powerful actors in the world economy. Venezuela therefore was able to show a Third World radicalism that would have been more difficult a few years earlier.[9]

Pérez officially resumed diplomatic, economic, and cultural relations with Cuba, and a new friendship soon developed between the two nations and their governments. Strict mutual nonintervention was the basis of the relationship: Pérez allowed no anti-Castro activities from Venezuela, and Cuba abstained from aiding the left-wing opposition in Venezuela. From there, Venezuela went on to supply petroleum to Cuba and to draw Castro into Caribbean consultations. Before that, Venezuela had been the main promoter of the decision to lift Organization of American States (OAS) sanctions against the Castro regime. In return for Cuban nonintervention in the West Indian islands close to the Venezuelan coast, the Venezuelan president accepted the role of intermediary between Havana and Washington. With full conviction, Carlos Andrés Pérez and his foreign minister, the talented and progressive Simón Alberto Consalvi, at the end of their term sought to convince the liberal sectors of the inter-American community of the possibility of gradually weaning Cuba away from the Soviet bloc. By means of the outstretched hand, they argued, the democracies of the Western Hemisphere should be able to induce Fidel Castro and his colleagues to assume an increasingly "Titoist" position.[10]

Pérez enjoyed the international game and was successful at it. On several occasions, he discreetly met other Caribbean and Central American heads of government on one or the other of the small Venezuelan islands located at some distance off the country's Caribbean coast to discuss problems of acute common interest, such as the recovery of the Panama Canal by Panama, the need to get rid of Somoza, and a promising scheme for a Venezuelan-Jamaican-Mexican joint aluminum venture.[11] He also talked with Guyana's Forbes Burnham about a possible frame of reference for the settlement of the territorial controversy between the two countries.[12] The bond of somewhat similar, left-nationalist or democratic socialist political philosophies helped make these encounters fruitful. Fidel Castro participated in some of them, and to some degree the groundwork was laid for a gradual rapprochement between social democratic and Marxist currents in the Caribbean area. President Pérez warmly defended that policy and rejected the right-wing accusation of being "soft on communism." He defended the viewpoint that democracy, to win the fight with communism in the long run, should compete with it positively, in terms of liberating oppressed people in the Third World from tyranny and exploitation. Even Cuba itself, he argued, might thus be drawn back gradually into the camp of social and political pluralism.[13]

A New Confrontation with Cuba (1979–1982)

Both the Venezuelan and the international scenes looked far less appealing in March 1979, when President Luis Herrera Campins was sworn in, than it had been five years earlier at the time of Carlos Andrés Pérez's rise to the presidency. The great boom in oil prices had occurred in 1974; 1979 was marked by worldwide "stagflation," turning into sharp recession. Venezuela had been subjected to an excessive spending spree by the Pérez government, and cuts in expenditures and austerity measures were urgently needed.

In addition to local and worldwide economic difficulties, there were the international political crises pointing to the end of détente and renewed East-West conflict. The NATO decision to install new missiles in Europe, the Soviet invasion of Afghanistan, and the election of Ronald Reagan in the United States had resulted in a climate of tension. The North-South dialogue and the Third World's chances of success in the search for a New International Economic Order were weakening. Conservative governments in the United States, Britain, and other Western countries were again viewing the problems of the developing world from a strictly East-West perspective.

All these factors were conducive to a switch toward more conservative politics in Venezuela. In order for the country to stay in tune with trends in the Western world as a whole, a few steps to the right were inevitable. Furthermore, Luis Herrera Campins had to "live down" a reputation of "radicalism" or "leftism" within the ranks of the Christian Democratic party. Caldera, who had a reputation as a conservative, had been able to turn leftward during his term of government without any fear of being suspected of being "red," whereas President Herrera needed to win the confidence of an initially distrustful business community.

Finally, there existed and still exists among leading politicians of both COPEI and AD the notion that in order to get elected and to govern successfully, a party needs a minimum degree of U.S. support. COPEI felt in 1978–1979 that the United States was still doubtful about Luis Herrera and COPEI's trustworthiness and that a decided effort should be made to gain the full confidence of the Washington and New York establishments.[14]

All these elements encouraged the rise and dominant influence of conservative persons and groups within the governing party. In the shaping of foreign policy particularly, traditional Christian Democratic tendencies toward extreme anti-Marxism and strong identification with the "Christian West" have played a decisive role since 1979.[15]

The Herrera government from the beginning viewed the Caribbean area as "leftist dominated" and threatened by a constant expansion of Cuban influence. In this it obviously concurred with the view of the Reagan administration. The democratic socialist government of Michael Manley in Jamaica, the leftward trends in Dominica and St. Lucia, the success of the Sandinistas in Nicaragua, and the revolution of the New Jewel Movement in Grenada, as well as Forbes Burnham's "Marxist-Leninist" gestures in Guyana, all looked alarming to the new Venezuelan government.

At the beginning of September 1979, the Sixth Summit of the Movement of Nonaligned Nations was held in Havana. Venezuela attended as an observer. (In order not to offend U.S. sensibilities, no Venezuelan administration has dared to assume full membership in the nonaligned group.) The Venezuelan delegation to the Havana meeting was headed by the foreign minister, Luis Alberto Zambrano Velasco, to demonstrate the importance the Caracas government assigned to the event (previously, the delegations to nonaligned meetings had always been at mere ambassadorial level).

At this stage, Venezuela still intended, apparently, to maintain the friendly relations with Cuba that had been established during the Carlos Andrés Pérez administration. The Cuban authorities were extremely cordial toward the Venezuelan foreign minister, who, furthermore, was approached in a friendly and expectant spirit by many representatives of the Afro-Asian world. The private talks that were held on that occasion, however, between the Venezuelan foreign minister and the Cuban authorities were somehow not satisfactory. On the Venezuelan side there was an ingredient of ideological anti-Marxism and suspicion of Havana's motives that tended to impede complete understanding. Furthermore, the representatives of the Venezuelan Christian Democratic administration were dismayed to see how immensely popular their heartily disliked predecessor, Carlos Andrés Pérez, was in Cuba and among the nonaligned countries.

Immediately after the Havana conference, a Venezuelan mission was sent to the smaller and least developed islands of the English-speaking East Caribbean (Grenada, St. Vincent, St. Lucia, Dominica, Antigua, and St. Kitts-Nevis). The purpose was to inform the islands' governments of Venezuela's intention not only to continue but to improve and expand existing cooperation programs. During the visit to Grenada, the Venezuelans were impressed by the intellectual patriotic dedication of the members of the People's Revolutionary Government, but at the same time slightly dismayed by the Cuban influence that was already obvious.

The more thoughtful Venezuelan advisers were, however, conscious of the fact that the Cuban penetration in Grenada was due mainly to Venezuelan negligence. Immediately after the overthrow of the Gairy dictatorship on March 13, 1979—the same day on which President Herrera was sworn in—the revolutionaries of Grenada had turned to Venezuela, asking it for urgent aid in both defense and development matters. The Cuban government was in full agreement with this, for on various occasions Havana and Caracas have discreetly agreed on mutual noninterference in areas located in close proximity to one or the other and in 1979 the Castro regime was highly interested in maintaining good relations with Venezuela. Caracas, however, failed to comply with Grenada's requests, and months passed without any positive response from Venezuela. This was due in part to the normal difficulties encountered by a new administration in getting organized and settling down to work, but to the Grenadians it seemed like indifference and rejection. In any case, after waiting for a suitable period and with previous notification to Venezuela, the Cubans finally felt free to move in and take over assistance to Grenada on a grand scale.

In spite of these facts, Venezuelan conservatives both within and outside COPEI thereafter came to regard the Cuban presence in Grenada as part of a global "expansion of Soviet-Cuban influence" in the Caribbean and a possible threat to Venezuelan security. They also cast a jaundiced eye at the presence of supposedly pro-Cuban elements in the governments of St. Lucia and Dominica and joined the United States in opposition to Michael Manley's democratic socialist (and friendly to Cuba) government in Jamaica.

During 1980, deterioration of Cuban-Venezuelan relations was swift and thorough. This was undoubtedly encouraged by the global atmosphere of growing East-West tension. The worsening of stagflation and the turn toward clear and painful economic recession tended to increase intransigence and aggressiveness on the part of public and private decision makers. "Détente is dead" was the new slogan, and a second cold war seemed in the making.

By April 1980, the U.S. State Department was moving toward the conclusion that Fidel Castro had given up his previous line of moderation and of peaceful coexistence with Latin American capitalist regimes and was again thinking of exporting revolution to other Caribbean countries. The Venezuelan government and ruling party were willing to accept the prevalent State Department opinion, which tended to confirm the ideological prejudices and predispositions of conservative Christian Democrats. Advisers supposedly close to the Opus Dei movement within the Catholic Church had long been fanning the inherent anti-Marxism of the Herrera administration's leaders, and the U.S. government's opinion conveniently supported their thesis.

In its first year, the Herrera administration had been hesitating in its foreign policy decisions between an "occidentalist" or anti-Marxist perception and an "autonomist" or Third World orientation advocated by advisers belonging to the liberal wing of COPEI or to those from the noncommunist left. By April 1980, a definite decision had been taken in favor of the former more conservative option. Thereafter, the left-of-center advisers were increasingly ignored and eventually removed.[16]

One of the results of that decision was the absolute commitment of COPEI and the Venezuelan government to support Duarte and the Salvadoran junta against their enemies and critics. This policy caused a profound division of opinion within Venezuela. For ten years—ever since Caldera had launched his independent foreign policy and proclaimed the objective of "international social justice," and continuing throughout the Pérez administration—there had been virtual national unanimity in regard to foreign policy. Now, as a result of the Salvadoran issue, the opposition (both the social democrats of

AD and the groups of the Marxist left) began radically to criticize and attack the government's line in international affairs. COPEI and conservatives generally responded bitterly and more and more tended to stress the supposed "Soviet-Cuban offensive" or "Soviet-Cuban encirclement" as an excuse for Venezuelan aid and comfort to the Salvadoran government.[17]

The more concrete issues that brought Cuban-Venezuelan relations to the brink of a total break concerned incidents at the Venezuelan Embassy in Havana and the handling by the Caracas authorities of the trial of a group of men accused of destroying a Cuban civil airplane, with the resultant death of its passengers and crew.

The incidents at and around the Venezuelan Embassy began in December 1979, when a group of people seeking asylum crashed the gate and nervous Cuban guards fired into the embassy grounds. It would have been easy to smooth over the incident, but Venezuela chose to protest loudly and angrily, calling for the removal of the guards from the embassy. Thereafter, incident followed incident: The Venezuelan and the Cuban press began to attack each other's government, and reprisals were taken against the Cuban Embassy in Caracas that caused the departure of that mission's chief.

But still more serious was the "affair of the Cuban airplane." In October 1976 a Cuban civil aircraft full of inoffensive people proceeding from Caracas was blown up by a powerful bomb shortly after taking off from Barbados. This singularly foul deed was apparently planned by anti-Castro terrorists. The first investigations showed the alleged culprits to be Venezuelans and Cubans resident in Venezuela; arrests were made in various cities, and the group of suspects was brought to trial before a Venezuelan military tribunal, as cases involving explosives and war weapons are subject to martial justice according to the laws of the republic.

The Carlos Andrés Pérez administration had clearly shown its belief in the guilt of the accused and had promised to seek their conviction and their exemplary punishment. The Cuban government had expressed its appreciation of that attitude and its confidence in Venezuelan military justice. Because of the much-criticized slowness of Venezuelan judicial procedure, the case dragged on into the Luis Herrera period. From the beginning of 1979, certain suspicions were heard of the new administration's alleged softness toward the accused. In 1980, while the quarrel over the embassy incidents was going on, the military prosecuting attorney, who until then had been trying to convict the accused, suddenly changed his position and announced his belief that the defendants' guilt could not possibly be proved. Immediately, Fidel Castro recalled the Cuban diplomatic personnel still residing in Caracas and stated that he would break off diplomatic relations officially and fully in case of a formal and definite acquittal.[18]

Even though the Luis Herrera government has occasionally used apparently radical rhetoric, basically its Western alignment alongside the anti-Soviet bloc has been clear. Nonetheless, relations with the United States were negatively affected by the Malvinas/Falklands crisis, in which the support of the Venezuelan government for that of Argentina was complete and very vocal. For the moment, in this particular contingency, Cuba and Venezuela found themselves on the same side under the same flag of anticolonialism. The Venezuelan government's decision to back Argentina strongly and to criticize the United States severely for "turning their back on the Rio Treaty" is due to a number of factors, not to any single one.

The next elections will be held in Venezuela at the end of 1983, and by January 1983, COPEI was running behind AD in all the public opinion polls. A strong stand for Latin American continental nationalism against Anglo-Saxon intervention or aggression is bound to improve the image of the government and the ruling party. Moreover, Venezuela, like Argentina, has a territorial claim against a Commonwealth country. Although President Herrera has stated clearly that Venezuela does not intend to use force against Guyana,[19] the Malvinas/Essequibo analogy obviously makes for mutual sympathy and support between Argentina and Venezuela. In connection with this issue, the Herrera administration wished, furthermore, to demonstrate to right-wing patriots that it is not "soft" when it comes to facing a United Kingdom that, for extreme Latin American conservatives, has never ceased to be "perfidious Albion." At the same time, the strong censure by President Herrera of the U.S. attitude improved his party's image in the eyes of the Marxist left, which saw the Malvinas/Falklands crisis as an opportunity to create anti-imperialist consciousness and praised the administration's position on this issue.

Last but not least, genuine identification with the Latin world as against Anglo-Saxon imperial arrogance is strong and massive in Venezuela, and the government is truly reflecting a national mood. Not only did Venezuela and Cuba suddenly find themselves objectively allied in favor of Argentina and against Anglo-Saxon intervention, but concrete steps were undertaken to improve relations. Discreet contacts were resumed between the two governments, including a visit to Havana by the Venezuelan minister of state.

Toward a Rapprochement?

A veritable rapprochement and a return to the friendliness between Cuba and Venezuela of the 1974–1979 period is perfectly possible.

But much will depend on the shifting overall trends of international, Venezuelan, and Cuban politics. If East-West tension prevails at its present level of intensity, or grows worse, improvement of Venezuelan-Cuban relations will be difficult. In cold war situations, the political pressures of the ruling centers tend to align the lesser members of their respective spheres of influence in rigid confrontation with those of the other bloc. A lessening of East-West tension, on the other hand, opens the way to "the flowering of a hundred flowers" within each imperial area. Some of its members feel encouraged to drift away from rigid conformity toward positions of increasing autonomy vis-à-vis the ruling center and to establish bonds of friendship and cooperation with countries of the other sphere. Thus Venezuela and Cuba were in a phase of reconciliation during the détente period of the 1970s.

Even without a return to détente, a mere change in the United States toward a more liberal type of administration could have a positive effect on Venezuelan-Cuban relations. Democratic victory in 1984—even with a relatively conservative Democratic president—would probably mean a more flexible U.S. policy toward leftist forces in Latin America, a greater understanding that being on the "left" does not automatically mean being communist or pro-Soviet. This might in turn lead to a rebirth of the (currently disregarded) thesis of a gradual reintegration of Cuba into the Latin American community, the eventual rise of a "Titoist" orientation in Cuban foreign policy, once the Havana regime no longer felt threatened by foreign hostility and encirclement. If such should be the future tendency in the United States, it would encourage a more positive and friendly attitude by Venezuela toward the Cuban government.

In Venezuela, the return to power of Acción Democrática in 1984 might (and most probably would) have a positive effect on relations with Cuba, independent of the external factors mentioned above. It is true that it was under an AD president, Rómulo Betancourt, that the sharpest conflict with the Castro regime originally arose and that relations began to improve under President Rafael Caldera of COPEI, but these events were due to unique circumstances: the rise and fall of the absurd and destructive "armed struggle" of the Venezuelan far left.

In contrast to COPEI, which has consistently included in all its ideological documents, since its pioneer days of 1939, the explicit aim of fighting Marxism as a hostile and negative social doctrine,[20] AD has never accepted the idea of an anti-Marxist ideological crusade. Its own method of sociopolitical analysis is based on historical materialism with a national-revolutionary and social democratic twist.[21] Betancourt and his relatively conservative sector within AD were vehemently opposed to the Soviet and Cuban governments because of these regimes' aggressive and repressive nature. But this rejection was never couched in fundamentally ideological terms. Carlos Andrés Pérez and his wing of AD established a distinction between the "democratic left" and the "Marxist left." AD, as a part of the democratic left, or social democracy, is to compete positively with the Marxist left to gain the confidence and leadership of Latin American liberation forces.[22]

In spite of the presence in the AD leadership of some vehemently anti-Cuban figures (the secretary-general, Manuel Peñalver, has blasted the Castro regime violently in some of his statements), all in all, there is no doubt that a future dialogue between Castro and AD would have a greater chance of success than one between the Cuban government and COPEI. An important factor in the possibility of a positive AD-Castro relationship would be constituted by the personal influence of Carlos Andrés Pérez: The former Venezuelan president enjoys his international reputation as a Third World progressive and does not intend to jeopardize that prestige (which also serves as an element of strength in internal party struggles).

A decisive improvement of the Caracas-Havana rapport would certainly require, in addition to better East-West relations and more open attitudes on the part of the United States and Venezuela, an evolution of the Cuban authorities' attitudes toward greater independence from the Soviet Union. Such an evolution seems possible. The Cuban Communist party is even less monolithic than other communist parties, in part because of its origin as a fusion of several heterogeneous groups, with national liberation and social democracy as their initial aims. It has been pointed out that even after 1968, when identification with the Soviet bloc became more pronounced, Cuba had on occasion shown a will of its own.[23] Reportedly, Castro himself has expressed privately his desire for greater Cuban autonomy vis-à-vis the USSR. Leading figures of the Venezuelan AD have the impression that a more relaxed international climate and the end of reprisals against Cuba would certainly lead to initiatives of a "Titoist" type on the part of the Havana regime.

Venezuela possesses a permanent, nonpolitical foreign service that constitutes the solid foundation of its diplomatic and consular corps. Top officials change with governing parties, but the middle and lower echelons remain stable. By and large, these personnel are capable. The reports and analyses they prepare tend to be neither excessively conservative nor daringly progressive. Often, Venezuelan permanent foreign service officials show far greater sense than their politically appointed chiefs. In regard to Cuba, they would advocate neither hostility nor guileless trust.

The business community of Venezuela is obviously inclined to be hostile toward the Cuban regime, as toward any leftist regime. One of its most sophisticated sectors is that of the export-minded nontraditional manufacturers, grouped together as the Asociación Venezolana de Exportadores (AVEX). To a large degree, AVEX members trade with the Caribbean or invest in the area, and they consider it the number one natural export market for Venezuela. They watch Caribbean political developments with a good deal of attention. In regard to Cuba, they tend to be wary but not hysterical. On the one hand, they support a policy of "containment" of eventual Cuban expansion; on the other hand, they would not be averse to doing business with socialist Cuba on a mutually beneficial basis.

The military constitutes a professional sector of increasing culture and sophistication. Officers usually attend university and study a second profession in addition to their specific military training. The idea that national defense and security involve a wide range of areas, including the economic, the social, and the cultural, is not foreign to them. Strategic thinking in terms of geography, history, sociology, economics, and psychology, in addition to armed might, is taught in military schools and advanced training courses. Ideologically, the military leaders are anti-Marxist, anti-Soviet, and anti-Castroite, but they are not necessarily antisocialist. The idea of some sort of moderate and "national" socialism, based on a mixed economy and intended to eliminate social injustice, appeals to many of them. The Malvinas/Falklands crisis has caused an estrangement between many of them and the United States. Undoubtedly, the concept of a neutral Latin America between East and West is gaining ground in the armed forces of Venezuela, as in those of the rest of the subcontinent. In regard to Cuba, this means a vigilant defensive attitude, but it by no means signifies a disposition to aid the United States in any crusade to stamp out leftist political ideas and practices in the Caribbean to preserve the status quo.

Thoughtful political, business, and military groups in Venezuela today agree on the enormous importance of the Caribbean for the country's security and development. Disagreement arises among Venezuelan foreign policy thinkers when the question of Cuba is raised as a part of the overall Caribbean perspective. Persons with a right-of-center orientation see Cuba as a permanent subversive menace that must be isolated as much as possible. Left-of-center analysts believe that a stable peaceful coexistence with Cuba is possible and should be sought on the basis of frank, explicit agreements regarding mutual noninterference in and respect for each other's vital interests. Those who share the more liberal view of Venezuelan-Cuban relations believe that the Caribbean basin has three main internal actors: Mexico, Cuba, and Venezuela. They understand that if the area is to become increasingly autonomous within the international system and liberated from outside domination and cold war involvement, a sensible and stable balance between these three "middle powers" will have to be established.

Notes

1. See Julio Portillo, *Venezuela-Cuba, relaciones diplomáticas 1902–1980* (Caracas: Editorial Arte, 1981), pp. 11–12.

2. See John J. Johnson, *Political Change in Latin America: The Emergence of the Middle Sectors* (Stanford, Calif.: Stanford University Press, 1958). Also, Boris Goldenberg, *The Cuban Revolution and Latin America* (New York: Praeger Publishers, 1966), pp. 17–96.

3. During 1958, the ideas expressed in *Tribuna Popular,* the Venezuelan Communist party newspaper, were remarkably moderate. The basic idea was this: The time is ripe for the class rule of the national bourgeoisie, not the proletariat.

4. This fellowship was particularly clear at the fifth consultation meeting of the foreign ministers of American states at Punta del Este in 1961.

5. The so-called Betancourt Doctrine (nonrecognition of de facto governments arising from coups d'etat against democratically elected regimes) was firmly applied by both Betancourt and Leoni, even when right-wing support seemed needed against leftist subversion.

6. See Rafael Caldera, *Habla el presidente* (Caracas: Ediciones de la Presidencia de la República, 1969–1974), 5 vols. Also, *Justicia social internacional y nacionalismo latinoamericano* (Madrid: Seminarios y Ediciones, 1973).

7. Demetrio Boersner, *Venezuela y el Caribe; presencia cambiante* (Caracas: Monte Avila, 1978), pp. 99–105.

8. For an informative and interesting account, accompanied by a possibly biased interpretation, see Eloy Lanza, *El subimperialismo venezolano* (Caracas: Fondo Editorial "Carlos Aponte," 1980), pp. 139–150.

9. It should be pointed out, however, that this radicalism was often more verbal than effective. Nevertheless, I think Lanza, *Subimperialismo,* exaggerates in considering Pérez's "*tercermundismo*" as a mere façade for "subimperialist" cooperation with the United States.

10. See Alfredo Peña, *Conversaciones con Carlos Andrés Pérez, Vol. 2* (Caracas: Ateneo, 1979), pp. 272–284, for Pérez's evaluation of Castro and the Cuban revolution.

11. On Carlos Andrés Pérez's top-level initiative, see Michael Manley, *Jamaica's Struggle in the Periphery* (London: Third World Media, Ltd., 1981), pp. 98, 114–115, and 182. See also John D. Martz, "Venezuelan Foreign

Policy Toward Latin America," in Robert D. Bond, ed., *Contemporary Venezuela and Its Role in International Affairs* (New York: Council on Foreign Relations, New York University Press, 1977), pp. 156–195.

12. Ibid.

13. Peña, *Conversaciones,* pp. 272–284.

14. Based on conversations of the author with COPEI leaders in February 1979.

15. The Advisory Commission on External Relations, a body of political and technical outside advisers to the Foreign Ministry, is one of the main channels of right-wing advice.

16. A decision to exclude independent advice was taken during the "reflection meeting" held by a small band of Christian Democratic leaders together with the foreign minister in the first week of March 1980.

17. The attacks on the government's foreign policy were particularly sharp in the *Diario de Caracas,* beginning in February 1980.

18. For two contradictory versions of the case, see Alicia Herrera, *Pusimos la bomba, ¿y qué?; confesiones de los terroristas a la periodista Alicia Herrera* (Valencia, Venezuela: Vadell Hermanos Editores, 1980); and the weekly magazine *Zeta,* December 13 and December 20, 1981.

19. Press conference on April 19, 1982; see *El Universal* and *El Nacional,* April 10, 1981.

20. See J. E. Rivera Oviedo, *Los socialcristianos en Venezuela: historia e ideología* (Caracas: Centauro, 1977); and Paciano Padrón, *COPEI, documentos fundamentales de 1946* (Caracas: Centauro, 1981).

21. This is particularly evident in the "Tésis Política del PDN" of 1939, reprinted in *Acción Democrática: doctrina y programa* (Caracas: AD, 1962), pp. 11–41.

22. Carlos Andrés Pérez has stated these ideas on many occasions, most recently on May 4, 1982. See *El Nacional,* May 5, 1982.

23. For example, see Pierre Schori, "Cuba in Africa," *Nueva Sociedad,* no. 36 (May-June 1978):94–104.

7

Cuba and the Latin American Communist Parties: Traditional Politics and Guerrilla Warfare

Luis E. Aguilar

Any effort to understand the arduous relations between Cuba's Revolutionary Government—Castro's government would be a better term—and the Latin American communist parties must take into account the evolution of three interrelated but not coincidental factors: (1) Castro's ideas as to which revolutionary tactic should be applied in Latin America, (2) the Soviet Union's international strategy and its influence on the continent and especially in Cuba, and (3) the communist parties' real capacity to act as a "revolutionary vanguard."

An Uneasy Rapprochement (1959–1962)

Castro's victory in January 1959, and the rapid transformation of his regime into a socialist dictatorship, caught the Latin American communist parties by surprise. Even the Cuban Communist party, which had moved from initial criticism of Castro as a petty bourgeois adventurer to limited support, had failed to foresee the imminence and magnitude of his triumph. As late as November 1958, barely one month before Batista's downfall, the Cuban Communist party had stated that "the tyranny has failed in its attempt to dominate the struggle of the masses, but *it would be wrong to suppose that this alone implies the imminent possibility of its overthrow.*" Echoing the international communist political strategy, the party asked for the formation of a "democratic coalition government."[1]

Latin American communist parties understood the tactical error of their Cuban comrades and the reasons for it. They themselves had failed to play a prominent role in the "revolutionary" episodes that shook the continent in the 1950s: the Bolivian revolution, the rise and fall of Jacobo Arbenz in Guatemala, the collapse of Colombia's and Venezuela's military dictatorships. Consequently, their propaganda focused on the only aspect of the Cuban experience that could enhance their importance: The victory and survival of the "glorious" Cuban revolution had been made possible because the military might of the Soviet Union had bridled U.S. imperialism. Cuba had demonstrated that the international balance of power had tilted in favor of the Soviet Union and its socialist allies.

But the impact of the Cuban revolution on Latin America proved to be too deep for this limited demonstration of solidarity. A revolutionary fever swept the continent. Emerging Marxist groups, lumped together under the denomination of the "new left," announced their readiness to follow the examples of Castro and Guevara and vented their contempt for the communist parties, which they called "a revolutionary rear guard." Sensitive to this criticism, young and impatient sectors inside the communist parties demanded radical action. By 1961 the majority of the communist parties had been forced to at least discuss the possibility of "armed struggle" in their respective countries. Two went beyond theoretical discussions. At the beginning of 1962, the Guatemalan Communist party (known as the Partido Guatemalteco del Trabajo, or PGT) sent groups to fight in an already developing guerrilla campaign. At the end of that year the Venezuelan Communist party, which had joined the Cuban-modeled Movement of the Revolutionary Left (MIR) to create the Forces of National Liberation (FLN), decided to launch an urban terrorist and rural guerrilla offensive against the democratic government of Rómulo Betancourt. Castro, who was violently anti-Betancourt, applauded the decision of the PGT and the Venezuelan Communist party, but sent material support only to the Venezuelan rebels, exalting the Venezuelan communists as the example to be followed by all true Latin American revolutionaries.

But even during this period of "rapprochement," the relations between Castro and the communist parties were tense. Marxism was not enough to overcome their basic differences. A man of action more than of ideas, Castro seemed never to have overcome his suspicion of, or contempt for, the revolutionary capacity of Latin American communists. His relations with the Cuban Communist party did nothing to allay that mistrust. In April 1961, on the eve of the ill-fated Bay of Pigs invasion, Castro proclaimed the socialist nature of the Cuban revolution. A few months after his spectacular victory over the invaders, he confessed his Marxist-Leninist convictions and announced the formation of a single party (Partido Unico de la Revolución Socialista) that would fuse the communists, the 26th of July movement, the Student Revolutionary Directorate, and other minor organizations. Encouraged by Castro's public conversion to Marxism, the communists used their experienced cadres to gain control of the new organization (eventually called ORI, Integrated Revolutionary Organizations). In March 1962 an alarmed Castro made a scathing denunciation of veteran communist leader Aníbal Escalante and other comrades, "ambitious sectarians" who had tried to turn ORI into an instrument for personal power. Selecting terms that could fit almost all Cuban communists, he called them arrogant "high school Marxists" who hid under the bed while true revolutionaries were fighting in the Sierra Maestra. Following this attack, Castro tightened his control over the new "socialist" regime, reduced the so-called "Old Guard" of the Communist party to a subordinate role, and flaunted his uncompromising revolutionary principles.[2]

On their side, neither the Soviet Union, by then defending the doctrine of "peaceful coexistence," nor the Latin American communist parties felt at ease with Castro's and Guevara's images of victorious guerrilla fighters, increasingly demanding revolutionary action. The Latin American communists, naturally, were in a weaker position. Numerically small, with limited experience of or capacity for violent tactics, guided by leaders who had loyally followed Moscow's instructions, the Latin American communist parties were jolted by a strategy that seemed to them unrealistic and full of dangers for their own future. The fate of their Cuban comrades, forced to march behind this new type of improvised "socialist" leader, was enough warning. Even before Castro transformed his call for guerrilla war into the essential issue of his policy, the communist parties were cautioning their members to study the peculiarities of the "Cuban model," avoiding a mechanical and precipitate application of its guerrilla tactics.

This latent discord between Castro and the Latin American communist parties burst open after the missile crisis of 1962. Feeling betrayed by the Soviet Union's decision to withdraw the missiles from Cuba without even consulting him, Castro felt free to follow his dream of becoming the leader of a new international revolutionary movement. There were no third alternatives, no peaceful roads to socialism, no compromises with imperialism. "The duty of a revolutionary is to make revolution." Those who hesitated were charlatans or traitors. Anticipating communist objections, Castro warned the parties, "Who will make the revolution? . . . the people, with or without the party."[3] A period of rural guerrilla warfare (1963–1968) and ideological confrontation followed.

Guerrillas Versus Communist Parties (1963–1968)

Coming in the wake of the increasingly bitter Sino-Soviet dispute, which had already split several Latin American communist parties, Castro's radical challenge intensified their internal crises and made them more vulnerable to the new left's attacks. The expanding popularity of the Cuban guerrilla formula was an obvious threat to the parties' existence. With their greatest strength located in the cities, considering themselves the only true vanguard of the proletarian revolution, the majority of the parties closed ranks against a tactic based on rural struggle and peasant support. Worse still, from Guevara to Régis Debray, whose book *Revolution in the Revolution?* became a sort of bible for the new left and anathema for the communists, the new theoreticians asserted that during the revolutionary struggle the guerrillas should have full control over political and military affairs. The communists viewed this as heresy that had to be quashed.

Castro's relations with the Soviet Union and his international prestige restrained the communists. They aimed their arguments at the "adventurous extremists of the left" who had misread the real lesson of the Cuban experience. In Latin America, the communists argued, objective conditions for revolution were not ripe. To hasten into action, believing small heroic groups alone could spark a revolution, was to disregard Marx's teachings, to disdain the masses, and to provoke military and imperialist reactions. Once again Lenin's famous text about extremism being the infantile disease of communism became a favorite topic in Latin American communist publications. The polemic was clouded by Marxist rhetoric and by the fact that Castro too was obliged to fight with oblique arguments. Unwilling to risk a direct attack on the Soviet Union, the Cuban leader and his spokesmen concentrated their criticism on certain "reactionary elements" in the communist parties. Only once, at the peak of the polemic, did both sides openly exchange insults.

Caught in the middle of this "fraternal" quarrel, Soviet leaders moved with extreme caution. Communist China had already made some inroads in the Latin American left, and now loyal communist parties were being confronted by the only Marxist government in the hemisphere. In February 1963 Brazilian communist leader Luis Carlos Prestes visited Havana and angered the Cubans by declaring that to promote armed struggle in his country (then under a democratic regime) was a disastrous mistake. Shortly after, Khrushchev invited Castro to Moscow and received him with full red-carpet treatment. Nevertheless, the joint communiqué published after the visit implied a victory for the Latin American communist parties. After the usual celebrations of Cuba's revolutionary achievements, Castro paid homage to the "generous economic aid" provided by the Soviet Union, promised Cuba's support for the "Leninist principle of peaceful coexistence," and agreed that "the unity of international Marxist-Leninist movements was essential for the anti-imperialist cause." Castro also promised that Cuba's communist party would continue "to struggle for the unity and fraternal solidarity of workers and communist parties" and agreed to hold a congress of Latin American communist parties in Havana in November 1964. The only paragraph making concessions to Castro's ideological position was a masterpiece of vagueness: "The question of the peaceful or nonpeaceful road toward socialism in one country or another, will be definitively decided by the struggling people and the degree of resistance of the exploiting classes to the socialist transformation of society."[4]

The continuous emergence of guerrilla groups in Latin America and Castro's commitment to their cause made this Moscow compromise nothing more than a truce. Soon an odd political scandal gave Castro another opportunity to turn the screws on the Cuban communists. In 1957 the Student Revolutionary Directorate had stormed Havana's Presidential Palace but failed to kill Batista. The few leaders who survived the attempt were killed in their hiding place by the police. They had been betrayed by one Marcos Rodríguez, a member of the Communist Youth, who nonetheless after the triumph of the revolution received a scholarship to study in Czechoslovakia. Suddenly, in 1964, a few months after Castro's return from Moscow, the strictly controlled Cuban press leaked information about Rodríguez's betrayal to the public. The uproar was followed by a sensational trial, in which the most prominent leaders of the Communist party were forced to explain publicly their participation in the sordid affair. Significantly, Castro testified as a witness—a witness who, with no one objecting, began his lengthy testimony by proclaiming that Rodríguez was guilty and that some comrades had not acted correctly. After the trial, the defendant was executed and some communist leaders, including Joaquín Ordoqui, vice-minister of the Armed Forces, were deposed and placed under house arrest. Only two members of the communist Old Guard survived the purge with some measure of power: Carlos Rafael Rodríguez and Blas Roca. As a political force, the prerevolutionary Communist party had ceased to exist.[5]

Under such inauspicious circumstances, the promised Congress of Latin American Communist Parties was held in Havana in September 1964. Even if the final communiqué condemned "factionalism inside the parties," nothing much was accomplished. The "fraternal" spirit was probably absent. The Soviet, Cuban, and Latin American communist press made few and brief comments on the event. After the meeting, Castro and the Latin American communist parties went back to their respective trenches. The truce had ended.

In December 1964 Che Guevara was sent to the General Assembly of the United Nations as the leader of the Cuban delegation. Before departing, he made a speech in Santiago de Cuba repeating the charge that Latin American communists were "dragging their feet in the revolutionary struggle." One month later, in January 1965, on the sixth anniversary of his triumph, Castro reiterated his commitment to the armed struggle and hinted at the possibility of Soviet reprisals. "Nothing will check our will," he declared; but, he added somberly, "the Cuban people should be ready to fight alone, to resist imperialism even if absolutely no aid whatsoever could reach Cuba from abroad." A short time afterward the disappearance of Che Guevara raised international speculation, Régis Debray published his arguments exalting guerrillas over communist parties, and preparation for a Tricontinental Conference began in Havana.

Castro based his strategy on the conviction that he could pull the Soviet Union to his side and overcome communist resistance by engulfing the parties in a continental revolutionary tide. By 1965, albeit with a touch of revolutionary intoxication, he appeared to be reaching his goal. A myriad of self-proclaimed Marxist groups had joined the armed struggle or announced their decision to do so. Reports of new guerrilla fronts, sometimes purportedly exaggerated by conservative or military sources, reached Havana from every corner of the continent. Even "progressive" Catholics seemed to be under the spell of what a skeptical Chilean communist called "a formula for instant revolutionary glory." "Christians for Socialism" groups multiplied, and the Colombian priest Camilo Torres solemnly declared that "for Christians, revolution is not only permissible, it is an obligation."[6] In January 1966 he joined the guerrillas. Significantly, he joined the ELN (Ejercito de Liberación Nacional), a minor pro-Castro guerrilla group. The Colombian Communist party criticized Camilo Torres's decision.

That month, at the peak of such high expectations, the so called Tricontinental Conference (the full name was First Conference of Solidarity of the People of Africa, Asia and Latin America) was held in Havana. With several Latin American communist parties excluded for their "revisionism" and a Soviet delegation concentrated on thwarting Chinese schemes, Castro and his host of new leftist radicals carried the occasion. After interminable discussions in and out of the sessions, the conference recognized the necessity of armed struggle in most of Latin America and promoted the organization of a regional permanent institution, OLAS (Organization for Latin American Solidarity), with permanent headquarters in Havana. The delegates left, never to meet again.

Castro was exultant. In his closing remarks he pointed out that "in spite of the short time available a document was drafted that is without doubt the most profound, the most far-reaching and the most radical of any that could have been drafted or decided on in a conference of this kind," promised "the Dominican people will not have to face the Yankee imperialists alone" (referring to the landing of U.S. troops in that republic in May 1965 to "prevent another Cuba"), and affirmed that conditions in the continent were ripe for armed revolution. He ended with a prophecy: "The struggle on this continent, in almost every country will take the most violent forms, and as we know this fact, the only correct course is to prepare for it."[7]

The prophecy was wrong, at least temporarily. Contrary to Castro's optimism, the guerrilla revolutionary tide was ebbing. The *guerrilleros* paid a heavy price for disregarding communist advice to study the peculiarities of the Cuban revolution. Of those peculiarities, one proved to be decisive. Batista's army, a corrupt, demoralized corps whose best officers disliked his dictatorship, was incapable of mounting a military offensive or even sustaining a good defense. Following Debray's teachings, Latin guerrillas assumed all Latin American armies to be in similar condition. They were dead wrong. Between the Tricontinental Conference and the first meeting of OLAS in Havana in August 1967, the situation in the continent changed drastically. The tide moved in favor of the communist parties' cautious tactics, not against them.

By the summer of 1966, the Peruvian guerrillas had been annihilated and Régis Debray captured in Bolivia. In Colombia, ex-priest Camilo Torres was killed in action and the independent "socialist" republics occupied by the army. Guatemalan Turcios Lima, a guerrilla leader hailed by Castro during the Tricontinental Conference, had perished and his group almost totally disbanded. Military regimes ruled in Bolivia, Brazil, Argentina, and Ecuador. And the Venezuelan Communist party had abandoned guerrilla operations.

The defection of the Venezuelan Communist party was a bitter blow for Castro. This was the party he had signaled as an example to follow, the one whose delegation appeared to be closest to the Cuban line during the Tricontinental Conference. At the first opportunity Castro reacted furiously. When the Venezuelan Central Committee suspended from command guerrilla leader Douglas Bravo and repudiated a terrorist action, Castro poured scorn and insults on the Venezuelan leadership, "cowards, traitors, opportunists," and sided with Bravo. Exasperated, Castro raised the polemic to the level of a decisive continental issue. "Communist parties must decide between the Venezuelan guerrilla fighters and the defeatists who want to surrender the entire guerrilla movement. This is the line of definition, and we are arriving at a time of decisions!" "Their attitude toward guerrilla struggle will define the communists in Latin America!" claimed *Granma*'s headline the following day.

To leave no doubt about the importance of the issue, Castro abandoned his caution and criticized the Soviet Union for dealing with oligarchic governments like Colombia, where a Soviet delegation was signing a commercial treaty "at the very moment that the entire leadership of the Communist party was arrested . . . and that same day Soviet Tass agency was assaulted, quite a spirit of reciprocity!"[8]

In August 1967, at the OLAS meeting, Castro made a new effort to turn the tide. The Venezuelan Communist party had not been invited and the Brazilian and Argentine parties had refused to attend, but those communist delegations in attendance did appear to be receptive, and there were enough representatives of the extreme left to create a favorable atmosphere. Once again Castro blasted the Venezuelans, criticized the Soviets, and called for a decisive revolutionary offensive. The conference agreed that guerrilla struggle should be considered the fundamental, but not the only, revolutionary way, and that *guerrilleros* ought to fight under the banner of Marxism-Leninism. To one friendly witness, Castro seemed perplexed by the results of the meeting, and by the attitude of the orthodox communists "who remained impassive and defiant amid a large crowd of frenetically cheering Castroites."[9] Perhaps those impassive communists knew that the guerrilla struggle was agonizing and that Castro's words were the last gasp of Cuba's inflexible guerrilla line. Two months after they adjourned, Che Guevara was killed by the Bolivian army.

Advantages and Limits of Reconciliation (1968–1979)

The death of Che Guevara after so many disasters was a devastating blow for Cuba's guerrilla theory. Castro accused the Bolivian communist leadership of cowardice and treason and reassured his followers that Guevara's sacrifice would galvanize Latin American youth into revolutionary action. Nineteen sixty-eight was named "the year of the heroic guerrilla fighter." But these were only brave attempts to stave off defeat. In October 1967, one month after Guevara's death, the Colombian, Venezuelan, and Ecuadorian communist parties issued a joint communiqué criticizing Castro for his attempts to interfere in the internal affairs of "fraternal" parties. With a remarkable lack of good taste, the Bolivian party dismissed the discussion of Guevara's failure, stating that "no one invited Guevara to Bolivia."[10]

A more formidable enemy then took an antiguerrilla stand. Castro's public criticism of the Soviet Union had not passed unnoticed in Moscow. His decline as a new revolutionary apostle, and the disastrous condition of Cuba's economy, convinced the Kremlin's leaders that it was time to check Castro's disturbing extremism by applying a weapon they had previously hesitated to use: economic pressure. On January 1, 1968, Castro informed Cubans that the Soviet Union "apparently" was not going to meet the increasing petroleum needs of the nation. Strict controls on the consumption of fuel had to be imposed. No outburst of revolutionary protest followed the announcement. Better than any of his listeners, Castro realized the precariousness of his position and the choking potential of the Soviets' grip.

Fearing that his opponents inside Cuba could be tempted to take advantage of his troubles, Castro, as usual, took the offensive. In February 1968 the Cuban government denounced the existence of a "micro-faction" inside the Communist party whose sinister plans coincided with those of the "pseudo-revolutionaries" and the Central Intelligence Agency (CIA), and that had had clandestine meetings with several Soviet and East German officials. The principal culprit was again Aníbal Escalante, who had been allowed to return to Cuba in 1964. Criticism of Castro as an erratic dictator who felt superior to Marx, Engels, and Lenin while pushing Cuba to economic disaster was one of the crimes of the micro-faction. Punishment of the conspirators crushed any potential opposition and stifled criticism in Cuba. But Moscow and the communist parties kept a stony silence.

In August 1968, one year after the first and last meeting of OLAS, Castro began his retreat toward conciliation with Moscow. In carefully selected words, he justified the Soviet invasion of Czechoslovakia. The speech stunned the new left and many of Castro's sympathizers, but it was warmly received in the Soviet Union. Castro's silences were as expressive of his new attitude as his words. In October 1968 Mexico was convulsed by a bloody repression of student demonstrations. Ironically, the students had begun their protest with a march in honor of the Cuban revolution. Their appeals for solidarity and the boycott of the Olympic Games in the capital received no answer from Havana. Two weeks after the so-called massacre of Tlateloco, Cuban athletes displayed their flag at the opening of the Olympic Games in Mexico City.

As his reconciliation with the Soviet Union gained momentum, Castro's relations with the Latin American communist parties, and with Latin America in general, steadily improved. In 1970 the Cuban leader applauded the Peruvian military government as revolutionary, treated the majority of Latin American governments with diplomatic respect, and traveled to Chile to help socialist President Salvador Allende in his efforts to calm Chilean radicals like the MIR (Movimiento de Izquierda Revolucionario), who accused Allende and the communists of betraying the "socialist revolution." On the centenary of Lenin's birth, Castro criticized the extremists of the new left with almost the same words that the Venezuelan Communist party had employed against him during the 1968 confrontation. "We all know that there are super-revolutionaries in theory, super-leftists, true super-men, capable of defeating imperialism in two seconds . . . with their tongues!"[11] Perhaps he was referring to Douglas Bravo, by then accusing Castro of betraying the guerrillas and selling out to the Soviet Union.

In 1975 Havana played host to the Conference of Communist Parties of Latin America and the Caribbean. Some of the delegates were the same ones who in 1967 had impassively listened to Castroites cheering. On this occasion no extremist organization, no members of the new left had been invited. Discussions and conclusions were impeccably pro-Soviet. At the end of the year, in his report to the Cuban Communist party, Castro summarized his new position: "We have an unlimited faith in Lenin's fatherland. . . . Only the existence of the mighty Soviet Union is capable of deterring imperialist aggression. . . . Those who criticize the Soviet Union are like dogs barking at the moon."[12]

For many analysts of the Cuban revolution, and certainly for the new left, Castro's ideological reversal and his constant praise of the Soviet Union represented a total surrender of his revolutionary principles. This statement requires qualification. Castro did surrender his independent line of action, his ambition to be the leader of a new revolutionary movement, but not his aggressiveness or his will to play an important role in international affairs. The polemic and crisis of the 1960s had taught him that he could not oppose the Soviet Union—and he acted accordingly. But by becoming an ally of the Soviet Union, by accepting its tutelage and control, he was able to solidify his power and intervene more effectively in the world arena. His willingness to send Cuban troops to Angola demonstrated simultaneously his reliability and his usefulness. And as a trusted Soviet partner in Latin America he became capable of influencing Moscow's policies in the hemisphere—which represented a sort of victory over the Latin American communist parties. They had opposed him as a Marxist heretic; now the heretic had become a representative and adviser of the Marxist Rome. His efforts to maintain close relations with Third World countries, and, principally, with noncommunist radical groups in Latin America are a measure of his capacity for independence and for influencing Moscow's strategy in Latin America.

Castro's relations with Latin American communist parties have remained correct if not "fraternal," but it is doubtful that he had changed his opinion about their revolutionary capacities or possibilities. Events in Latin America had certainly not enhanced the revolutionary prestige of the communists. By 1976 a military coup had ended Chile's socialist experiment, the Tupamaros had been crushed in Uruguay, and the Peruvian "revolution" was slowing down under a new, more conservative military government.

For the Soviet Union, Cuba, the only example of a Latin American revolutionary "socialist" model, became increasingly important. With full Soviet support, Castro multiplied schools for revolutionaries in the island, expanded anti-imperialist propaganda, and established contacts with all type of radical movements in the hemisphere, especially in the Caribbean and Central America, where Castro has concentrated his efforts since the early 1970s.

In this area, Cuba's role has been invaluable to the Soviet Union and the communist cause. Precisely because he tried to leave a door open for unorthodox Marxists, radicals, and populists, refusing to limit his relations to the communist parties, Castro could play the role of ideological guide and unifier for many of those movements. His influence and his material aid were probably determining factors in the formation of a revolutionary common front to fight Somoza's dictatorship in Nicaragua. The victory of the Sandinista Front for National Liberation in Nicaragua in July 1979 demonstrated the soundness of Castro's policies.

A New Revolutionary Offensive? (1980–?)

As has occurred in the rest of Latin America, in Nicaragua the Communist party failed to be the vanguard of the revolution. The initiative fell into the hands of a diversity of radical groups, mostly of middle-class extraction, who rallied around the memory of anti-Yankee guerrilla fighter Augusto César Sandino and began fighting the dictatorship of Anastasio Somoza Debayle. As early as 1968, more than a decade before Somoza's fall, an alert Nicaraguan communist expressed his concern about his party's passivity: "For whereas in words we did not accept that anybody could do so much as dispute our vanguard role, in practice we calmly relinquished it to other forces, even including the parties of the bourgeoisie."[13] The party did not or could not listen.

Contacts between Castro and the Sandinistas began in the early 1960s, but it was not until the middle 1970s that the rural and urban campaign against Somoza gained momentum. Cuba remained a source of material and moral support in the struggle. Immediately after their victory in July 1979, Sandinista leaders visited Havana and expressed their warm solidarity with Cuba. Since then, Cuban influence has grown in Nicaragua, guiding the new government along a cautious but steady Marxist course. Naturally, Nicaragua's revolution sent a violent tremor through Central America. The emergence of guerrilla movements in El Salvador, Guatemala, and Honduras opened a new revolutionary horizon in a region regarded by communists as "the backyard of U.S. imperialism."

This situation, so full of possibilities for Moscow and Havana, has stimulated a communist reevaluation of the guerrilla warfare theory. In the summer of 1980, one of the contributors to the Soviet magazine *Latinskaya Amerika* enthusiastically stated: "The Nicaraguan experience demolished the previous simplistic interpretation of guerrilla actions, confirmed the justice of many of Che Guevara's strategic principles and crystallized his idea of creating a powerful popular guerrilla movement."[14] Almost simultaneously, several Latin American communist leaders proclaimed "armed struggle" as the only way to reach socialism in Latin America. Curiously, Castro, perhaps relishing the irony of this communist reversal, has been less eager than his Soviet and Latin American comrades to open a discussion on a subject that provoked so many polemics and divisions in the past. Significantly, on the 15th anniversary of Che Guevara's death, neither Fidel Castro nor Raúl Castro made any speech. The principle speaker was Major Ramiro Valdéz, who paid a rather subdued homage to the memory of Guevara.

It is worth noticing, though, that Latin American communist parties' endorsement of guerrilla warfare is, like Moscow's, neither emphatic nor unanimous. Parties with remote possibilities for immediate action appear more inclined to bellicose statements than those already involved in armed struggle. Thus, whereas the Chilean Luis Corvalan and the Uruguayan Rodney Arismendy had called for armed struggle in their respective nations, in Central America, where the bloody strife has mobilized some radical and non-pro-Soviet Marxist groups, communist parties usually defend the use of "all methods, political, legal and clandestine" to fight imperialism, insisting on the need for unity of all revolutionary forces.[15]

As in the past, the communist parties' notion of their essential role as revolutionary vanguard is one of the obstacles to achieving that dreamed-of "unity" of revolutionary forces. In Guatemala, for example, the communist PGT's insistence on a dominant position has undermined the efforts of the so-called Unión Nacional Revolucionaria Guatemalteca, which includes several revolutionary groups and a dissident sector of the PGT. In January 1982 the Unión Nacional issued a "fraternal" call to the PGT "to begin discussions toward joining the revolutionary unity."[16] To this date (October 1982), that call has not been officially answered.

One factor that could explain present communist support for guerrilla campaigns, the favorite tactic of the new left, is precisely the new left's decline. Today's guerrilla fighters are usually better equipped, better trained, and certainly less ideologically diversified than those of the 1960s. Few of them have criticized the communist parties, none has proclaimed that a new revolutionary vanguard is replacing the old. Even the Chilean MIR, one of the most virulent critics of the communists in the past, today has adopted a conciliatory attitude toward Moscow and the Latin American communist parties.[17] Under these conditions it is much safer for the communists to encourage this new and more controllable guerrilla offensive. Some Soviet writers might try to rehabilitate Guevara's methods, but certainly not "Guevarism" as a doctrine—at least not as it was interpreted in the 1960s by the fiery prophets of the new left. The praise of Moscow and the communist parties for Che Guevara symbolize their control over the forces he had once thought would rise against them. It marks a defeat, not a posthumous victory, for the Argentine leader.

"There is a new revolutionary wave sweeping Latin America," announced Castro not long ago. The words have a familiar echo. But there can be no doubt about what kind of revolution he was referring to. "Today there is only one superior way to be a revolutionary: to be a communist. This is so because the communist embodies the idea of independence, the idea of freedom, the idea of justice. . . . That is what we want to be: communists. That is what we want to go on being: communists. That is our vanguard, a vanguard of communists."[18] That declaration, a far cry from Castro's independent radicalism at the Tricontinental, can be safely endorsed by all the communist parties of Latin America.

Notes

1. "Mensaje del Partido Socialista Popular Cubano al Partido Comunista Chileno," *XI Congreso Nacional* (Santiago de Chile: Publicaciones del Partido Comunista, 1959), p. 29.

2. The full text of both anti-Escalante speeches is in Fidel Castro, *El partido marxista-leninista* (Buenos Aires: Edición Rosa Blindada, 1965).

3. Régis Debray popularized that expression years later, but Castro used similar terms even before the Declaration of Havana (1962), in which it was stated: "This struggle will be carried out by the masses; by the people." See Castro, *El partido marxista-leninista,* p. 322.

4. "Declaración conjunta sovietica-cubana," *Cuba Socialista,* June 1963, pp. 14, 15–17. For an excellent background to the meeting, see D. Bruce Jackson, *Castro, the Kremlin and Communism in Latin America* (Baltimore: Johns Hopkins University Press, 1965), pp. 19–22.

5. Castro's testimony is in Fidel Castro and Janette Habel, *Proceso al sectarismo* (Buenos Aires: Jorge Alvarez, 1965), pp. 73–213. A good study on the trial and its consequences is Maurice Halperin, *The Taming of Fidel Castro* (Berkeley: University of California Press, 1981), pp. 22–70.

6. Camilo Torres, "Message to Christians," in Enrique López Oliva, *El camilismo en la américa latina* (Havana: Casa de las Américas, 1970). The booklet offers other texts of pro-Camilo groups in Latin America.

7. Of the available sources, I have used the English version published in Canada by the Cuban Embassy, *The Tricontinental Conference* (Ottawa: Embassy of Cuba, 1966), pp. 17–19.

8. This quotation and those in the preceding paragraph are taken from Fidel Castro, *Critica a la dirección del partido comunista venezolano* (Montevideo: Nativa Libros, 1967), pp. 9, 11–12. For the Venezuelan Communist party (PCV) answer, accusing Castro of pretending to be a "super-revolutionary," a "sort of revolutionary pope," see Luis E. Aguilar, *Marxism in Latin America* (Philadelphia: Temple University Press, 1978), pp. 391–395.

9. K. S. Karol, *Guerrillas in Power* (New York: Hill & Wang, 1970), pp. 381–383.

10. Quoted in *El diario del Che* (Mexico: Siglo XXI, 1973), p. 282. According to Che's diary, Castro sent him a message stating that the Bolivian delegation at OLAS "*ha sido una mierda.*" See ibid., p. 213. On September 8, in a rare expression of anger, Guevara noted: "A newspaper in Budapest criticizes Che Guevara, a pathetic and seemingly irresponsible figure, and hails the Marxist attitude of the Chilean Communist Party. . . . How I would like to reach power, if only to unmask all kind of cowards and lackeys and to rub in their snouts their swine remarks!"

11. *Proyección internacional de la revolución cubana* (Havana: Instituto del Libro, n.d.), p. 146.

12. Fidel Castro, *Informe central al primer congreso del PPC* (Havana: Ediciones Rocinante, n.d.), p. 48.

13. Luis Sánchez, "Nicaraguan Communists in Vanguard of the Liberation Movement," *World Marxist Review,* Vol. 11, no. 2 (February 1968):34–35.

14. Quoted in Robert Leiken's forthcoming book, *Soviet Strategy in Latin America.* I consulted the galley proofs by courtesy of the author.

15. See, for example, the declarations of Antonio Castro (leader of the Guatemalan Communist party) and Guillermo Torriello in *World Marxist Review,* Vol. 24, no. 3 (March 1981):66–68.

16. "Declaration of Revolutionary Unity," *Latin American Perspectives,* Vol. 9, no. 3 (Summer 1982):115–122; especially p. 120.

17. See the declarations in Havana of Martín Pascual Allende, secretary-general of the Chilean MIR, after returning from Moscow, quoted in *Foreign Broadcast Information Service,* September 16, 1982, p. Q4.

18. *Granma,* December 19, 1980.

8
Cuba and Africa:
Military and Technical Assistance

Aaron Segal

Fidel Castro noted in June 1982 that 120,000 Cubans had seen military service outside the country and that a further 30,000 doctors, teachers, engineers, and technicians had also worked abroad.[1] These are extraordinary figures, accounted for by eighteen African states, Grenada, Nicaragua, Iraq, Vietnam, and several national liberation movements.

How does one explain the fact that a poor Caribbean island nation, with a population of 10 million, has sent abroad since 1965 2 to 3 percent of its total labor force, 15 to 20 percent of its armed forces, and a substantial portion of its technical personnel?[2] The economic costs have been substantial, although oil-exporting countries such as Iraq are asked to pay in foreign exchange for Cuban assistance. It is important to underline the extraordinary magnitude of the Cuban aid to Africa.

A host of countries have provided African states with military assistance: Belgium, France, East Germany, Israel, Soviet Union, United States, Great Britain, North Korea, and China. These programs have been mostly military training and advice by small missions. Belgium, with U.S. air support, intervened with troops in Zaire in 1964; Britain sent troops to Kenya, Uganda, and Tanzania at the request of their governments in 1964 to quell army mutinies; Belgian, Moroccan, and French forces helped Zaire quell local rebellions in 1977 and 1978; and France has sent "firefighting" forces to defend allied African governments on several occasions. However, France is the only non-African power to maintain permanent forces on African soil, and these in recent years have dropped below 10,000 and have been spread over several countries (e.g., Djibouti, Senegal, Chad until 1979). Thus the 35,000 Cuban troops permanently based since 1978 in Angola and Ethiopia are several times greater than the total of all non-African troops in Africa. Indeed, the Cuban forces separately in Angola and Ethiopia are larger and better equipped than all but a handful of African armies.[3]

Similarly, the approximately 8,000 Cuban technical personnel who have been in Africa at any one time since 1976 are dispersed over eighteen countries, although about 90 percent are in Angola and Ethiopia.[4] This level of effort is second among non-African states only to that of France, which sends thousands of young men to Africa as "*coopérants*" for teaching and other purposes in lieu of military service. Although Cuba provides no financial aid or loans, its technical assistance program in Africa is comparable to that of the United States or the United Kingdom and greater than that of far more prosperous donor states such as Sweden and Spain.

The official Cuban view is that their involvement is prompted solely by "internationalism," that is, "international proletarian solidarity with the peoples of the Third World."[5] Where these peoples have defeated colonialism, imperialism, and feudalism (as in Angola and Ethiopia) there is a special commitment by Cuba, as a socialist nation that has followed a similar path, to provide assistance. The official view denies any material or economic interests, affirms that involvement is the result of Cuban responses to African requests, denies any pressure from the Soviet Union, and considers as objectives the defeat of the counterrevolutionary forces led by the United States and racist South Africa. Thus, in the official view Cuban motives and objectives are wholly ideological, have no trace of self-interest, and are an internationalist response to African legitimate needs.

At times Cuban officials have suggested additional supplementary motives. These include Cuba's "Afro-Latin" character and social structure, with black and brown Cuban soldiers returning to Angola to fight for the liberation of a country from which their ancestors might have been taken to Cuba as slaves.[6] Similarly, Africa is sometimes seen as an appropriate battlefield for the revolutionary spirit of Cuba, especially after the setbacks to Latin American guerrilla forces in the 1960s and the killing of Che Guevara in Bolivia in 1967. Finally, officials occasionally mention Cuba's surplus of young, trained technicians and its ability to earn foreign exchange by exporting their services to certain countries. As one official remarked, "We are educating people not only for Cuba, for also the entire Third World. If a country can't pay our internationalist aid is free, but if a country can pay, why shouldn't it?"[7] No figures are available, but Algeria,

Angola, and Libya are the only African recipients of Cuban aid likely to be providing any reimbursement.

Outside observers have cited other objectives and motives to explain Cuba's presence in Africa. One view is that Cuban involvement substantially enhances its bargaining power and leverage vis-à-vis the Soviet Union, its patron.[8] According to this view Soviet generosity since 1974, in its postponement of the repayment of Soviet loans to Cuba, in the terms of trade for Cuban sugar in exchange for Soviet petroleum, and in provision of weapons, transport, and other direct costs, has reflected the new role of Cuba and its value to the USSR. We shall consider later Soviet motives and objectives, but it is clear that Cuba has proved itself useful to the Soviets through at least some of its African involvements.

A related view maintains that Cuban motives also include bringing pressure to bear on the United States. Certainly there have been pronounced U.S. reactions to the Cuban presence in Angola and Ethiopia and a much greater recognition of Cuba's nuisance value in Washington. Whether or not this involvement has fundamentally altered the chances for a Cuban-U.S. détente is not yet clear. Cuba has added a condition and raised the price of any détente through its African presence. A U.S. government anxious to get Cuba out of Africa will have to make additional concessions in other areas. The immediate effect, though, has been to harden Cuban-U.S. relations, to add to existing collision courses new ones over Angola's future and the mode of independence for Namibia, and to make any Cuban-U.S. deal more difficult and unlikely. Certainly in ideological terms Cuba has succeeded in its objective of putting the "counterrevolutionary forces" on the defensive.

Other alleged Cuban motives include the need to provide combat experience for Cuban forces untested since the early 1960s. The Cubans have obtained in Angola and Ethiopia valuable combat experience with Soviet weapons in both fixed battles and counterinsurgency.

There is also the personal "Fidel" factor in Cuban motives and objectives. Largely isolated in Latin America and with a limited presence in the Caribbean, Castro may have been seeking an arena and a role for Cuba as a world power, albeit a middle-level one. Africa certainly provided both visibility and occasion for leadership. Castro used this skillfully to have Cuba designated the host of the 1979 meeting of the Nonaligned Movement with himself as chairman. Cuba moved to the forefront of the radical nonaligned states through its help for Africa, even if it antagonized some of the moderates. This style of world leadership is slippery and often ephemeral; battle-weary

Iraq was scheduled to replace Cuba in 1982 as Nonaligned Movement host, and the meeting was subsequently rescheduled for India. What matters, perhaps, is that Cuban involvement did elevate Cuba's importance on certain major world issues. The Chinese press has charged Cuba with being a Soviet surrogate and betrayer of Third World interests, but in this interpretation the Cuban desire for middle-power status was largely Castro's own doing.[9]

There is a final view that cites the element of sheer opportunism in Cuban motives and objectives. Ideology may help to explain the Cuban presence in Angola, but it does not account for Cuban aid to thoroughly sanguinary regimes in Equatorial Guinea and Uganda and to African petty tyrants elsewhere, or for its dumping of the Eritrean nationalist movement after years of support in order to take the side of a bloody Ethiopian military dictatorship. Similarly, in 1982 Cuba embraced Argentina in the Falklands/Malvinas War after spending years denouncing the same Argentine military government for its repressive treatment of Argentine radicals.

One suspects that as Cuba sought quick roads and visible successes in Africa it often paid little attention to the nature of its new allies. Some were bona fide communists or at least Marxists, others were what was available in a certain country at a given time. Cuban diplomats are quick to explain their withdrawal from places like Equatorial Guinea and Uganda once they realized the nature of the regimes.[10] What were their initial motives? To spread Cuba inexpensively across the map of Africa to the chagrin of Washington and the pleasure of Moscow? There was also opportunism in the massive involvements in Angola and Ethiopia, especially the latter.

African Motives and Objectives

African motives and objectives for involvement with Cuba have been largely the product of deep weakness. More than twenty years after independence, most of the fifty-two independent African states are doing poorly. There is little or no economic growth and continued dependence on non-African aid, investment, and technicians. There are few reliable or efficient security or military forces. Governments and ruling elites often have little or no legitimacy in the eyes of their citizens, and political tension, instability, and discontent are endemic. Out of this weakness has come an interest in Cuba.

First has been the desire to obtain another and relatively disinterested source of technical assistance. Cuban doctors, paramedics, engineers, and other technical personnel come free, are often colored black or brown, bear no taint of former colonial power, and are trained and accustomed to working under crude and difficult conditions. Although expatriates, they do not enjoy the high life-styles of other expatriates, including Soviet and Eastern European technicians. Alone in the Soviet bloc the Cubans are capable of providing African governments with low-cost, reasonably competent technicians who will not offend the local populations with their arrogant behavior. Keep in mind, though, that the majority of African states, like Tanzania and Zambia, that have accepted Cuban civilians have not been interested in the Cuban military. Moreover, civilian technicians in each country have numbered in the 200–500 range, and these are spread over the country. Such numbers in most countries make up only 5 to 10 percent of the total foreign technical personnel, who are still mostly from Western Europe.[11]

A handful of African governments—Congo (Brazzaville), Guinea (Conakry), Uganda, Equatorial Guinea, Sierra Leone, and Benin—have at one time or another sought Cuban security and/or military training and limited staff. These governments have been mostly personalist dictatorships of an extremely fragile and nervous nature. The leaders have turned to Cuba and East Germany out of despair at the state of their own security forces, riddled with plots and coupmakers. The Cubans are said to have aborted one coup in Brazzaville but not its successor. The Cubans have been seen as relatively disinterested security personnel, often to be discarded, as in Guinea (Conakry) at the first opportunity. Cuban security forces are said to have instigated the Mozambican government expulsion of alleged Central Intelligence Agency (CIA) agents. African governments with chronic security problems have been gradually turning to the more ruthless East Germans while relying on the Cubans for military training.

The principal Cuban military advantage for the Africans has been their familiarity with Soviet weapons, especially heavy armor. This training and combat role has proved critical in both Angola and Ethiopia, where local forces either were trained with Western equipment or had little experience with heavy weapons. The Cubans have stayed on as military advisers and trainers, as a deterrent against renewed outside attacks, and as useful supplements for still unreliable national forces. Essentially the Cuban forces provide guard, security, and internal police forces, freeing troops for combat. There is little evidence since the Ethiopian-Somali battles of 1978 or the 1975–1976 clashes in Angola that the Cubans have been used as front-line forces. Yet their presence is an important element of regime support in both countries, as the Cubans remain probably the most loyal and disciplined troops at the disposal of the regimes. They are not mercenaries but foreign troops committed to a certain national leadership, as seen in their participation in putting down a high-level Angolan coup in 1979.[12]

In essence, the Africans who have sought Cuban aid have seen it as another and relatively safe source of help. Cuban economic interests in Africa are virtually nil (Angola needs to export its oil for foreign exchange while Cuba trades sugar for Soviet oil). Cuban political motives are not great-power or neocolonial machinations, and if this were not so, why would the Cubans be any worse for the Africans than other aid donors? Cuban military intervention in Angola against South Africa was timely and popular—although Ethiopia was a less clear-cut case. The 1981–1982 exercise of the first African Peace-keeping Force in Chad put on display the weakness of the Organization of African Unity and the need for non-African intervention.

A number of African states prefer to rely on former colonial powers if intervention is needed or to organize pan-African forces. Nigeria, Kenya, Ivory Coast, Zaire, Botswana, Morocco, and others could all be labeled "pro-Western" or "neutral." These are among the thirty-four African states that have not sought Cuban aid. They were also the most hostile to Cuban forces in Ethiopia; they saw the situation there, unlike that in Angola, as a dispute between African states. The division is in part one between "radicals" and "moderates" but also one between those who think non-African intervention should be avoided whenever possible and those who consider it as a means to an end.

The debate is at its sharpest with respect to support for guerrilla movements. Cuba has consistently provided moral, material, and military support to a wide variety of movements considered as fighting anti-imperialist struggles. It helped many of the anti-Portuguese movements, the Eritreans, and Joshua Nkomo's forces in Zimbabwe; at present it aids SWAPO (Southwest African People's Organization) in Namibia and the Polisario movement fighting against Morocco for an independent Western Sahara. Understandably, given their own struggle, the Cubans have often shown greater affinity for the guerrilla movements than for government-to-government relations. However, they have insisted that each movement must win its own struggle and that Cuban support be only peripheral.

Support for guerrilla movements thrusts Cubans into domestic politics in a number of African states, although they managed not to back any side in the chaotic situation in Chad. However, they found themselves initially supporting the losing side in Zimbabwe, switching from the Eritreans to the Ethiopians in some haste, and encountering Moroccan hostility due to their help for Polisario.[13] As conflicts escalate in South Africa and Namibia one can expect that African moderates will call for the Cubans to keep out, while some of the radicals may seek their intervention. The prolonged negotiations during the 1980s over the independence of Namibia have apparently become stuck over a South African demand that such independence be conditioned on a Cuban withdrawal from Angola.[14]

Soviet Motives and Objectives

Some clarification of Soviet motives and objectives is needed at this point. Africa has been on the periphery of Soviet interests, but it is seen as a continent where imperialist and colonialist forces are so weak that the prospects exist—for example, in Ethiopia—for a rapid transition from feudalism to socialism. However, the Soviet experience with Africa has been fraught with setbacks. The Soviets have been expelled at various times from Egypt, Somalia, Sudan, Zaire, and Ghana. Even the so-called Afro-Communist regimes of Angola, Ethiopia, and Mozambique have preferred more efficient Western economic and technical aid and investments.[15] Problems of the Soviet economy have limited the Soviets' ability to provide financial aid and trade, and their technical experts have a reputation for being boorish and inept. The principal Soviet foreign policy instrument in Africa has become the sale or grant of military equipment—hence their interest in compensating for their own weaknesses through more flexible Cuban delivery systems and technicians. Cuba's revolutionary experience as a poor, racially mixed country is also much more accessible to Africans than is the ideology of the 1917 revolution.

The Soviets appear to be constructing a series of client states, both close to their borders, like Afghanistan, and distant, like Angola and Ethiopia. As Sovietologist Seweryn Bialer has pointed out, "Soviet leaders and writers seem honestly to believe that not only Soviet military assistance but even overt Soviet military action as in Angola do not constitute the export of revolution. The use of Soviet military power did not create a revolutionary situation; it merely altered the balance of forces in favor of revolutionaries against counterrevolutionaries who are actively supported by foreign reactionary interests." Bialer went on to argue that the Soviet definition of what is a "progressive" regime is very flexible and has little to do with "the likelihood or magnitude of Soviet military help or intervention. The decision to help or intervene is basically a situational, not a doctrinal one."[16]

Believing that Third World nationalism represents a "historic force" on their side, the Soviets are willing to engage in conflict, but not in direct military confrontation with the United States, in Africa. The convergence of Soviet and Cuban interests, although it is by no means complete, has made possible Cuban political use of Soviet military aid. Yet it is not clear that Angola and Ethiopia will be stable or reliable clients or that Cuban-Soviet convergence is possible elsewhere. Soviet opportunism rules out the use of Soviet troops.

Four Periods of Cuban Involvement in Africa

Cuba's involvement in Africa can be divided into four distinct phases. The first, 1959–1974, was a period of loose, informal, and limited ties, often with an emphasis on contacts with African nationalist movements rather than independent governments.[17] Fraternity and solidarity were the key phrases as Cuba sought support against the threat of U.S. overt or covert attacks. The institutional highlight of this period was the 1966 Tricontinental Conference, held in Havana. Ironically, this conference coincided wtih a series of setbacks for Latin American guerrilla groups aided by Cuba. However, the 1965 African visit of Ernesto (Che) Guevara, the Argentine revolutionary companion of Castro, also suggested that Africa was not ripe in Cuban eyes for revolution, in contrast to the assessment made by Zhou Enlai, then Chinese foreign minister, on his 1964 African tour. Hence Cuba continued to cultivate close ties with a few governments such as Congo (Brazzaville) while concentrating its moral and modest material support on several of the anti-Portuguese nationalist movements, especially the PAIGC (African Party for the Independence of Guinea and Cape Verde), led by Amilcar Cabral in Guinea-Bissau, and the MPLA (Popular Movement for the Liberation of Angola), led by Agostinho Neto in Angola. Many nationalist leaders visited Cuba during this period, and there were close ties with the ELF (Eritrean Liberation Front). However, there was little or no intimation between 1959 and 1974 of any conceivable future direct intervention in Africa.

The second and more controversial period of Cuban involvement was in 1975 and 1976, with the dramatic use of Cuban troops in Angola, their clashes with South African forces supporting a rival Angolan nationalist movement, Union for the Total Independence of Angola (UNITA), and the escalation into a United States–USSR confrontation.[18] Cuba backed the MPLA, with which it had had close contact since 1962, in a three-cornered pre-independence Angolan civil war. When the United States declined to intervene directly and U.S. congressional pressure terminated covert CIA intervention, the South Africans hastily withdrew to the Namibian border and the MPLA emerged victorious.[19] However, a continued large-scale Cuban military and civilian presence was needed to shore up the war-shattered economy and ensure Angolan internal and external security. Thus in 1976 Cuba became, with Soviet weapons, logistics and some financial aid, the effective guarantor of Angola's independence. It is unlikely that this role had been envisaged when Cuba acted opportunely to send troops in 1975 at the request of the MPLA when South African intervention was likely. Most of the evidence suggests that Cuba acted on its own initiative in 1975 in Angola but with tacit Soviet support, which became explicit in early 1976.

The focus of the third period of Cuban involvement, 1977–1978, was the Horn of Africa. Here events were precipitated by Somalia, which, after years of Soviet military aid and training, sought to take advantage of the 1974 Ethiopian revolution and press its claim to the Somali-populated Ogaden. Meanwhile, after a series of internal purges, Colonel Mengistu Haile Mariam emerged in 1977 as military ruler of a fractious Ethiopia. Ending the former emperor's close military ties with the United States, Mengistu approached the Soviets for help. Enticed by the prospect of a much more important African client state with an ostensibly "revolutionary socialist" regime, control over a slice of the Nile River, a naval base on the Red Sea, and several strategic borders, Moscow lost interest in equally socialist but recalcitrant and nationalist Somalia. The price of the Ethiopian client was the abandonment of both Somalia and the Eritrean nationalists seeking independence from Ethiopia.

Fidel Castro, on his lightning 1977 visit to the Horn, pressed the case for a vague federation of socialist states to reconcile the opposing forces.[20] There were no takers. Somalia expelled its Cuban and Soviet military and security advisers and other personnel and, perhaps mistakenly hoping for U.S. support, launched a military attack on the Ogaden. This time massive Cuban military intervention, using troops from Angola and Cuba, and Soviet military airlifts, weapons, and advisers were needed to help Ethiopia check the Somali advance and mount a counteroffensive that expelled the Somalis. There is little doubt that the Cubans and Soviets rescued Mengistu from a probable defeat, if not worse. Their aid also made it possible later for the regrouped Ethiopian forces to take the offensive against the Eritreans and other internal dissidents. Although Cuba carefully claimed to take no part in "internal" Ethiopian conflicts, it swiftly ended its material and moral support of the Eritreans and denounced their demands for independence.

As in Angola, the Cubans found themselves at the end of 1978 effective guarantors of Ethiopian security. Although the Ethiopian army is much larger and better armed than that of Angola, it is stalemated in a debilitating counterinsurgency war in Eritrea; harassed by paramilitary guerrillas in the Ogaden, Tigrinya, and elsewhere; and beset by enormous problems of internal political control.[21] The presence of well-armed Cuban troops and advisers may not be as critical to its survival as in Angola, but Cuban withdrawal had become a risky and highly sensitive matter.

The Cubans took the initiative in Angola; it was the Soviets who acted first in Ethiopia. The Soviets saw Ethiopia as a major prize and the Cubans as the instruments of delivery. Soviet financial generosity toward Cuba was helpful in ensuring Castro's interest, as was the prospect of another international triumph. Yet it was harder to explain to the Cuban people why soldiers were being committed to Ethiopia, a country with which Cuba had had little contact before 1977, and against former Somali and Eritrean allies. African states, which had almost uniformly defended Cuban intervention against South African forces in 1975, were deeply divided over Ethiopia. Most rejected Somalia's irredentist claim and its use of force but feared the Cuban-Soviet alliance as a new factor in African politics. Again, African diplomacy had failed to restrain the Somalis, and a threatened African state had resorted to major power intervention. The Cubans this time were seen by most as the tail rather than the dog.

The fourth period, since 1979, has been one of Cuban consolidation and stabilization. There have been no new military adventures and a real desire, if one that is difficult to implement, to reduce Cuban forces in Angola and Ethiopia. Elsewhere the emphasis is on civilian aid, preferably for pay. At the end of 1981 Cuba had diplomatic relations with thirty-two African states, provided civilian aid to fifteen, maintained 17,000 to 19,000 troops in Angola and 15,000 in Ethiopia, had military and security advisers in eight countries, and remarkably, was providing a secondary education in Cuba for 3,000 Angolans and Mozambicans and more than 10,000 youth from Congo (Brazzaville), Ethiopia, Namibia, and São Tome and Principe.[22]

Fidel Castro could celebrate the twentieth anniversary of the victory of the Cuban revolution on January 1, 1979, by citing its African triumphs.

> For 20 years we have held a trench in the first line, the closest one to the most aggressive and powerful imperialist metropole. Not only have we defended this trench with honour and dignity, sons and daughters of our people have fought and died in such distant places as Angola and Ethiopia to help other peoples defeat imperialism, neo-colonialism, racism, and fascism. Imperialism was dealt its first Girón in Cuba, but it was dealt another in Angola and still another in Ethiopia. Three Giróns in 20 years![23]

Yet the prospects seem limited during the 1980s for further Cuban triumphs in Africa, whether in the Western Sahara against seasoned and U.S.-armed Moroccan troops or in Namibia or South Africa. Instead, the revolution in 1979 in Nicaragua, the coup and radical regime in Grenada, the civil war in El Salvador, and even the Falklands War suggest that Cuba might find more fertile terrain in Latin America than in Africa.

It has tried to increase its civilian aid to Ethiopia and Angola while seeking a formula for troop reduction and eventual withdrawal that would not put its partners in jeopardy. The danger for Cuba is that its African triumphs could be reversed by the overthrow of fragile regimes. Yet its continued presence risks growing nationalist clashes with those same regimes and populations. As the costs of intervention grow, so must the appeal of withdrawal. It is worth noting that for the last few years Cuban troops in Angola have been confined largely to the cities and towns, away from raiding South African forces on the Namibian border and UNITA guerrillas in the vast interior. Similarly, in Ethiopia Cuban soldiers have not fought against Eritreans or other dissidents. Instead they have replaced regular Ethiopian forces on security duty in order to free them for combat. Like other armies of intervention, the Cubans would like to hand over and get out but dare not yet.

The Nature and History of Cuba's African Involvement

A more detailed look at each of these periods illustrates the nature of Cuban involvement. As early as 1960 Cuba found a "friendly" government in Ghana under President Kwame Nkrumah and in 1963 in independent Algeria under Ahmed Ben Bella. Cuba provided modest military and security contingents to both governments and then withdrew after the Algerian coup in 1965 and Nkrumah's ouster in 1966. Meanwhile a steady stream of African nationalist leaders had visited Havana in the early 1960s. Cultural, linguistic, and political ties were forged with the major movements from Portugal's African colonies and some military training initiated. Exceptions were FRELIMO (Front for the Liberation of Mozambique), then led by U.S.-educated Dr. Eduardo Mondlane, and Holden Roberto's FNLA (National Front for the Liberation of Angola), which was said to be U.S.-funded.

Tired of tackling Cuban economic problems, Che Guevara began in 1965 a quixotic search for world revolution. Several months of Central African travels were thoroughly disillusioning, and Guevara was to be killed in 1967 attempting to open another front in Bolivia.

What remained of his African journey was a Cuban military and security mission to the "radical" government of Congo (Brazzaville) which provided a base for the MPLA. The taking of power in Zaire in late 1965 by Mobutu Sese Seko, who established authoritarian rule and thus ended effective guerrilla action, was another setback to Guevara's and Cuba's hopes. Instead of training guerrillas, Havana received and filled another request for security advisers, this time from President Sékou Touré of Guinea (Conakry).[24]

During the period 1965–1974 Cuba was mostly receiving requests from friendly and ostensibly radical governments for help with internal security. Small missions were sent to Sierra Leone and to Equatorial Guinea, in spite of President Macias Nguema's reputation for corruption and violence. Technical military missions went to Somalia in 1974 and to Algeria and Tanzania in 1975. (The only breaks from this low-key pattern were a major Cuban military training mission sent in 1973 to South Yemen, and 500 to 700 Cuban armed troops allegedly sent to Syria at the time of the 1973 Arab-Israeli War.[25])

The Tricontinental Conference held in Havana in 1966 provided Cuba an opportunity to rally support, to proclaim its global revolutionary commitment, and to meet with a number of political leaders. As a result Cuba intensified its ties to the MPLA and the PAIGC. Both movements were led by extremely intelligent intellectuals, Dr. Agostinho Neto and Amilcar Cabral, respectively, who were conversant with Marxist theory and capable of talking to the Cubans in ideological terms.

After 1966 the Cubans consistently provided military training, propaganda facilities, and some small arms to both these movements. Cuban assistance was provided in Cuba and at times in Congo (Brazzaville). However, these and other movements were at the same time receiving Soviet, Czech, Algerian, Tunisian, and other aid.[26] The Cubans were not the principal donors or sources of advice. For instance the Eritrean movement, ELF, had received Cuban military training off and on since 1967 and Cuban public support in 1969 for its anticolonial struggle, but it did not depend on the Cubans, who took a neutral position in 1976.[27]

The April 1974 military coup ending the fifty-year Salazar-Caetano corporatist regime in Portugal brought swift changes in Africa and Portugal. Previously, Portugal's African wars had been bogged down, with no quick outcome foreseen. Cuba had sent officers to fight with the PAIGC in Guinea-Bissau, perhaps to gain insurgency experience, and had continued its aid to the flagging MPLA, which was having problems with the Soviets in 1973–1974. Now the prospect of transfers of power negotiated with Lisbon transformed the political and military situation.

Cape Verde and Guinea-Bissau, Mozambique, and São Tomé and Príncipe had clearly dominant nationalist movements with which Lisbon would negotiate, but Angola had been living through an anticolonial and a civil war since 1961 contested by three broadly based movements. The FNLA, based in Kinshasa, had its strength among the Bakongo peoples of northern Angola and the refugees in Zaire. UNITA, led by Jonas Savimbi, drew its support from the Ovimbundu people of the Southern Plateau, but also from disillusioned former supporters of the other movements. The MPLA was a primarily mulatto and Umbundu movement of the cities and the Central Plateau. Its sophisticated multiracial leadership, years of contact with the underground Portuguese Communist party, and radical rhetoric made it a natural ally of the Cubans.

Each movement raced to strengthen its military forces and to build an urban political base before the November 11, 1975, date set for independence. The FNLA began to receive Chinese military help in June 1974 and clandestine aid from the United States in July. UNITA also received some covert U.S. aid, as well as aid from South Africa, whose troops lined the Angola-Namibia border, a UNITA zone of operations. Soviet aid to the MPLA was resumed in November 1974 after a six-month cutoff.[28]

The escalation of the Angolan arms race in 1975 initiated the second period of Cuban involvement. As political talks between the three movements and the Portuguese faltered, the search for external help intensified. The MPLA requested in May 1975 and received Soviet weapons and 230 Cuban instructors. The pattern for future cooperation had been established.

As Angola careened more deeply into civil war, U.S. covert and South African overt aid to the FNLA and UNITA were stepped up.[29] South African troops crossed the border on August 9 and secured the South African–funded Cunene hydroelectric project. The MPLA failed to get the additional Soviet help it requested, but Cuba sent additional troops.[30] None of the movements achieved military superiority, and each was riddled with indiscipline, irregular forces, poor command structures, and feeble logistics.

Perhaps seeing an opportunity to put their allies in power with a quick armored strike, 5,000 South African troops based in Namibia struck north for Luanda, the Angolan capital, on October 23, 1975. Lightly armored and moving rapidly, they came within a few miles of Luanda, which was being attacked from the north by the FNLA and a few mercenaries. It is probable that the South African government had reason to believe that the United States would support its move to forestall an anti-Western MPLA government in a country with impressive oil, natural gas, diamond, iron ore, and other resources.

The MPLA on November 4 asked for further help. Air and sea battalions were immediately dispatched, and the first Cuban combat troops landed in Angola on November 8. By mid-December 1975 Angola was independent, with a solely MPLA government headed by President Agostinho Neto. FNLA forces had been routed and had fallen back across the border into Zaire. The advance of South African and UNITA forces had been turned back. The South Africans retreated in an orderly manner into Namibia while UNITA disappeared into the vast bush of southern Angola and resumed guerrilla war. The South Africans claimed that they had inflicted heavy losses on the better-armed Cubans and MPLA. Their withdrawal coincided with the uproar in the United States over the covert CIA involvement. The aftermath of the Vietnam War resulted in the victory of the amendment by Senator Richard Clark (D-Iowa), with its ban on any U.S. overt or covert military intervention in Angola. The South Africans claimed that they had been deceived and would not have acted without the promise of U.S. support.

The Cuban intervention in Angola in 1975–1976 was an impressive logistical and military operation. Between 18,000 and 24,000 Cuban troops arrived in Angola from November 1975 to March 1976.[31] Part of the Cuban fishing fleet had to be redeployed to transport troops. Denied landing rights for air transports by once-friendly Guinea (Conakry), Cuba had to improvise routes using Georgetown, Guyana, and other points. Soviet logistical support had to be offloaded on congested Angolan docks. Throughout, the initiative was Cuban, not Soviet. Cuban Vice-President Carlos Rafael Rodríguez was quoted in 1978 as saying, "We started it in a risky, almost improbable fashion, with a group of people packed in a ship and in those British Britannia aircraft of ours. Eventually, the operation was coordinated with the Russians, who were beginning to send military supplies. . . . But the thing started off as a purely Cuban operation."[32] Soviet transport aircraft were not made available until January 1976, after U.S. diplomatic pressure had closed several stops to the Cubans.[33]

Cuba saved the day in Angola. But Angola as early as 1976 became its client. Cuban instructors were needed to train a new national army. A July 1976 agreement provided for thousands of civilian Cuban teachers, engineers, doctors, and so on. UNITA continued to harass government forces over a wide area, and the Cubans were needed for counterinsurgency. The SWAPO forces based in southern Angola needed arms and training and were frequently subject to raids by

South African forces. Worst of all, the MPLA racial-ethnic coalition showed increasing signs of strain, and Cuba would have to provide presidential security. Negotiations began in 1976 between the two governments on Cuban troop withdrawals, but invariably a continued Cuban presence was considered necessary. The Angolan economy was a shambles, with U.S. oil companies providing most of the foreign exchange. Large sections of the country were out of control, including part of the border with Zaire, where numerous Zairean insurgent refugees had gathered. There was no way that the Cubans could be allowed to go.

Cuban intervention in Angola in 1975 may have been unexpected; the 1977–1978 third period, marked by Cuban involvement in the Horn of Africa, was even more so. For the first time two states, Ethiopia and Somalia, switched sides in the United States–USSR conflict. And Cuba switched also.

The aftermath of the 1974 Ethiopian revolution was a series of internal purges and bloodlettings. Armed by the Soviets and frustrated diplomatically, the Somalis believed the moment ripe to strike at a weakened Ethiopia. The United States, traditional suppliers of weapons and training to the emperor, refused to feed an arms race in the Horn of Africa. Addis Ababa in December 1976 asked the Soviets for military assistance. Cuba and Ethiopia had established low-profile diplomatic relations in July 1975, and Castro had been the first to congratulate Colonel Mengistu on his seizure of power in January 1977.[34]

During March 1977 Castro undertook an extensive seven-nation tour of Africa and South Yemen. He conferred with Colonel Qadaffi in Libya, the first Cuban recognition of Libya as a "progressive" state. There were also stops in Addis and Mogadishu and an attempt by Castro to conciliate Mengistu and Somali President Siad Barre at a meeting in South Yemen. Castro's proposal of a loose anti-imperialist federation, including Ogaden and Eritrea as semi-autonomous entities, drew no takers. Mengistu maintained that Eritrea and the Ogaden were domestic Ethiopian problems while Barre insisted on Somali claims.[35]

Castro's highly informal visit coincided but was not coordinated with a March 1977 African visit of then Soviet President Nikolai Podgorny, the most senior Soviet official ever to visit Africa. Podgorny, too, shuttled between Addis and Mogadishu without success as guerrilla activity by pro-Somali forces in the Ogaden escalated.

Beginning in April 1977, the Soviets and Cubans coordinated their activities in the Horn based on Soviet strategy. Castro visited Moscow at the end of his African trip. So did Mengistu in May 1977, requesting

Soviet weapons and Cuban instructors.[36] Cuban instructors were sent in May, as guerrilla forces moved into the Ogaden, to train Ethiopians in the use of Soviet arms. Eritreans formerly considered "anti-imperialists" were reclassified as "secessionists."[37]

The next moves were made by the Somalis. They increased their support of the guerrillas, expelled the Cubans and Soviets from Somalia in November 1977, and launched in December 1977 a regular army offensive into the disputed territory. Meanwhile the Ethiopian army was taking severe losses at the hands of the two Eritrean movements and from other domestic insurgents. Moscow and Havana continued to press conciliation formulas as late as August 1977, which failed due to what they later called Somali chauvinism and intransigence.

Reeling from Somali and Eritrean drives and deeply divided politically, the Ethiopians turned in January 1978 to Moscow and Havana for weapons, instructors, and combat troops. The alternative was the dismemberment of Ethiopia and even the possibility of a Somali drive on Addis. Having opted for Ethiopia, and perhaps fearing that the United States would eventually support Somalia, the Soviets moved quickly. This time they mobilized a massive military airlift to supplement the 400 Cuban military instructors in Ethiopia in January 1978 with 17,000 regular Cuban troops by April 1978, drawing on island reserves and redeployment from Angola.[38] Cuban Vice-Minister Raúl Castro, brother of Fidel, visited Addis Ababa and Moscow in January 1978 to coordinate the aid. Soviet military instructors were also provided, and it is said that four Soviet generals directed the major battles against the 40,000-man, Soviet-trained Somali army.[39]

The Ethiopian-Somali War was over by April 1978, when all regular Somali forces had been pushed out of the Ogaden. However, the guerrilla war continued, fed by hundreds of thousands of Ogaden Somalis who fled into Somalia as refugees. The Somalis had taken several major Ethiopia cities (Dire Dawa, Harar) but had overrun their supply lines and fighter planes and were particularly vulnerable to a heavily armored counteroffensive. The Ethiopians provided the foot soldiers; the Cubans manned the artillery, missiles, tanks, and armored cars; and Cuban and Ethiopian pilots flew the U.S.-made jets of the former Royal Air Force. The Somalis fought well but were outgunned and outmanned, and casualties on both sides were heavy. Mengistu did not admit to the presence of Cuban troops until March 2, 1978, although the Somalis had taken Cuban prisoners.

As in Angola, military victory in Ethiopia marked the beginning rather than the phaseout of Cuban intervention. Mengistu wanted to move swiftly against the Eritreans with Soviet support. The Cubans refused to place their troops in battle against their former allies, although *Pravda* claimed that "the Eritrea rebellion has become a plot serving foreign interests."[40] Mengistu visited Havana in April 1978 and pressed the anti-Eritrean case, as well as seeking further Cuban civilian and military support. Castro told Cubans that "Ethiopia also needs internal peace. Cuba therefore equally supports a peaceful and just solution, based on Leninist principles, to the national question, within the framework of an Ethiopian revolutionary state that would safeguard as an inalienable right its unity, integrity, and sovereignty."[41] Cuban pressures to establish a single Ethiopian Marxist party were rebuffed, and two Cuban diplomats were expelled from Ethiopia for smuggling a dissident Ethiopian Marxist politician into the country.[42]

Cuban relations with Ethiopia were from the first much more difficult than those with Angola. Lacking a common language or culture, the two proud, nationalistic peoples could go no further than a marriage of convenience. Desperately poor Ethiopia soon began to complain about the terms of Soviet aid and trade and to ask for free Cuban technicians. Mengistu's harsh military rule seems perilous to the Cubans, who would prefer political institutions. Much less developed economically than Angola, Ethiopia has a minuscule working class, few economic growth prospects, and enormous needs. Cuba fears being drawn into Ethiopia's internal conflicts but cannot withdraw its forces unless and until the Ethiopian army can take over. Training by Cubans of both the Angolan and Ethiopian armies has gone very slowly while the worst danger is that politicized armies will seek to topple the regimes. The longer the Cubans stay the more it seems that they fulfilled their initial military objective but have since become Soviet and Ethiopian pawns.

Castro's desire for a political rather than a military settlement in Ethiopia was reflected during his September 1978 visit to Libya, Ethiopia, and Algeria. Speaking in Addis Ababa he stated his confidence that Ethiopia's leaders "will be able to preserve not only the territorial integrity of the country, but also the unity of all [revolutionaries] in a great revolutionary Ethiopia."[43]

The action for Cuba was in the Horn during 1977–1978; there were also serious problems elsewhere. A May 1977 coup attempt nearly toppled the Angolan government, which received Cuban security help. The coup involved a clash between Africans and mulattoes in the government and the MPLA, with the plotters perhaps being encouraged by the Soviets. The Cubans defended a multiracial, ideological government, which had inherited a damaged economy that it further mismanaged, thus alienating itself from many Angolans. Race, ethnicity, and nationalism are three cornerstones of African and Angolan politics, and the Cubans risked being caught in the middle.[44]

Later they were to advise President Neto against a loosening of the restrictions on the private sector in the interests of economic efficiency.

A further Cuban headache in Angola during the period was the presence of several thousand partly armed refugees in western Angola along the border with the mineral-rich province of Shaba, Zaire. Dating as far back as 1963 and the Katanga secession effort, these refugees were mostly Luba, with close ties on both sides of the border. Armed by the MPLA during the Angolan civil war, and perhaps having received some Cuban training, the insurgents were beyond the control of the Angolan government. Acting probably on their own initiative, several thousand invaded Shaba Province in March 1977, overrunning several small mining towns, causing panic among the European technicians and their families, and threatening the government of Zaire and the rule of President Mobutu.

Cuba was quick to deny any involvement in the March 1977 invasion of Shaba.[45] The United States acted with several of its European allies to fly in 1,500 Moroccan troops with French and Belgian advisers. The invaders were soon routed and withdrew to Angola. The Moroccan troops were to stay until they could be replaced by trained and reliable Zairean forces, and Angola and Zaire were to initiate quiet talks aimed at resolving their several disputes.

Nothing was done during the interim and, in May 1978, a second and similar cross-border invasion occurred. This time the insurgents captured and destroyed the mining town of Kolwezi, killed Africans and Europeans alike, and terrified the Zairean army. Again Mobutu charged Cuban and Angolan complicity in the invasion, a charge that was echoed this time in Washington; Castro personally denied the charge. A French and Belgian force flown in U.S. planes routed the invaders. Since then the border has been relatively quiet, although Angola and Cuba have done little to disarm the insurgents or Zaire to strengthen its forces in Shaba Province. However Cuba and Zaire did reestablish diplomatic relations in 1979 after their earlier break, and Angolan-Zairean relations and trade were established. It is doubtful that Cuba would encourage an armed rabble to invade Zaire, an act so different from all its other conduct in Africa. Moreover, the overthrow of the Zairean government could only worsen Angolan security along its poorly patrolled borders. It has been suggested that East German security personnel were involved in the Shaba invasions. If so, it is unlikely that the Angolans or Cubans were aware of it; a reflection of their lack of control of this vast country.

Cuba had by mid-1977 come up with a powerful new rationale for its African policies. Castro, after visits to Algeria, Libya, Ethiopia, Somalia, South Yemen, Tanzania, Mozambique, and Angola, declared "the continent of Africa is the weakest link in the chain of imperialism." In South America progress was impeded by the middle class—"that bastion of fascism." Africa, however, has no middle class, and it is therefore possible for developing African peoples—"victims of capitalist imperialism"—to pass directly "from tribalism to socialism."[46] Contacts were made with Joshua Nkomo, Sam Nujoma of SWAPO, and Oliver Tambo of the African National Congress (ANC) of South Africa, and Cuba promised the eight front-line states of Southern Africa defense against a South African invasion should they request it.[47] Two U.S. administrations publicly fulminated against the Cuban presence in Africa to little avail.

What slowed the Cubans down and initiated the fourth period, from 1979 to the present, was the very consequences of their African involvement. They refused to let their troops in Ethiopia be used against the Eritreans but were attacked within the Nonaligned Movement for their stand anyway. They barely averted a coup against President Neto but were unable to pressure the Angolans to control the western border with Zaire. Mengistu insisted on retaining Cuban troops but resisted Cuban efforts to broaden his regime with civilians. Elsewhere, in Congo (Brazzaville), Uganda, and Equatorial Guinea, pro-Cuban governments were toppled. Cuba was blamed by the Chinese and the Americans for the Shaban invasions. Its turn to host the Nonaligned Movement conference in 1979 was unsuccessfully challenged by thirty member states. Although Soviet aid had risen, total Cuban military expenditures had doubled between 1973 and 1978, and unreported casualties from Angola and Ethiopia were rising.[48]

Beginning in 1979, Cuba conducted much of its diplomatic relations with its African friends through the Nonaligned Movement. Here too Cuba's influence was limited, and there were sharp disappointments. At the Havana meeting, Yugoslavia and another group of "moderate" states attacked Castro's definition of nonalignment as compatible with belonging to the communist bloc. At the U.N., on votes involving Afghanistan and Kampuchea, only Angola, Ethiopia, and Mozambique voted with Cuba; its other African aid recipients took the other side or abstained.[49] During the prolonged voting to fill a Security Council seat more than one-third of the nonaligned club voted for a nonmember (Colombia) rather than Cuba. Except for its three "core" African allies, Cuba's African friends appeared to be pragmatic and relatively uninfluenced by Cuba in their foreign and domestic policies. Mounting Cuban economic problems prompted some Cuban technocrats to question the African priorities of their leaders.

Cuba's political and military profile in Africa was lower in 1979 than it had been since 1975, and it has remained low. The 19,000

Cuban troops and 6,500 technicians in Angola were indispensable for the stability of the Angolan government, especially during the illness and death of President Neto in 1980 and the succession by José Eduardo dos Santos. Cuba restrained its arms and instruction to the SWAPO camps in Angola, did not commit troops to defend these camps against South African raids, and advised SWAPO to accept the U.N. plan for Namibian independence. Although there were already fifteen times as many Cuban technicians in Angola as in Ethiopia, Cuba sought to phase down its military presence and increase technical aid. Similarly, in Mozambique and Zambia Cuba emphasized technicians, although it did respond to a Mozambican request for security advisers in 1981. The new directions were indicated by a 1979 construction contract between Cuba and Libya to provide for more than 2,000 Cuban workers and a $115 million Libyan payment.[50] The most significant Cuban provocative act since 1979 was the diplomatic recognition afforded to Polisario, the Western Sahara independence movement, in 1980, in spite of good relations with Morocco since the early 1960s. Moroccan planes strafed a Cuban fishing trawler off Western Saharan waters in June 1980, although Polisario relies on Algeria and Libya rather than Cuba for its arms.

Table 1, based on British intelligence sources, provides a picture of the Cuban presence in Africa in 1979. There have been only slight changes since that date.

Writing in 1981, two veteran observers of African affairs noted the changing Cuban role. "Except for involvement in counter-intelligence service, Cuban bulls and cows, teams of doctors and engineers and agricultural specialists became the main feature of Cuba's active involvement."[51] As Cuba continues to train surplus technicians and many African states experience shortages, this involvement should continue, limited perhaps by the growing Cuban desire to be paid in foreign exchange. Similarly a small-scale African need for military and security training should continue, although the Cubans have shown no better results in this area than most of the other purveyors.

Further Cuban military intervention is unlikely. The protracted desert war in the Western Sahara is not suitable for Cuban troops or Soviet equipment and, if escalated, could result in a United States–USSR confrontation. Cuba shows no signs of wanting to again take on the South Africans, another case risking Western involvement. SWAPO is relying more on diplomacy than insurgency to gain Namibia, and further Cuban involvement could jeopardize the negotiations. South African exile movements have received aid from a variety of sources but have yet to sustain a guerrilla offensive. Thus Cuba remains as a possible guarantor of Angola and Mozambique against South

Table 1. Cubans in Africa, 1979

	Military Personnel	Civilians
Angola	19,000 (mostly combat troops)	6,500
Ethiopia	15,000 (approximately; mostly combat troops)	450
Guinea (Conakry)	350	50
Congo	Up to 300	75
Mozambique	200	600
Guinea-Bissau	50–100	30
Equatorial Guinea	200 (until recently)	50
Zambia[1]	Up to 100 military advisers with ZAPU	
Tanzania	Up to 50	150
São Tomé and Príncipe	Up to 50	100
Madagascar	Up to 50	—
Benin	Up to 50 (security advisers)	—
Sierra Leone	Up to 50 (security advisers)	—
Cape Verde	—	10–15

[1]Cuban military advisers were withdrawn from Zambia after the independence of Zimbabwe. Reprinted from *Africa Contemporary Record, 1979–1980,* edited by Colin Legum. By permission of Holmes & Meier Publishers, copyright 1981 by Holmes & Meier Publishers, Inc., New York, N.Y.

African invasions, although it is helpless to assist against the kinds of raids that South Africa has preferred.

Africa is riddled with scores of border disputes and cases of ethnic unrest and demands for secession. Cuba has formally promised not to use its soldiers to aid one African state to violate the border of another, as well as to stay out of domestic conflicts. Its experience in Ethiopia has probably strengthened this resolve. Although it is possible that an African government might request Cuban aid against external aggression or internal conflict aided by counterrevolutionaries, Cuba is overcommitted in Angola and Ethiopia and gun-shy about further African wars.

Cuba's combination of calculation and ideology in Africa has kept two governments in power, both closely tied to Cuba and the USSR. The price of these successes has been becoming stuck in an African quagmire; the clients are afraid to stand on their own feet. Cuba's triumphs have appreciably increased its importance vis-à-vis Moscow and brought much more generous Soviet aid, no small consideration in an economy as dependent as that of Cuba. Soviet aid, though, has not generated economic growth, and Cuba's economic prospects for the 1980s are gloomy, with persistent shortages of foreign exchange, poor prices for sugar, and unchanging living standards.[52] Demands to rationalize the African operations should increase.

Cuba's stunning political triumphs in Africa have returned Fidel Castro to the world's center stage, at least briefly. The 55-year-old former revolutionary was able to offer two fresh revolutions to boost sagging Cuban morale. However, the leadership devoted enormous amounts of time to African problems at the expense of the sick Cuban economy. There can be no future African triumphs unless the leadership somehow manages a safe disengagement from Angola and/or Ethiopia. Understandably, the attractions of strife-ridden Central America or isolated Caribbean islands look tempting compared to those of Africa.

Cuba's African involvement has of course impeded a possible normalization of relations with the United States. The Cubans have considered their African presence as nonnegotiable, both for its ideological and its leverage value. Instead, between 1975 and the present, quiet steps were taken to restore a minimum of diplomatic but not commercial relations between Cuba and the United States. As Cuba is unable to afford to buy U.S. goods—with or without a trade boycott—it is unlikely to agree to U.S. demands to withdraw from Africa in exchange for full diplomatic relations. Too much has been invested in its African presence, which has value in Moscow, in the Nonaligned Movement, and in Africa, to offer it as a bargaining counter.

Cubans and Africans over the course of twenty years of interactions have learned to use each other. Cuba's ideology needs possible African revolutions, Cuban prestige and leadership need an active role in Africa, and Cuban national interests support such a role. A dozen or more African states and movements need Cuban technical, military, or security aid, generally available on generous terms with few strings. Angola and Ethiopia need Cuba for their survival; Cuba needs them as political triumphs in an austere economy and society. Cuban and Soviet objectives often but not always converge in Africa. The United States is unable to thwart major Cuban moves except by seeking to rally African opinion. The Cubans are in Africa to stay, although probably at lower levels of commitment than from 1975 to 1980.

Notes

1. *New York Times,* June 13, 1982.
2. Carmelo Mesa-Lago, *The Economy of Socialist Cuba* (Albuquerque: University of New Mexico Press, 1981), p. 53.
3. *Annual Survey of the World's Armed Forces* (London: International Institute for Strategic Studies, 1981).
4. Mesa-Lago and June S. Belkin, eds., *Cuba in Africa* (Pittsburgh: University of Pittsburgh Latin American Monograph Series, 1982), pp. 43–44.
5. Excerpt from speech by Fidel Castro, in Ezzedine Mestiri, *Les cubains et l'Afrique* (Paris: Editions Kaethala, 1980), p. 196.
6. Ibid., p. 188.
7. *New York Times,* June 23, 1982.
8. Mesa-Lago and Belkin, *Cuba in Africa,* p. 201.
9. "Vu par la presse chinoise," in Mestiri, *Les cubains,* pp. 223–224.
10. Personal discussions with members of the Cuban Liaison Office in Washington, D.C., 1979–1980.
11. Colin Legum, ed., "Cuba and Africa in 1980," *Africa Contemporary Record 1980–81* (New York: Africana, 1981), pp. A118–124.
12. G. Bender comment, in Mesa-Lago and Belkin, *Cuba in Africa,* pp. 149–159.
13. *New York Times,* July 15, 1980. Morocco broke diplomatic relations with Cuba in April 1980 over Cuban recognition of Polisario.
14. *New York Times,* July 1, 1982.
15. David Ottaway and Marina Ottaway, *AfroCommunism* (New York: Africana, 1980).
16. Seweryn Bialer, *Stalin's Successors* (New York: Cambridge University Press, 1981), p. 528.
17. William LeoGrande, "Cuban-Soviet Relations and Cuban Policy in Africa," in Mesa-Lago and Belkin, *Cuba in Africa,* p. 18.

18. John Marcum, *The Angolan Revolution,* 2 vols. (Cambridge, Mass.: M.I.T. Press, 1978).

19. John Stockwell, *In Search of Enemies, A CIA Story* (New York: Norton, 1978).

20. Nelson Valdés, "Cuba's Involvement in the Horn of Africa," in Mesa-Lago and Belkin, *Cuba in Africa,* pp. 63–94.

21. Ibid.; and David Ottaway and Marina Ottaway, *Ethiopia* (New York: Africana, 1979).

22. Legum, *Record 1980–81,* pp. A118–119.

23. Colin Legum, ed., *Africa Contemporary Record 1979–80* (New York: Africana, 1981), p. A162.

24. LeoGrande, "Cuban-Soviet Relations," p. 19.

25. Ibid., p. 20.

26. Marcum, *Angolan Revolution.*

27. Valdés, "Cuba's Involvement in the Horn," pp. 78–79.

28. LeoGrande, "Cuban-Soviet Relations," pp. 22–26.

29. Stockwell, *In Search of Enemies.*

30. LeoGrande, "Cuban-Soviet Relations," p. 24.

31. Ibid., pp. 24–25.

32. Colin Legum, ed., *Africa Contemporary Record 1977–78* (New York: Africana, 1979).

33. LeoGrande, "Cuban-Soviet Relations," p. 26.

34. Valdés, "Cuba's Involvement in the Horn," p. 67.

35. Legum, *Record 1977–78,* pp. A107–108.

36. Valdés, "Cuba's Involvement in the Horn," p. 68.

37. Ibid., p. 80.

38. LeoGrande, "Cuban-Soviet Relations," p. 39.

39. Colin Legum, ed., *Africa Contemporary Record 1978–79* (New York: Africana, 1980).

40. Valdés, "Cuba's Involvement in the Horn," p. 83.

41. Ibid., p. 84.

42. Ibid., p. 86.

43. Ibid., p. 89.

44. Bender, in *Cuba in Africa,* p. 156.

45. LeoGrande, "Cuban-Soviet Relations," pp. 30–31.

46. Legum, *Record 1977–78,* p. A116.

47. Ibid., pp. A113–114. Cuba switched its aid to Mugabe's forces in 1978.

48. Mesa-Lago and Belkin, *Cuba in Africa,* p. 203.

49. Jorge Domínguez, "Political and Military Limitations and Consequences of Cuban Policies in Africa," in Mesa-Lago and Belkin, *Cuba in Africa,* pp. 105–140.

50. Sergio Roca, "Economic Aspects of Cuban Involvement in Africa," in ibid., p. 171.

51. Colin Legum and Zdenanek Cerzenka, in Legum, *Record 1980–81,* p. A118.

52. Carmelo Mesa-Lago, *The Economy of Socialist Cuba* (Albuquerque: University of New Mexico Press, 1981); and U.S. Congress, Joint Economic Committee, *Cuba Faces the Economic Realities of the 1980s* (Washington, D.C., March 22, 1982).

9
Cuba and the Third World: The Nonaligned Nations Movement

H. Michael Erisman

Foreigners were drawn to prerevolutionary Havana by its brothels and casinos. Now they come for summit conferences. This transformation from vice capital to diplomatic center reflects the island's meteoric rise to prominence in world affairs. As one scholar has pointed out, "Cuba is a small country, but it has a big country's foreign policy. It has tried to carry out such a policy since the beginning of the revolution, but only in the second half of the 1970s did it have the conditions . . . to become a visible and important actor actually shaping the course of events."[1] In short, Havana has developed a capacity to exert international influence, becoming for the first time in its history a player rather than a pawn in interstate politics.

Traditionally Cuban diplomacy was concerned mostly with responding to other nations' initiatives in the Caribbean. Two countries in particular—Spain and the United States—dominated Havana's foreign affairs agenda, the former as its imperial overseer from 1511 to 1898 and the latter through a neocolonial relationship during the period 1898 to 1958. This pattern extended into the revolution's early years as Castro's government fought for its life against Washington's attempts to destroy it.

Increasingly, however, Havana took the lead in trying to influence the dynamics of the international system and by the late 1970s had displayed a significant capacity to do so. An anonymous U.S. observer recognized this, saying, "Don't overlook the realities. In competition with the world's strongest nation, the leader [Fidel Castro] of a weak island country has outwitted the United States, broken out of isolation to renew diplomatic ties with almost the entire world and has helped win two wars in Africa."[2] Cuba's global prominence has been a consequence of its expanding role in the Third World and its efforts to assume leadership in nonaligned circles. It is thus important to trace the evolution of Havana's Third World policies, which can be divided into four broad developmental phases: (1) consolidation of the revolution, 1959–1962; (2) hemispheric *fidelismo,* 1962–1968; (3) incipient globalism, 1968–1975; and (4) mature globalism, 1975 onward.

Consolidation of the Revolution, 1959–1962

Castro's government, like most new revolutionary regimes, was initially concerned with internal problems: consolidating its control and implementing its program of radical social change. Internationally, Cuba was preoccupied with the U.S. security threat and with establishing closer economic and military ties with Moscow to counteract it. These more pressing matters prevented Havana from devoting much time or energy to Third World affairs.

In 1961, however, two events heralded Cuba's future activism. First, it was one of the twenty-three countries gathered in Belgrade to found the Movement of Nonaligned Nations. Havana's presence signaled that Cuba's international perspective was undergoing change; the hemispheric parameters that historically had defined its sphere of concern were being replaced with a vision of itself operating in concert with kindred Afro-Asian states on the larger world stage. Second, this altered self-image assumed concrete dimensions when, in response to an invitation from President Kwame Nkrumah, Cuban military advisers were sent to Ghana to train both its troops and guerrillas from other African countries.

Despite such innovative policies, U.S. hostility remained Havana's top concern. The task of countering this hostility was complicated by the 1962 missile crisis, which sparked a process of deterioration in Soviet-Cuban relations that was not reversed until 1968. Outraged by Moscow's willingness to negotiate a unilateral settlement with the Kennedy administration and convinced that they could not rely on the Soviets to deter Washington, the Cubans explored other options in their quest for security. This search, as well as their intense, ideologically rooted commitment to leftist solidarity, led them into the thick of radical Third World politics, especially in Latin America.

Hemispheric *Fidelismo*, 1962–1968

Although Havana was oriented primarily toward the Western Hemisphere, its interest in Africa continued to grow. In 1963 Cuba made an unprecedented move, sending combat troops to Algeria to assist Ahmed Ben Bella's socialist government in a border dispute with Morocco. These units did not, however, see action, as a ceasefire was implemented shortly after their arrival.

Cuba likewise expanded its presence in sub-Saharan Africa, dispatching military aid missions and supporting national liberation struggles, especially the Popular Movement for the Liberation of Angola (MPLA), the African Party for the Independence of Guinea and Cape Verde (PAIGC), and the Front for the Liberation of Mozambique (FRELIMO). But perhaps nothing better symbolized Havana's affinity for Africa than the appearance there of a legendary figure from the revolution's ranks—Che Guevara.

> In April 1965, . . . Guevara arrived in Congo-Brazzaville to lead a force of 200 Cuban "internationalist fighters" against the Congolese regime of Moise Tshombe. From September to December, the Cubans fought with the Congolese guerrillas, but when Joseph Mobutu's coup overthrew Tshombe in November 1965, the Cubans' Congolese allies requested their departure so that an armistice with the new regime could be arranged.[3]

Che's sojourn demonstrated a Cuban commitment to sub-Saharan Africa that was reiterated when Havana established formal military missions in Congo (Brazzaville) (1965) and Guinea (Conakry) (1966).

These initiatives notwithstanding, Cuba did not then develop a major or positive Third World thrust in its foreign policy. In fact, Havana was often bickering with many developing states. With respect to the Nonaligned Movement,

> Cuban foreign policy was sharply at odds with the then-prevailing consensus within the movement. While the non-aligned summits focused on easing international tensions between the superpowers, Cuba remained deeply skeptical about the prospects for peaceful coexistence unless and until it extended to coexistence between big and small powers. . . . Indeed, for the Cubans, the problems of cold war, colonialism, and underdevelopment all sprang from the same root—imperialism—and hence could not be successfully addressed in isolation or by the movement's continued neutrality toward the West.

> In advocating a staunchly anti-imperialist view of non-alignment, Cuba had little tolerance for the movement's heterogeneity or its proclivity for papering over ideological rifts with bland generalities.[4]

Such disharmony was magnified when Havana's foreign policy took on more strident ideological overtones. As its relations with other Latin American governments (except Mexico) unraveled, given their support for Washington's policy of isolating the island with an economic and diplomatic boycott, the Castro regime began to define its friends and enemies on the basis of their adherence to its political philosophy. Because most Third World governments, including many in the Afro-Asian delegation that numerically dominates the Nonaligned Movement, did not meet Cuba's stringent standards of radicalism, Havana found it difficult to establish close ties with them and frequently showed little interest in actually doing so. Instead Cuba concentrated on supporting leftist insurgencies in Latin America, hoping to ease U.S. pressure on the island by creating diversions on Washington's flanks (i.e., the "two, three, many Vietnams" strategy) and ultimately to break the U.S. economic and diplomatic blockade. Havana's radicalism was clearly motivated by security concerns: "Paradoxically, Cuba's efforts to export revolution in the 1960s were largely defensive in nature. . . . Cuba's promotion of revolution in Latin America was primarily an attempt to break out of . . . isolation by helping to create other revolutionary governments in the hemisphere."[5]

Pursuing this policy of hemispheric *fidelismo,* Cuba in 1963 helped to organize the Colombian Army of National Liberation. In Venezuela the authorities discovered a three-ton rebel arms cache that had been smuggled in by Havana. By mid-decade the cult of the guerrilla *foco* was in full bloom; throughout the continent young leftists attempted to replicate the success of Castro's revolutionary struggle. Although encouraging them all in one way or another, Cuba became most closely attached to the movements in Venezuela, Colombia, Guatemala, Peru, and Bolivia, supplying them with arms, money, training facilities, and in some cases in-country advisers.

Eventually Havana decided to go beyond simply extending bilateral assistance and to try to unify the traditionally fragmented left so that aid from various sources could be used to maximum advantage by having coordinated multilateral programs. This approach demanded an institutional mechanism to ensure effective implementation. The Nonaligned Movement was not, in the Cubans' opinion, a viable possibility; they considered it too ideologically heterogeneous and too moderate to act decisively. Most existing communist organizations were dominated by the Soviets, whom Havana did not fully trust and with whom its relations at this time were quite strained. Thus, the Cubans opted to form new internationals. In January 1966 they convened a conference at which the Organization of Solidarity of the Peoples of Africa, Asia, and Latin America (commonly known as the Tricontinental) was established to promote worldwide cooperation among revolutionaries. Then in August 1967 they founded the Organization for Latin American Solidarity (OLAS) to coordinate guerrilla campaigns throughout the hemisphere. Beyond the obvious immediate goal of spreading Castroism, Havana hoped to use these groups to free Latin American nations from U.S. hegemony so that they could join the nonaligned bloc. In other words, hemispheric *fidelismo* was to be the vehicle for incorporating a radicalized Latin America into the Third World behind Cuban leadership.

But all these efforts failed. Neither the Tricontinental nor OLAS lived up to initial expectations. The Castroite insurgencies in Latin America were smashed or rendered impotent by a Washington-sponsored counterattack. The most demoralizing blow for the Cubans occurred in Bolivia, where Che Guevara was captured and killed in October 1967. As the 1960s drew to a close, right-wing elements led by the military had emerged more firmly entrenched than at the beginning of the decade.

Incipient Globalism, 1968–1975

One might have expected, given the failure of hemispheric *fidelismo* combined with the deterioration of Havana's relations with Peking,[6] increased pressure from Moscow to behave more moderately,[7] and an economy reeling from poor performances in 1968–1969 and the severe disruptions caused by the unsuccessful 1970 attempt to bring in a record 10-million-ton sugar harvest, that the Cubans would abandon aspirations for nonaligned leadership and adopt a low profile. Instead, they did exactly the opposite: They stepped up their international activity to recoup their setbacks in Latin America and to become recognized as a power in Third World affairs. Havana was particularly anxious to establish itself as a broker between the Soviet camp and the developing nations, seeing such a linkage role as a means to enhance its leverage with the USSR as well as its influence in nonaligned circles.

To achieve these goals, Havana made some pragmatic adjustments in its foreign policy geared to establishing cordial ties with as many developing nations as possible. Havana was even willing to become more ecumenical in defining its friends. Rather than relying on the strict criteria that in the past had tended to limit its political partners to like-minded radicals, Cuba became more flexible, placing greater weight on such considerations as "nationalistic," "anti-imperialistic" credentials than on ideological beliefs. Accordingly, Havana proclaimed its willingness to cooperate with regimes that, although not revolutionary, were "progressive" (i.e., strongly committed to socioeconomic reform and independent from Washington). This tolerance for diversity meant that Havana now looked on most developing states as potential allies. It opened the way for Cuba to play a more active role in Third World–nonaligned affairs.

To promote this offensive, Castro, whose trips abroad had been mainly to the Soviet Union and Eastern Europe, began numerous visits to developing countries. In November and December 1971 he went to Chile, Peru, and Ecuador; he toured ten African nations during May and June 1972; and in September 1973 he embarked on a worldwide journey that included Guyana (where he also met with the leaders of Jamaica, Barbados, and Trinidad and Tobago), Guinea, (Conakry), Algeria, Iraq, India, and finally North Vietnam (where he was the first head of government to visit North Vietnamese–controlled areas in the South). The highlight of these travels was the 1973 Nonaligned Summit Meeting in Algeria. Cuba had previously sent lower-ranking officials to these gatherings. Fidel's presence was proof of the significance Havana attached to its Third World policies. Castro was at his charismatic best in Algiers, focusing attention on the national liberation struggles raging in Africa and the developing countries' deteriorating position in the international economy as central themes in his call for a more unified, more militant organization. When the conference adjourned, it was evident that his performance had enhanced Cuba's stature and its Third World leadership prospects.

> The prominence of international economic issues and the anti-colonial wars in Africa were moving the political center of non-alignment toward the left just when Cuban policy was adopting a more global orientation. Long on record as emphasizing colonial and developmental issues, Cuba became a leading voice in the [nonaligned] movement when these issues came to the fore.[8]

From 1972 to 1975 Havana instituted diplomatic relations with the following Latin American countries: Barbados, Trinidad and Tobago, Guyana, Jamaica, and Peru in 1972; Argentina, 1973; Venezuela, 1974; and Colombia, 1975. Mexico had never severed its ties with Cuba, and Chile under Salvador Allende had restored them in 1970. This new hemispheric respectability led to sentiment to lift the sanctions which the Organization of American States (OAS) had imposed on

Cuba in the 1960s. Peru first proposed such action in 1972, and it was finally approved in 1975.

Concurrent with its political initiatives, Havana stepped up its military aid programs. New advisory and training missions were dispatched to Sierra Leone (1972), South Yemen (1973), Equatorial Guinea (1973), and Somalia (1974). Moreover, Cuba once again sent combat troops overseas, this time to Syria when the October 1973 Yom Kippur War broke out. Exactly what they did there is unclear; most were withdrawn by February 1975.

By 1975 Havana's Third World influence was stronger than ever. It had preserved its standing as a leader in radical circles and had also achieved greater prestige in the eyes of nonaligned moderates, as evidenced by its choice as coordinator for agenda items concerning national liberation movements at the February 1975 conference of developing nations in Dakar; its selection as a working-group member of the U.N. Special Committee on Decolonization in February 1975; and its designation as host of the March 1975 Third Ministerial Meeting of the Nonaligned Movement's Coordinating Bureau.

Mature Globalism, 1975 Onward

During the crucial years 1975–1979, Havana's Third World activities reached unprecedented proportions, expanding not only geographically but also functionally. Developmental aid was given equal billing with military assistance. These programs complemented a strong diplomatic campaign that brought more and more Third World dignitaries to Havana for consultations. A review of the Cuban press reveals that in 1974 only three Third World heads of state and one national liberation movement leader visited the island. But over the next few years these figures rose steadily. Such summitry paid large dividends, enhancing Havana's reputation as a major international center, providing excellent opportunities to showcase the revolution's achievements in socioeconomic development, and guaranteeing a dialogue through which Cuba could generate support for its foreign policies.

The Angolan conflict marked the turning point for Cuban globalism. By demonstrating that it had the ability and the will to project its strength and influence thousands of miles, Havana changed from a regional power to a significant actor in international macropolitics. The process began in late 1975 when Cuba, with Soviet logistical backing, dispatched to Angola elements of an expeditionary force that would ultimately total approximately 20,000 to help the MPLA defeat its Western-backed opponents. What was unique was not the action itself—Havana had previously sent troops to Algeria and Syria—but rather its magnitude, its impact on the struggle, and the long-term presence that ensued. From the time its first regulars arrived in October or early November 1975 until the February 1976 triumph, Havana's buildup was swift and massive. It was also decisive, with the Cubans spearheading most assaults (especially against the South Africans, who in October 1975 had thrown into the fray more than 10,000 men with heavy artillery and armored vehicles). Finally, instead of standing down after the war, Havana strengthened its ranks and settled in for an extended stay.

This pattern was repeated two years later in Ethiopia when the survival of Col. Mengistu Haile Mariam's socialist regime was threatened by a Somali invasion of the Ogaden Desert. During the pro-U.S. Haile Selassie's reign the Cubans had supported Addis Ababa's two arch enemies—the secessionist Eritreans, who were attempting to break away to form their own independent state, and the Somalis, who were claiming the Ogaden. In the early 1970s, Havana furnished aid to left-wing Eritrean rebels and also operated, along with the USSR, a security assistance program in Somalia. Both Cuba and Moscow had then strongly backed Somalia's territorial claims, although Castro, adhering to the insistence of the Organization of African Unity (OAU) that African borders not be altered by force, stressed that the dispute should be settled peacefully.

Cuba's pro-Somali, pro-Eritrean stance changed after Haile Selassie's army overthrew him in September 1974 and the radical Mengistu faction gained the upper hand in February 1977. While Havana and the Kremlin applauded these developments, the Somalis became increasingly angry, feeling that they had been betrayed by the Soviet-Cuban rapprochement with their adversary. Consequently Mogadishu began to mend its fences with the West.

As the situation became more tense, Castro tried repeatedly during a March 1977 African tour to mediate a resolution of the Ogaden and Eritrean disputes by proposing the creation of an anti-imperialist federation composed of South Yemen, Ethiopia, Somalia, an autonomous Ogaden, and an autonomous Eritrea. When these efforts failed, Cuba backed Mengistu.

Serious fighting broke out in July 1977. Responding to Mengistu's pleas for help, Havana and Moscow launched a closely coordinated counteroffensive in late 1977. The Cubans provided 15,000 troops while the Kremlin supplied logistical support and Soviet officers commanded the overall joint campaign. The struggle was for all practical purposes over by March 18, 1978, when the Somali army, which had taken a terrible pounding from Cuban artillery and air attacks, began a final retreat back within its prewar boundaries.[9]

The Angolan and Ethiopian operations were the largest, most controversial manifestations of Havana's expanding military presence in the Third World, which peaked in 1978. The approximately 39,600 troops that Cuba had stationed overseas that year represented 19 percent of its standing and ready reserve forces. Despite a significant percentage decline in 1979, Cuba's overall military strength abroad remained remarkable for a small country.

Although there were misgivings in some Third World quarters about Havana's military exploits, the general post-Angolan response was positive. In both the U.N. General Assembly and the OAU the developing nations took positions indicating that they were sympathetic to Cuba's contention that it was fulfilling its international obligations by helping governments to defend themselves against external aggression and by supporting insurgents whose national liberation struggles had been deemed worthy of solidarity (e.g., in U.N. or OAU resolutions). The Nonaligned Movement endorsed Havana's Angolan policy at its 1976 summit in Sri Lanka and then voted unanimously to hold its 1979 meeting in Cuba, which meant that as host Castro would serve as the organization's chairman and chief international spokesman from 1979 to 1982.

Havana's prestige was not, however, based solely on its military ventures. It was also the result of its developmental assistance, which although not producing many headlines did generate substantial goodwill. Particularly after the 1976 Sri Lanka summit, Cuba began a quiet but dramatic buildup of its economic and technical personnel overseas. In fact, in terms of percentage increases of personnel abroad, Havana's developmental aid programs were growing more rapidly than its military ones in 1978 and 1979.

There were also those who wanted to keep Havana's influence to a minimum because they felt that its links to Moscow were too strong and that the Kremlin had expansionist tendencies that had to be countered to preserve international peace and their own independence. Their opposition to Cuba's policies and their misgivings about the *fidelistas'* leadership qualifications exploded at the July 1978 Ministerial Conference of the Nonaligned Movement in Belgrade, with Ghana, Morocco, Somalia, and Senegal accusing Havana of aggression in Africa and insisting that it withdraw its troops. Moreover, Somalia and Egypt demanded that the 1979 nonaligned summit be moved from Havana and threatened to boycott it otherwise. But these efforts to derail Cuba's momentum failed.

Even before the Sixth Nonaligned Summit in Havana (September 3–8, 1979) began, it was producing sensational news copy. *Time* reported that the delegates "were preparing for a fierce showdown over the

. . . very soul of the Third World" and that the conference "promised to be the most critical ideological tug-of-war in the quarter-century-old identity crisis of the emerging Third World."[10] The struggle revolved around two broad issues: the question of defining nonalignment and the imperialist enemy/bloc relations controversy. Cuba's stance reflected its desire to transform the Nonaligned Movement from an ideologically diffuse, cumbersome body with little capability to influence international events into a streamlined organization operating as a unified radical force committed to solidarity with the Soviet-led socialist bloc. To the more moderate faction, which coalesced behind Yugoslavia's Tito, Castro's willingness to tilt toward the East and his contention that the USSR is the developing states' natural ally were anathema. Thus the stage was set for a Cuban-Yugoslav confrontation, while behind the scenes both the United States and Peking, although not members of the movement, worked hard to prevent a *fidelista* victory, which they feared could shift the global power balance in Moscow's favor.

The Sixth Nonaligned Summit: Cuba's Policies Debated

Defining Nonalignment. The most fundamental question for the Nonaligned Movement is how nonalignment should be defined. High stakes are involved in the definition; the perspective that prevails will delineate the movement's essential nature and its role on the international scene.

The moderates, following the precedent set at the 1955 Bandung Conference, insisted that the determination as to whether a state is nonaligned should be based solely on its military ties. Any country that is not "a member of a multilateral alliance concluded in the context of great power conflicts"[11] should be considered nonaligned. Because this view is totally nondoctrinal, those who espoused it were committed to the principle that the movement should be highly eclectic, accepting as members Third World countries ranging from the most conservative feudal monarchies to the most radical Marxist-Leninist regimes. Implicit in this position was the idea that the movement would not regularly play a partisan role in Cold War bipolar politics and therefore had no natural superpower allies.

The more vociferous anti-Cuban nations argued that Havana, although not a formal party to the Warsaw Pact, was nevertheless a Soviet ally helping to facilitate Moscow's military expansion into Africa. At the core of this analysis stood the "surrogate thesis," which holds that the Soviets have capitalized on Cuba's economic and strategic vulnerabilities to create a dependency relationship that gives them a predominant role in Havana's decision-making processes.[12] In other words, the roots of Cuban foreign policy were seen as lying in the Kremlin, thus making the *fidelistas* the "Gurkhas of the Russian Empire."[13] According to this logic Havana was not nonaligned and therefore was not fit to lead the movement. Indeed, Cuba's most intransigent critics hinted that it was not even worthy of membership.

Havana, assuming an unorthodox stance that generated heated opposition, sought to broaden significantly the traditional notion of nonalignment by injecting political factors into the equation. Cuba wanted the movement to state forcefully its basic objectives (eradication of U.S.-Western imperialism and neocolonialism), to formulate a clear action program to achieve them (cooperation with the Soviet bloc), and to regard only those countries that enthusiastically supported these goals and policies to be nonaligned. This position was alluded to by Fidel Castro in a speech to the Fourth Nonaligned Summit and was developed more fully at the Fifth Summit by Cuban Vice-President Carlos Rafael Rodríguez, who said,

> We must stress the fact that to abstain from being a member of a military bloc is not enough to merit belonging to the Movement; membership also implies adhering to a program of change that will make it possible for the peoples to overthrow colonial or neocolonial slavery and open up the road to development and well-being.
>
> Cuba feels it necessary to repeat at Sri Lanka something it said at Algiers; if we really want to have moral and political force in the eyes of the peoples, quality and not quantity is what should matter to us. That is the only way that the admission of new members will mean a true increase in our influence and political power.[14]

At Belgrade the Cubans presented their most forceful defense of these views, arguing that to achieve a higher degree of unity and hence greater international leverage, the movement had to require all participants to back its political action program and to recognize such loyalty rather than mere military nonalignment as the paramount consideration in determining its makeup because " 'non-alignment' is not the essence of our Movement; it is a sine qua non for being a member of the same. . . . The Movement is a specific movement whose members are non-aligned countries that objectively subscribe to the program and goals for which it was set up."[15] The Cubans maintained that despite their close ties with the USSR, they were unquestionably nonaligned in the fullest sense of the term because their foreign policy had invariably conformed to the movement's goals.

Once Cuba had demanded political consensus in the Nonaligned Movement, the question arose as to how to achieve it. It could not be attained by simply screening new members more carefully because the number of potential recruits was rather small; most Third World countries had already joined. Accordingly it would have to be shaped from within. But what about those members who refused to support the organization's program? Rodríguez alarmed many of the Belgrade conferees with Havana's reply: "The head of state of Libya . . . proclaimed the need for a periodic revision of the membership of the Non-Aligned Movement so as to see who abides by the principles and who doesn't. We are of the opinion that this is important."[16] Stated bluntly, the Cubans were endorsing the idea that "nonprogressive" states be purged.

The membership issue was brought to a head by the Arabs' demand that Egypt be banished from the movement for its separate peace with Israel. The Arabs pointed out that the organization had repeatedly condemned Zionism as a form of racism and Israel as an imperialist power, calling on its members to support the Arab struggle to obtain a comprehensive Middle East settlement that would allow the Palestinians, led by the Palestine Liberation Organization (PLO), to exercise their right of national self-determination. Sadat, they complained, had broken ranks by concluding a treaty with the Begin government based on the Camp David accords. This was, they insisted, grounds for expulsion. The traditionalists rejected this rationale because, given their idea of nonalignment as nonparticipation in great power alliances, Cairo qualified for membership no matter what its posture was toward Israel.

In principle, Havana stood behind the radical Arabs. But in practice the furthest the Cubans went was to call for censuring the Sadat regime and to promote sanctions short of ejection; they knew that the votes to expel were not there because most black African states were strongly opposed. Thus Havana avoided an all-out confrontation and Egypt escaped ouster (although Cairo was placed on probation for eighteen months, during which its foreign policy was to be monitored by a special committee empowered to recommend future punitive action). Although this decision constituted a step toward more stringent membership criteria by establishing the precedent that the movement expected its participants to support its stands on specific important matters and might apply sanctions, conceivably including expulsion, to those who did not comply, it certainly was not an unequivocal endorsement of Cuba's politicized definition of nonalignment. In fact, the conference's Final Declaration reaffirmed the moderates' conventional conceptualization, stating that a country qualifies for membership if it tends toward an independent foreign policy based on coexistence of states with different sociopolitical systems, consistently supports national independence movements, and does not have military relationships concluded in the context of great power conflicts.

The Imperialist Enemy/Bloc Relations Controversy. Unquestionably the issue of bloc relations was the summit's centerpiece controversy; it permeated the battle over the content of the Final Declaration and was at the core of practically every disagreement between the pro- and anti-Cuban factions. The dispute revolved around two interrelated questions: Which of the great powers pursue imperialist policies that threaten Third World states, and what type of relations should the Nonaligned Movement establish with the two superpowers? In the media and among the conferees themselves the issue was stated more bluntly: Should the nonaligned nations consider the Soviet-led socialist bloc their natural ally in a campaign against U.S. imperialism?

The Yugoslavs contended that both Moscow and Washington pose a potential danger to Third World countries. At first, they pointed out, the movement concentrated on exposing and combating Western imperialism because most members were Afro-Asian states that had long suffered under, and only recently escaped from, European colonialism. But it must be recognized, they said, that the USSR is also prone to expansionist impulses and has attempted to enlarge its sphere of influence by pursuing a systematic global policy of political and military intervention. Thus the organization must strike a balance by supplementing its traditional anti-Americanism with concern for "hegemonism," the code word used to refer to Soviet imperialism. Tito wanted to tilt a bit to the West to put the Eastern bloc into perspective. Seeing such a realignment as imperative for maintaining the movements's integrity, he pushed hard to have the Final Declaration condemn bloc politics in any form and commit members to opposing Soviet hegemonism as well as U.S. imperialism. This would also, he hoped, convince Castro that it would be futile, given the majority's expressed preference for an evenhanded posture, to try to use his leadership prerogatives to nudge the nonaligned closer to the Kremlin.

Cuba's position was predicated on making a sharp distinction between anti-blocism (opposition to the existence of great power alliance systems) and anti-superpowerism (regarding those who head these alliances to be ipso facto your adversary). Havana felt that an anti-bloc attitude was sound, supporting fully the demand for an end to the division of the world into hostile armed camps. But it insisted that the Nonaligned Movement had to evaluate the great powers on the basis of their actual behavior toward the developing nations. And as far as Cuba was concerned, the conclusion was obvious—the Western states have a long history of imperialist buccaneering while Moscow had always stood behind national liberation movements and continued to do so. The movement should, therefore, recognize the socialist bloc as its natural ally in its struggle against the continuing machinations of the United States and its capitalist cohorts. Accepting and acting upon this idea would not, Havana contended, make one aligned with, or a puppet of, the Soviet Union. Rather it would simply mean that one is a political realist who, understanding that nonalignment is not and was never intended to be synonymous with neutrality, will move prudently to maximize the organization's capacity to confront and overcome its true imperialist enemy—the Western neocolonialists who seek to dominate the Third World.

The focus of the clash between these contending perspectives was the Sixth Summit's Final Declaration. The Cubans had written a working draft strongly ratifying their line on bloc relations. In particular, it included the controversial "natural ally" concept and, said its detractors, analyzed all key questions from a blatantly Soviet rather than an impartial viewpoint. The Tito faction was determined to rework it so that the version finally accepted as the movement's official policy would clearly reflect its views.

Initially the Final Declaration reads like a Yugoslav treatise. In its first twenty paragraphs, dealing mostly with general principles, hegemonism and blocism were routinely included in its list of evils. For instance, paragraph 11 states that the organization's essential objectives include

> elimination of imperialistic and hegemonistic policies and all other forms of expansionism and foreign domination

and then goes on to say that

> the Sixth Conference reaffirmed that the quintessence of non-alignment, in accordance with its original principles and essential character, involves the struggle against imperialism, colonialism, neo-colonialism, apartheid, racism including zionism and all other forms of foreign aggression, occupation, domination, interference, or hegemony, as well as against great power and bloc policies.

Also, Havana's opponents succeeded in preventing the term "natural ally" from entering the movement's vocabulary; nowhere in the entire declaration is that particular phrase used or even strongly alluded to.

The tone, however, changes as one moves into the latter 265 paragraphs, becoming overwhelmingly anti-Western and anti-U.S. The United States was repeatedly singled out, sometimes by the use of code words such as imperialist or neocolonialist and often by name, for criticism on specific issues. Washington was, among other things, denounced for supporting the Pretoria regime, thereby incurring responsibility for the maintenance of racist oppression and the criminal policy of apartheid (paragraph 74); playing a major role in preventing a just and comprehensive Mideast peace settlement (paragraph 100); becoming through its military aid programs a party to Israel's attacks on southern Lebanon, which were labeled tantamount to genocide of the Lebanese and Palestinian peoples (paragraph 117); perpetuating Puerto Rico's colonial status (paragraph 152); and unjustly blockading and otherwise acting in a hostile manner toward Cuba (paragraph 155). The Soviet Union, on the other hand, was never condemned by name; it was sometimes implicitly chided, but always in a manner encouraging it to refrain from following a certain course in the future rather than castigating it for its past or present behavior. And occasionally the Eastern bloc was actually praised, as when, during a discussion of the need for solidarity with African liberation movements, the declaration applauded the role that "the socialist countries . . . play in supporting this struggle, especially in terms of the aid given to the peoples of Zimbabwe, Namibia, and South Africa" (paragraph 36).

Certainly anyone reading the Final Declaration cannot but conclude that on the whole it was much harder on Washington than on the Kremlin. Hence the Cubans basically got what they wanted—an affirmation of the contention that the capitalist West in general and the United States in particular still constituted the enemy against which the developing nations must concentrate all of their anti-imperialist energies. The Yugoslav faction may have won a few semantic skirmishes regarding bloc relations, but Havana emerged triumphant in the overall substantive war by preventing any serious anti-Soviet attitudes from creeping into the movement's official policy statement and by preserving, if not intensifying, the nonaligned's traditional anti-Western stance.

The Cubans made similar, though less publicized, gains on the economic front, focusing on the demand for a New International Economic Order (which is one of the few issues on which practically all Third World countries agreed). Analyzing the Final Declaration's economic sections, one scholar concluded that

> most of the specific recommendations contained in the [1979] document conformed with those of the declaration issued by the Colombo [Sri Lanka] Conference. But where the 1976 declaration had blamed the *policies* of the developed market economies for the failure to achieve a New International Economic Order, the Havana declaration defined the

> problem as a *structural* one resulting from the dominant position of the developed market economies in the global economic system. This difference is more than mere nuance. The linchpin of Cuba's position that the interests of the non-aligned and the Communist camp coincide (hence the basis of the "natural alliance" thesis) is the argument that an objective (i.e., structural) conflict of interest exists between the Third World and the West. Thus, the Havana summit's Economic Declaration took a quiet but not inconsiderable step closer to Cuba's view of non-alignment as anti-imperialism.[17]

Basically, then, the Sixth Summit went well for Havana. The Cubans did not win every encounter or achieve maximum satisfaction on all issues, but they generally created momentum toward their positions on crucial questions and seemed to have laid a solid foundation within the movement on which to build their influence. This rosy scenario was, however, quickly dimmed by the Afghanistan crisis.

Afghanistan and Beyond

By intervening with thousands of troops in late December 1979 to ensure a pro-Moscow regime in Kabul, the Soviets seriously undermined Havana's carefully nurtured Third World prestige and its macro-strategy of attempting to maximize its international influence and independence by functioning as a connecting bridge between the developing countries and the socialist bloc. Within the Nonaligned Movement, to which Afghanistan belongs and whose cause Cuba, as the organization's head, was therefore expected to champion, strong anti-Soviet sentiment emerged. This was demonstrated on January 14, 1980, when its members voted fifty-six to nine (with twenty-six abstaining or absent) for a U.N. General Assembly resolution condemning the USSR's invasion. Twenty-four other developing countries not in the movement reacted to the resolution, bringing the Third World total to seventy-eight for censure, nine against, and twenty-eight abstentions and absences. Recognizing that a ballot against the Soviet Union or even an abstention would be seen as an admission that communist states can be imperialist and would therefore emasculate the natural ally thesis, which was important to its linkage role, Havana opposed the resolution. It then tried to placate its nonaligned constituents by indicating that it had done so not because it supported the Kremlin's intervention,[18] but because it viewed the United Nations exercise as a self-serving U.S. ploy to resurrect the cold war. Raúl Roa, Cuba's U.N. ambassador, explained his government's position as follows:

> As far as Cuba is concerned, this debate poses a need to take a stand in the face of an historic dilemma. The gross manipulation of events in Afghanistan by the U.S. imperialists and their efforts to capitalize on events there to conceal their cynical backing for the worst forces on the international scene [and] to promote their warlike policy . . . while once again giving vent to their primitive hatred of socialism leaves no room for niceties.
>
> We will not vote against socialism. . . . We are well aware of what socialism and what imperialism mean, and we fully appreciate the historic roles of both the Soviet Union and U.S. imperialism. We therefore cast our vote today against that imperialism.[19]

This rationale, however, elicited little sympathy. Instead, Havana's negative vote, which seemed to lend credibility to the surrogate thesis, created a backlash that destroyed its bid for a seat on the U.N. Security Council.[20]

Cuba entered the 1980s with a reordered set of Third World priorities. Specifically, it shifted its geographical focus from Africa and the Middle East to the Caribbean basin and clearly downplayed military in favor of developmental aid programs. Beginning in late 1978, Havana had become optimistic about the prospects for radicalizing the Caribbean basin. The catalyst for this reevaluation was the revolution in Nicaragua, where the left-wing Sandinista National Liberation Front (FSLN) was waging an increasingly effective war against the Somoza dynasty, Washington's oldest, most trusted ally in Central America.

> The uprisings in Nicaragua's cities in September 1978, even though they failed to unseat Somoza, were so massive that they persuaded the Cubans to reassess their opinion of Nicaragua's revolutionary potential. Cuba's leaders seemed to conclude that they had underestimated the strength of the left in the northern tier of Central American (Nicaragua, El Salvador, Honduras, and Guatemala). In late 1978 Cuba began once again to provide material aid to guerrilla movements in those countries. The Sandinistas were the first beneficiaries of this new policy.[21]

This optimism was rewarded in March 1979 when, in a dramatic departure from the Commonwealth Caribbean's tradition of parliamentary democracy, a group of young rebels led by Maurice Bishop staged a successful uprising in Grenada and began implementing their brand of socialism on the small island. Although Havana played no part in the coup, it quickly demonstrated its solidarity with the new government by furnishing arms, security advisers, doctors, and fishing trawlers as well as agreeing to build and pay one-half the cost of a new $50 million airport.

Despite these gains, Havana's support for the Latin American left has remained more circumspect than it was in the 1960s. Cuba has encouraged and aided radical elements, but in a manner designed to minimize the possible political and economic risks to itself and to its ideological brethren. It has cautioned against moving too far too fast in attempting to make revolution. Also, Havana has sought to reassure the hemispheric community that it will not systematically export *fidelismo* or take the initiative in directly interfering in the affairs of other states. Following the Angolan victory, Castro asserted:

> No Latin American country, whatever its social system, will have anything to fear from the Armed Forces of Cuba. It is our most profound conviction that each people must be free to build their own destiny; each people and only the people of each country must make their own revolution. The government of Cuba has never thought of taking revolution to any nation in this hemisphere with the arms of its military units.[22]

He reiterated this theme in comparing the Cuban and Nicaraguan experiences:

> They themselves [the Sandinistas] will by no means say that the two revolutions are exactly alike. They are both profound revolutions, alike in many ways and in many ways different, as all true revolutions must be.
>
> This is important for our people, important also for world opinion. Each country has its own road, its own problems, its own style, methods, and objectives. We have our own; they have theirs. We did things one way, our way; they will do things their way.[23]

For Havana, its Moscow connection, which because of Afghanistan had become a serious liability in the eyes of many African and Middle Eastern states despite Cuba's efforts to mediate a Soviet withdrawal,[24] is less scandalizing to nonaligned radicals in the Caribbean. They have customarily considered the United States the more menacing superpower and thus are more willing to accept Havana's aid programs as fraternal help against a common enemy than to condemn them as vehicles for Soviet subversion.

Conclusion

Whether Cuba's shifts in emphasis to the Caribbean and developmental assistance will enable it to regain its pre-Afghanistan momentum remains to be seen. Havana seems to be counting on the fact that its new priorities facilitate portraying Washington as the arch-villain who poses a dire threat to the developing nations. Cuba's reputation as a state dedicated to combating U.S. imperialism has been an asset in its attempts to secure a prominent niche in nonaligned circles; its current policies seem geared to revitalizing that tradition. Recognizing the developing nations' fear of Western neocolonialism and presenting itself as their David challenging the U.S. Goliath, Havana hopes to destroy any lingering doubts produced by Afghanistan about its Third World status and its right to a vanguard role in the bloc's affairs.

Cuba's resurgent Caribbean orientation is consistent with this grand strategy. Allying itself with the Sandinistas in Nicaragua, Bishop in Grenada, the leftist guerrillas in El Salvador and Guatemala, and radical nationalists throughout the basin, Havana has embarked on a high-visibility campaign against what it claims are ongoing U.S. efforts to exercise exploitive hegemony over the area. Such behavior aims not only at enhancing its influence in the Caribbean but also at refurbishing its standing among the nonaligned as an anti-imperialist leader.

Cuba is also trying to increase tension between Washington and the Third World by focusing attention on the controversy surrounding the question of a New International Economic Order (NIEO). Its stress on developmental assistance is part of this larger scenario. Most nonaligned nations contend that they are underdeveloped primarily because the present global economic system is manipulated by the large Western industrialized countries. Unless the existing relationships between the haves and the have-nots are radically redefined, the underdeveloped states do not think that they can ever modernize and prosper. The NIEO they foresee would entail such change, and hence practically all of them strongly defend the concept. Conversely, the United States has been conspicuous in its opposition. By accentuating these antagonisms and encouraging the developing nations to mobilize to confront Washington on NIEO issues, thereby making the United States rather than the Soviet Union and its friends the main target for the Third World's hostility, Havana could contribute to the emergence of conditions conducive to its resuming its central role in nonaligned politics. In any case, its Third World relations will remain a pivotal dimension in Cuban foreign policy for the foreseeable future.

Postscript

Due to the continuing Iran/Iraq war, the 7th Nonaligned Summit was not held in Baghdad (which would have conferred leadership on Iraq's radical president Saddan Hussien). It was transferred to New Delhi, where it convened in March 1983. This turn of events was another demonstration of Havana's inability during the preceding three and one-half years to effectively radicalize the Nonaligned Movement. Cuba experienced other frustrations as well. For instance, it could not command a role in mediating the conflict in Afghanistan nor the one between Iraq and Iran. Also, the New International Economic Order remained as elusive as ever.

At New Delhi, the movement did not significantly alter its fundamental positions on most issues. Its general tone was decidedly more positive toward the West as global recession led most members to advocate a détente-like posture emphasizing the need for North-South conciliation rather than confrontation. Castro's summit speech was hardly a call to the barricades. It explained the problems that his government had been unable to overcome, summarized the 7th Conference's final resolution, reviewed the impact of the ongoing international economic crisis on the developing states, and took a few jabs at Reagan's Central American policy. In short, once more Castro opted not to throw down the gauntlet before the nonaligned moderates, but rather to quietly transfer the movement's leadership to them.

Notes

1. Jorge Domínguez, "Cuban Foreign Policy," *Foreign Affairs,* Vol. 57, no. 1 (Fall 1978):83.

2. Quoted in Frieda M. Silvert, "The Cuban Problematic," in Martin Weinstein, ed., *Revolutionary Cuba in the World Arena* (Philadelphia: Institute for the Study of Human Issues, 1979), p. 7.

3. William LeoGrande, "Cuban-Soviet Relations and Cuban Policy in Africa," paper presented at the 1979 convention of the International Studies Association, Toronto, p. 9.

4. William LeoGrande, "Evolution of the Non-Aligned Movement," *Problems of Communism,* Vol. 29 (January-February 1980):39–40.

5. William LeoGrande, "The Dilemmas of Cuban Policy in the Third World," unpublished draft manuscript, p. 5.

6. Initially Sino-Cuban relations were quite good, reinforced by the considerable affinity between the two governments on ideological issues and by their quarrel with the Soviet Union. When Havana refused to break completely with Moscow and become the People's Republic of China's ally in the Sino-Soviet dispute, Peking's friendliness waned. In 1966 developing

tensions broke into the open when Cuba accused China, which had refused to increase its rice sales to the island, of economic blackmail. Castro went so far as to call Mao a senile idiot.

7. Regarding this pressure, see H. Michael Erisman, "Cuban Foreign Policy and the Sino-Soviet Split," paper presented at the 1980 convention of the International Studies Association, Los Angeles, p. 14: "In what seemed a none too subtle reminder of Cuba's economic vulnerability and the danger of overly antagonizing Moscow, irregularities and delays occurred in the Soviet Union's deliveries of oil to the island in early 1968. This, combined with Havana's other problems abroad and its sagging economy, contributed to what was the watershed event in the Russo-Cuban reconciliation—Castro's support for the USSR's 1968 armed intervention in Czechoslovakia and the subsequent Brezhnev Doctrine."

8. LeoGrande, "Evolution," p. 42.

9. Cuba's willingness to fight the Somalis did not extend to the Eritreans. Both Mengistu, who refused to compromise with the insurgents, and the Soviets pressured Havana to suppress the rebels. Advised by friends (e.g., Algeria, Guinea [Conakry], the PLO) to stay out, Havana preferred to forego further cooperation with the Soviets rather than anger many Third World states.

10. *Time,* September 10, 1979, p. 34.

11. *New York Times,* August 16, 1976, p. 10.

12. Cuba's dependence on the USSR is described by Jiri Valenta, "The Soviet-Cuban Alliance in Africa and the Caribbean," *World Today,* February 1981, pp. 46–47.

13. This phrase, apparently coined by U.S. Senator Daniel Moynihan, is quoted in "Castro's Globetrotting Gurkhas," *Time,* February 23, 1976, p. 25.

14. Carlos Rafael Rodríguez, "Speech at the Plenary Session of the Fifth Summit Conference of the Movement of Non-Aligned Countries," *Granma Weekly Review,* August 29, 1976, p. 7.

15. Cuba, "Statement Distributed at the Conference of Non-Aligned Countries in Belgrade, July 1978," *Granma Weekly Review,* August 13, 1978, p. 11.

16. Carlos Rafael Rodríguez, "Comments at a Press Conference Held at the July 1978 Belgrade Conference of Non-Aligned Countries," *Granma Weekly Review,* August 13, 1978, p. 10: "We see the Non-Aligned Movement as an association of countries with differing social and political ideas, belonging to different socioeconomic, religious or lay systems but with a bond that characterizes the participation of all in the Movement: that of not being involved in any of the global military pacts and of accepting the program of the movement."

17. LeoGrande, "Evolution," p. 50.

18. Although Havana never publicly criticized the Soviets on Afghanistan, it was unhappy about the whole affair. Seweryn Bialer and Alfred Stepan, "Cuba, the U.S., and the Central American Mess," *New York Review of Books,* Vol. 29, no. 9 (May 27, 1982):17, noted that: "Cuban-Soviet relations were among the most fascinating topics in our talks. Whenever the subject of the

Soviet Union came up, the Cubans expressed respect for and gratitude to their patrons; but had little to say in defense of Soviet actions . . . with regard to Afghanistan, the Cubans say they voted with the USSR on the U.N. resolution because they had no choice. But a senior official was at pains to stress that 'we did not applaud the sending of Soviet troops' and that 'we have been constantly trying to find a political solution that would lead to the withdrawal of Soviet troops.' "

19. *Granma Weekly Review,* January 27, 1980, p. 12.

20. Long before the Afghanistan crisis broke out, Cuba had been involved in an electoral battle with Colombia for the vacant Latin American seat on the Security Council. Bogotá's bid was strongly backed by the United States as a means to check Havana. Neither candidate was able to muster the required two-thirds majority in the General Assembly. When it appeared that the backlash from Afghanistan was generating growing opposition to its Security Council campaign, Havana gave up and supported Mexico, which easily won as a compromise candidate on the first ballot.

21. LeoGrande, "Dilemmas," p. 18.

22. Fidel Castro, *Angola: African Girón* (Havana: Editorial Ciencias Sociales, 1976), p. 24. Note, however, that he rules out only the deployment of regular Cuban forces against Latin American governments, thus leaving open the possibility of providing other forms of assistance to revolutionary groups.

23. Fidel Castro, "26th of July Speech," *Granma Weekly Review,* August 5, 1979, p. 2.

24. In his capacity as chairman of the Nonaligned Movement, Castro tried to mediate a Soviet withdrawal from Afghanistan and negotiate a settlement to the Iran-Iraq war. None of his initiatives succeeded. For details, see *Facts on File,* Vol. 40, no. 2057 (April 11, 1980):271; *Granma Weekly Review,* April 13, 1980, p. 1; ibid., October 12, 1980, p. 1; *Facts on File,* Vol. 40, no. 2090 (November 28, 1980):895; and *New York Times,* March 15, 1981, p. 8.

10
Cuba and the United States: What Happened to Rapprochement?

Max Azicri

The year 1977 was the only one in which Cuba and the United States moved toward rapprochement.[1] Contrariwise, under Reagan, relations between the two countries deteriorated badly, returning to the level of open animosity that characterized the 1960s. This turn of events was no accident. Reagan came to the office determined to confront and contain once and for all what he understood to be unacceptable, unrestrained subversive Cuban activity in the region. Havana was accused of acting as a Soviet surrogate in what was seen as a particularly dangerous East-West conflict. Immediately after Reagan's inauguration, Alexander M. Haig, Jr., then secretary of state, announced that the line had been drawn in El Salvador by the United States, implying rather clearly that further revolutionary gains in the area would not be tolerated. Reagan favored a collision course with Cuba as the most advisable path to contain Castro.

The restrained antagonism of the 1970s gave way to unrestrained hostility. Originally, the nature of the Cuban socialist regime was the focus of U.S. objections, but with time Washington centered on Cuban activity in the Third World, particularly Latin America and Africa. Today, under President Reagan, it appears that the Castro regime is very much under attack for both its domestic and its international policies.

The Cuban-U.S. "problem" was removed from its original bilateral context. It became clear that an eventual accommodation between Reagan and Castro, a total impossibility on a strictly ideological basis, was an equally elusive commodity at a rational, pragmatic level of decision making. It was not only the inimical character, to the United

States and Western interests, of the closely scrutinized Cuban actions in Central America, the Caribbean, and Africa that mattered. The fact that the Cuban regime had aligned itself with the Soviet Union was equally unacceptable. For all of this Cuba was to be punished diplomatically and economically, with military action if everything else seemed to fail.

Cuba's justification of its actions in terms of proletarian internationalism (meaning that country's historical duty to support wars of national liberation and anti-imperialist struggles) made no difference to Reagan, Haig, and their Latin American advisers. Indeed, it is precisely this activity among Third World countries that provided the grounds for a carefully thought-out set of policies outlining drastic responses to Cuban threats to U.S. interests in the region and elsewhere that had not heretofore been properly checked. The blueprint, calling for a U.S. commitment to thwart political gains by revolutionary movements and regimes, was drafted by an ad hoc group of conservative Latin Americanists (the Santa Fe Committee) for the benefit of then presidential candidate Reagan. It was from the ranks of this group and other long-established conservative think tanks that the Reagan administration chose some of its top- and middle-level Latin American decision makers, as well as other officials of its foreign policy bureaucracy, including both the State Department and the National Security Council.

During the first months of the Reagan administration, public denunciations by Haig, Assistant Secretary of State for Inter-American Affairs Thomas O. Enders, and to a lesser degree Reagan himself aimed to isolate Cuba diplomatically in the hemisphere. The economic embargo of the island, originally announced by President John F. Kennedy on February 3, 1962, and enforced so far by six U.S. presidents, was more strictly applied. All of this gave a clear picture of the extent of Reagan's hard-line policy toward Castro.

Nonetheless, the United States might "reconsider" if only Cuba would both disassociate itself from the Soviet Union, "returning to the Western Hemisphere," and be willing to put an end to its long-standing objective of subverting Latin America and the Caribbean. According to this scenario, Castro would then be rewarded with open access to the U.S. market; the economic embargo would be lifted, and an undetermined amount of economic aid and credit would follow. As far-fetched as this may seem, given the nature of present U.S.-Cuban relations, the "sellout of Fidel Castro" was weighed by some in Washington as an unlikely alternative, but one worth considering, one that could even emerge from the "get-tough-with-Cuba" approach.[2]

Castro's Reaction to Reagan

On July 19, 1980, the first anniversary of the Sandinista victory in Nicaragua, Castro attended the commemorative rally held in Managua. As Castro reminded the more than 350,000 people packed at the Plaza of the 19th of July, it was from Puerto Cabezas, Nicaragua, that the 1,200 Cuban exiles, financed and trained by the Central Intelligence Agency (CIA), departed for their 1961 Bay of Pigs invasion. Condemning presidential candidate Reagan as a threat to peace, Castro denounced what he called dangerous political developments in Washington. Taking issue with the recently adopted platform of the Republican party, he characterized it as a "threat to peace," as a document advocating that the United States "apply the 'big stick' policy in Latin America."[3]

Castro repeated the same theme a few days later in Cuba. With an increased sense of urgency, recognizing the probable victory of Reagan in November, he stated that "there is a real possibility of the party that approved such a platform winning the U.S. election." Later, in December 1980, at the Second Congress of the Cuban Communist party, Castro discussed the implications of Reagan's victory for Cuba and Latin America. Recognizing that it was difficult to evaluate a president before he had actually been inaugurated, Castro insisted that the danger posed by Reagan and his policies was very real and, therefore, could not be omitted from his report, which reviewed the most important events and problems faced by the country since the First Party Congress in 1975. Acting rather carefully and in a guarded fashion, Castro communicated his own sense of foreboding about these events.

Throughout the winter, summer, and spring of 1981, in marked contrast with the anti-Cuban outcry coming out of Washington, Havana's actions were remarkably restrained by its own standards—indeed, they were practically out of character. Mainly, Cuba seemed concerned with publicly denying the accusations voiced by Haig, Enders, and others of its involvement in the civil war in El Salvador. At the 1981 celebration of the July 26 anniversary Castro avoided attacking Reagan directly.

It did not take long for things to change. Confirming that the grace period granted to the Reagan administration was over, the official Communist party newspaper, *Granma,* published in early September a front-page editorial, "Haig and the U.S. Government Are Lying Through Their Teeth," refuting a series of recent accusations made by Haig. According to *Granma,* the secretary of state had said before the U.S. Senate Armed Forces Committee that the supply of

Soviet arms to Cuba had reached record proportions in 1981; moreover, that there was serious evidence that some of these arms had been redistributed in Central America; and that an undetermined number of Cuban military advisers were acting with the guerrillas in El Salvador, seeking to overthrow the military–Christian Democratic junta headed by José Napoleón Duarte.

Cuba admitted receiving in 1981 "a considerable number of arms" destined for defense only—"in view of the plans for aggression against our country which have been openly proclaimed by the United States." The weapons were needed for the newly organized Territorial Troop Militias, half a million strong. All the other accusations were rejected as "completely false, 100 percent false." The editorial ended, reflecting the official position of the Cuban government, challenging Haig "and his government before the world and the U.S. public opinion to produce even a little bit of proof of such allegations."[4] Just eleven days later, the Cuban foreign minister, Isidoro Malmierca, was accusing the United States before the United Nations General Assembly of launching bacteriological warfare against Cuba—by then there were 113 deaths, 81 of whom were children, caused by the dengue fever epidemic, which affected a quarter of a million people.

At the opening session of the Inter-Parliamentary Conference held in Havana on September 15, 1981, Castro finally made public his own perception of the Reagan administration:

> The U.S. system is not fascist, but I am deeply convinced that the group which constitutes the main core of the current U.S. administration is fascist; its thinking is fascist; its arrogant rejection of every human rights policy is fascist; its foreign policy is fascist; its contempt for world peace is fascist; its intransigent refusal to seek and find formulas for honorable coexistence among states is fascist. . . . Never will I say that the people of the United States are fascists, nor would I ever say so of their legislative institutions, their press, their many creative social organizations. . . . Our hopes are founded on the certainty that fascism can succeed neither in the United States nor the world, although it is true that at present, a fascist leadership has established itself in the United States on the basis of a structure of an imperialist bourgeois democracy. And this is extremely dangerous.[5]

Castro's indictment of Reagan and his administration was harsh; it undermined any chance for future negotiations with the U.S. president. It reflected, however, Castro's anger and frustration in the face of endless U.S. anti-Cuban statements, policies, accusations, special task force reports, CIA and military operational plans, and many innuendos and constant threats of forthcoming punitive measures. It also was a deeply felt reaction to Reagan's ideology. It was meant too, as a warning to fellow revolutionaries from a leader who was engaged in direct confrontation with a U.S. president pursuing a militant brand of right-wing politics. And yet, Castro's remarks seemed to capture not only past events, but future developments as well.

Only a month later, at the Second Congress of the Committees for the Defense of the Revolution, Castro denied what he saw as a particularly disturbing and unfounded news report coming from the United States. It was reported on October 19 by syndicated columnists Roger Evans and Robert Novak, said Castro, that "Cuba has sent 500 to 600 elite soldiers to Nicaragua with a view to taking over El Salvador and establishing a revolutionary Marxist government there." After characterizing this as nothing but fabricated lies, he focused on the request made by both journalists at the end of their article for additional measures by the U.S. government to prevent this from happening. Castro concluded by saying that this meant a "call for measures against us, such as attacks and a blockade against us."[6]

After Castro's speech events gathered their own momentum. It was reported first on November 3 by the Mexican newspaper *Uno Más Uno,* whose Havana correspondent is usually well informed on Cuban affairs, that without officially saying so, Cuba had mobilized its armed forces and reserves, fearing a U.S. invasion: "Tension was rising in the Cuban capital with loudspeakers blaring 'revolutionary marches' and government-contolled newspapers urging Cubans to defend their independence." The national mobilization was prompted by a list of "concrete measures" that the United States could take against Cuba (the list was contained in a report given by Haig on October 30 to President Reagan). Generalized fears of a U.S. attack against Cuba and Nicaragua would not wash away easily. The French newspaper *Le Monde* reported that Cuban Minister of Culture Armando Hart had said in Paris that "the United States was looking for a 'pretext' to intervene. We are bombarded with threats. We read in the American press that American leaders are coldly preparing an armed intervention in Cuba and Central America. . . . We will not remain inactive. We are preparing to resist an armed American intervention."[7]

An intriguing dimension of such a volatile situation was that precisely in November a secret meeting between Haig and Cuban Vice-President Carlos Rafael Rodríguez took place in Mexico City; other top-level meetings would follow in 1982 with a similar lack of success, including a reported quiet visit in March to Havana by Ambassador-at-large (and diplomatic troubleshooter for Reagan) Vernon Walters, a retired army general. Whatever sensitive issues were included in the Haig-Rodríguez agenda, evidently discussing and going over them did not lead the parties to a commitment to further negotiations. Probably this was too much to expect from a single meeting, given the level of mutual hostility that had been reached and particularly given the depth of Reagan's anti-Castro feelings, which were central to his own ideological convictions. Thereafter, the state of military mobilization continued in Cuba for several months. If the Haig-Rodríguez talks were not able to reverse the rising tide of confrontation, at least they avoided any further escalation. Cuba's position, in all likelihood mentioned by Rodríguez at the meeting, that whatever arms and military assistance were provided to the Salvadoran rebels' Democratic Revolutionary Front (FDR) and its military arm, the Farabundo Martí National Liberation Front (FMLN), had stopped before Reagan's inauguration—probably lasting until, and in preparation for, the so-called final offensive launched in early January 1981—could have had a somewhat positive, even if not fully convincing, effect. This position, however, has never been publicly accepted by Washington; what has been recognized is that seemingly the rate of the alleged flow of weapons reaching El Salvador from Cuba via Nicaragua had declined later in 1981.[8]

And so went the Cuban response during the first year of Reagan's Cuban policy. Basically, Cuba appeared to be trying to cope with—by manipulating to some extent and placating as much as possible—an aggressive, militant U.S. president, while still pursuing its revolutionary political goals and interests in the Central American–Caribbean region. The military assistance component of Cuba's relationship with Salvadoran, and possibly Guatemalan, revolutionary forces was denounced by Washington, but its existence was never fully confirmed. It was mainly a question of Washington's applying to the current upheaval in the region well-known patterns of Cuban behavior in some Latin American countries in the past. That Cuba was playing an important card in the area was never questioned by any objective political analyst; the problem has always been to ascertain the nature and extent of such Cuban policies and to determine the means used in their implementation.

The Reagan Offensive

In pursuance of its anti-Castro campaign, the United States has put pressure on different fronts at the same time. The options, policies, and different fronts invoked by the Reagan administration include the following:

Military Warfare. In April 1981 an interagency task force under Haig considered different policy options that were expected to persuade

Castro "to give up the pretense that his little island with its 10 million inhabitants is a superpower." The options under study included instituting a total air and naval blockade (of Cuba, perhaps also of Nicaragua); fomenting a popular uprising inside Cuba against Castro (working on the assumption that the 1980 Mariel boatlift that brought 125,000 disaffected Cubans to the United States was a strong indication of public discontent with the regime); intercepting aircraft and ships transporting Cuban troops (stopping further Cuban support for national liberation movements, especially in Central America); bleeding some of the Cuban troops stationed in Africa by supporting South African–backed Savimbi guerrillas in Angola; and invading the island (using U.S. troops or Cuban exiles, or both).[9]

Reinforcing the public perception of the administration's willingness to apply military options, other important voices offered similar signals. On February 22 presidential adviser Edwin Meese warned Cuba that the United States was willing to implement a naval blockade to stop the Cuban arms flow into El Salvador. On March 18 Under Secretary of State for Political Affairs Walter J. Stoessel, Jr., stated before the Senate Foreign Relations Committee that the United States had not ruled out the use of force to stop the flow of Cuban arms to El Salvador. On June 3, Enders (not yet confirmed as assistant secretary for inter-American affairs) stated before the Council of the Americas in Washington: "Cuba has declared covert war on its neighbors—our neighbors. The United States will join with them to bring the costs of that war back to Havana."

On August 28 Haig, while accusing Salvadoran rebels of practicing "straight terrorism," affirmed that Soviet arms were still being shipped from Cuba to El Salvador. On October 29 Haig, speaking to a foreign policy conference with out-of-town journalists, affirmed that " 'extensive studies' have been completed within the government about ways to thwart . . . Cuban subversion and terrorism in the Western Hemisphere," which were still under review before being presented to President Reagan for approval. On November 4 Haig, in the face of a stalemate in the civil war in El Salvador, suggested that the Pentagon should consider taking action against Cuba and Nicaragua (given both countries' support for the rebels). On November 23 Secretary of Defense Caspar Weinberger announced that the two-year-old Caribbean Command housed in southern Florida—which was instituted in 1979 by President Carter in response to the then "discovered presence" of the controversial brigade of Soviet troops stationed in Cuba—had just been upgraded (the timing of this announcement, especially in conjunction with Haig's on October 29 and November 4, is particularly significant; most likely their compounded impact played a significant part in increasing Cuban fears of an imminent military attack by the United States).

Another source of militant anti-Castro sentiment and activity was the Cuban exile community in the United States. Reverting to what had been rather common practice in the 1960s, and to a lesser degree in the 1970s, action-oriented underground groups and organizations started their forays once again to the island on sabotage missions. Their training camps in southern Florida now included Nicaraguan exiles seeking to overthrow the Sandinista revolutionary Government of National Reconstruction in Managua. On July 4, 1981, five Alpha 66 (a Cuban exile organization with a long history of hit-and-run sabotage attempts against the Castro regime) commandos infiltrated the island on a mission to assassinate Castro on July 26; however, by July 9 all had been captured by Cuban security forces.

Suddenly, in March 1982, the pseudo-military conflict between the Reagan administration and the Cuban government became dangerously escalated, reminiscent of the October 1962 Cuban missile crisis. Soviet President Leonid Brezhnev threatened retaliation against the United States if it deployed new missiles in Europe. In a fast and equally threatening reply, referring to what was in many people's minds—that the Soviet statement meant that Cuban soil would be used once again for missile installations as in 1962—Weinberger declared that "the United States would do whatever was necessary to keep Russian missiles out of Cuba." The Cuban-U.S. conflict seemed fertile soil for another missile crisis—an unequivocal signal of how easily the current level of animosity could get out of hand. The global implications of the Cuban-U.S. problem, highlighted all along by the Reagan administration's approach, put both countries back into the East-West conflict.

Reasserting its military presence in the region, particularly in and around Cuba, on May 3, 1982, the United States, as part of the "Ocean Ventura 82" war games, landed 400 Marines at the U.S. Guantánamo Naval Base and evacuated 300 Americans in what Cuba characterized as "an intimidating show of strength." The military exercise sent a clear message to all involved: U.S. might was still very much a part of the Caribbean basin.

Psychological Warfare. The case could be made that most of the Reagan administration's policy studies and options, and statements by its leaders, amounted to an exaggerated form of psychological warfare rather than to military plans as such. It is not that the military option was not seriously considered—quite the contrary; but there is more to it than that. A nation-state can have an unmistakable intimidating effect on its adversary by making him know that the military alternative is there and that it is willing to use that alternative if necessary. This experience by itself could be psychologically devastating—especially in a situation such as this one, in which the correlation of military might is totally unbalanced. In some ways, the benefit that could be obtained from playing such a psychological warfare–military game may obviate having to use force to achieve national objectives. Simply put, it is an application to international regional politics of what governments do with their own police to gain compliance from the population with its own system of law and order. The idea behind it is similar: Most law-abiding states, like most law-abiding citizens, never see the force behind law and order applied to them. Compliance takes place simply because of the knowledge that force may, if necessary, be used; on the other hand, there may be other rewards as well for those who comply.

The political consequences, however, could be quite the opposite of what is intended. Rather than weakening the adversary's resolve, such a course may harden it; instead of causing more internal cleavages, such a course may unify its social body within its political system and may increase the people's support for their leaders. Psychological warfare has been used by Reagan not only against Cuba but also against Nicaragua. Both countries may undergo a similar internal process reacting to Reagan's threats, but Nicaragua may experience a more lasting reaction. That is, while Cuba today has an already institutionalized political system—a Marxist-Leninist state—Nicaragua is still state-building, developing its own revolution. Further radicalization of Nicaragua, and increased support from the revolutionary segments of its society, may occur as a consequence of the psychological warfare. Although Reagan may not be able to put an end to either revolution, he may be able to increase their similarities. In reality, the U.S. president is ruling out the possibility of the revolutionary pluralist experiment Nicaragua claims to be trying to carry out—combining the private and public sectors under revolutionary organization and leadership. Paradoxically, Reagan is telling revolutionaries in the region that radicalization aiming at the Cuban way is the only possible alternative if they want their revolutions to survive.[10]

Nevertheless, there were other means contemplated to put even further pressure on Castro: telling the Cuban people the truth about what its government is doing by setting up a radio station (Radio Martí, named after Cuba's national hero) with specialized programming emphasizing antirevolutionary propaganda. The idea as such goes back to the Santa Fe Committee; it was one of the committee's proposals about how to respond to Castro and his regime. The idea behind Radio Martí is an indication of how profoundly the Reagan administration believes in the reality of the alleged inequities of the

Cuban socialist system and the way in which the regime has to rely on force to sustain itself in power. But above all, it represents a firm belief in the universal goodness of the U.S. system, of the political and economic system based on liberal democracy and capitalism. Hence, if only the Cuban people could know the truth—and the instrument to accomplish this would be Radio Martí, with its powerful broadcasting towers aimed full-time at the island—they would eventually rise up against Castro.[11]

Economic Warfare. Another proposal made by the Santa Fe Committee was that the Reagan administration should find ways in which the U.S. economic embargo of Cuba could be made more effective, thus increasing the level of economic pressure against the Castro regime. In the 1970s, first under President Ford and later under President Carter, the economic embargo had been relaxed. Ford allowed U.S. subsidiaries in Third World countries to sell their manufactured goods to Cuba, and Carter lifted travel restrictions, allowing U.S. citizens to spend U.S. dollars visiting Cuba. Reversing this trend, the Reagan administration considered measures "aimed at stopping the illegal flow of American goods that seep into Cuba through third countries." This includes checking the operations of some import-export firms in third countries suspected of buying U.S. goods and having them shipped to Cuba (where most of the time they are sold in stores for tourists who pay in U.S. dollars). Defending policies necessary to take away this edge from the Cubans, Haig advocated " 'looking at further tightening' of U.S. trade restrictions against Cuba because of its conduct around the world."[12]

In May 1981 the U.S. Treasury Department ordered customs officers in Boston to block the delivery of Cuban books, magazines, and newspapers addressed to individuals, libraries, organizations, and scholarly institutions until they obtained a license from the Office of Foreign Affairs Control allowing them to receive such publications. This measure represented a rather restrictive application of the Cuban Assets Control Regulations, which were promulgated in 1963 pursuant to the Trading With the Enemy Act of 1917—the legal foundation for the Cuban economic embargo. After a group of concerned individuals and institutions took legal action in federal court, the Treasury Department rescinded its order (allegedly over the opposition of the State Department), again allowing delivery of Cuban publications without license (as long as no payment is made).

On April 18, 1982, new restrictions were imposed. This time tourism and business travel to Cuba were banned after May 15. The announcement of the decision was couched in political terms with a high dose of anti-Cuban rhetoric: "Cuba will not be allowed to earn hard currency from American tourists at a time when Cuba is actively sponsoring armed violence against our friends and allies,"[13] said John M. Walker, assistant secretary of the treasury for enforcement and operations. In reality, however, very few U.S. tourists were visiting Cuba, although the potential for an increment in the amount of U.S. tourism was always there. Those who have been visiting Cuba in large numbers are the members of the Cuban-American community. They have done so since 1979, although lately at a much lower rate than in that year, when more than 100,000 Cuban-Americans visited their homeland. This was possible, first, because of the Carter decision lifting the travel ban to Cuba, and second, because of the agreements reached at the 1978 Dialogue Conference held in Havana. At that conference, a special governmental committee presided over by Castro met with representatives from the Cuban community living abroad. The approved agenda included such points as releasing more than 3,000 political prisoners, allowing Cubans living abroad to visit their homeland, and instituting a family reunification program.

Obviously, the Cuban regime made political points with such an agreement, improving its international image. It also developed a new source of tourists. It is against this type of gain accruing to Cuba (primarily political but with some economic significance) that the new travel restrictions are aimed. Parenthetically, Cuban-Americans are still allowed under this new policy to travel to Cuba and visit their relatives, as can U.S. journalists and academics for research and scientific purposes. The net effect then is that what Cuba earns will be similar to its past earnings from this type of travel. As a consequence, the restrictions end up as harassment for the Castro regime and additional government control for U.S. citizens, limiting their freedom to travel wherever they may wish.

Diplomatic and Political Warfare. The Reagan administration's diplomatic and political approach to the turmoil in Central America and the Caribbean is based on a modified version, adjusted to the administration's conservative ideology, political program, and rhetorical style, of the Truman Doctrine (which was used in Greece in the late 1940s at a time of communist-inspired subversive activity in that area) and of the Alliance for Progress (in recognition of the still pressing socioeconomic and developmental needs of the region's countries). This combined approach updates the Monroe Doctrine and the 1947 Rio Treaty, whose enforcement was much in the mind of Reagan's Latin American policymakers.

The Reagan administration's approach was based on the notion that not only was East-West détente dead for all practical and ideological purposes, but that, instead, a rather critical confrontation between the "free world and Soviet aggressive expansionism" was taking place right at the center of the United States's weakest frontier: the Caribbean basin. In this struggle, Cuba, to a lesser degree Nicaragua, and even Grenada, were surrogates for the Soviet Union. Such a situation had to end. Cuba, the source of problems in the Caribbean, would have to abandon its activity in the region, its meddling in the internal affairs of neighboring states—as it did in Latin America in the 1960s and in Africa in the 1970s—or face the consequences of its actions.

Cuba's utilization of the principles of proletarian internationalism to justify its international behavior, in the eyes of Reagan, was nothing but a meaningless, thin license to rationalize its becoming a Soviet proxy in the Third World. The logical outcome of looking at this political problem from such a perspective was placing Cuban-U.S. relations in regional and hemispheric contexts and a global East-West context as well. It is not that the outstanding issues separating both countries for many years had been solved, but that, relatively speaking, they have lost some of their urgency, given the magnitude of the regional political problems under consideration.

This shift from a bilateral to a regional or even global approach under Reagan has made the Cuban-U.S. problem even more intractable than it had been previously. Cuban international behavior ("exporting its revolution") has always been a major concern for policymakers in Washington. It was, after all, in 1962 that a defiant Che Guevara said before the Organization of American States, meeting in Punta del Este, Uruguay, that the U.S.-sponsored Alliance for Progress had the name of the Cuban revolution written all over it; for it was U.S. fear that the Cuban example would be followed by other Latin American countries that caused the economic development program to be instituted. In this sense, Kennedy's alliance was not much different from Reagan's Caribbean Basin Initiative, as in both cases hemispherically inspired U.S. cold war motivations and intentions were behind them.

Assistant Secretary for Inter-American Affairs Enders summarized in June 1981 the administration's steps against Cuba as part of a set of U.S. tasks in the hemisphere. The measures to be applied to Cuba follow a sequential, logical order, underscoring their punitive character and avowed intention of stopping Castro from committing additional subversive acts at whatever cost. According to Enders, the United States was prepared to (1) "help threatened countries to defend themselves"; (2) "help threatened countries to preserve their people's right to self-determination"; (3) help countries of the basin to achieve economic success"; and (4) "focus on the source of the problem . . . Cuba . . . [thus] the United States will . . . bring the costs of [this] war back to Havana."[14] A May 1982 State Department informational reference explains that U.S. interests in the Caribbean basin are represented by a complex policy including the following categories: (1) "support for free elections and broadly based democratic institutions as the best way for each country to pursue its development according to the wishes of its people"; (2) "the Caribbean Basin Initiative, to help Basin economies overcome structural underdevelopment"; and (3) "collective security efforts and security assistance to help democratically oriented governments resist violence, externally supported insurgents who would impose totalitarian regimes hostile to the U.S."[15]

Reversing another trend aimed at initiating rapprochement with Cuba—such as when several Latin American countries reestablished relations with Havana following the 1975 decision by the Organization of American States (OAS) to annul its earlier agreement under U.S. auspices to impose a trade embargo and break off diplomatic relations with Cuba—a new U.S. campaign to again relegate Castro to hemispheric isolation was launched. After developing friendly relations with the Castro regime just a few years earlier, Ecuador, Venezuela, Panama, and Costa Rica began to reverse such relations, putting considerable distance between their own political positions and Havana's.

Colombia, on March 23, 1981, and Jamaica, on October 29, 1981, broke diplomatic relations with Cuba. After defending the so-called New International Economic Order as its champion at the United Nations in 1979, Cuba found itself excluded from the North-South Conference held in Cancún, Mexico, in October. Twenty-two representatives from developing and developed nations met for two days to discuss how industrialized countries from the West could help the world's poorest countries overcome their socioeconomic misery and underdevelopment. Reagan, preaching the economic wonders of the marketplace as a formula for development and industrialization, had no use for state-oriented, socialist rhetoric at the meeting. He made rather clear to Mexico, the host and organizer of the meeting, that Castro could not be invited if it was expected that he, Reagan, would attend the Cancún gathering.

Consistent with its chosen regional approach, the administration enunciated its Cuban policy, denouncing Cuba's threats to its neighbors. Once Cuban subversive actions were well known, it was believed, Washington's policies would be supported by both U.S. public opinion and U.S. friends in Latin America and elsewhere. The first of these public relations attempts to win public opinion was the so-called White Paper on El Salvador (February 23, 1981). In addition to Cuba, Nicaragua was accused of playing a major part in the communist-inspired subversive actions in El Salvador and elsewhere in the region. The White Paper was based on evidence gathered by security agents from the United States and allied countries. However, once the evidence was closely examined by political analysts, charges were made that the conclusions drawn in the report were not warranted by the evidence upon which they were supposedly based. These critical evaluations were published in magazines and newspapers (*Nation, In These Times, Wall Street Journal,* among others), with the immediate effect of turning the White Paper into an embarrassment for the administration.

Nevertheless, other major State Department reports followed, such as "Cuba's Renewed Support for Violence in Latin America" (December 14, 1981), "Cuban and Nicaraguan Support for the Salvadoran Insurgency" (March 20, 1982), and "Cuban Armed Forces and the Soviet Military Presence" (August 1982). Pleading the administration's case before the Subcommittee on Western Hemisphere Affairs of the Senate Foreign Relations Committee, Enders stated that Cuba was now committed to a "strategy for uniting the left in the countries of the region, committing it to violence, arming it, training it in warfare, and attempting to use it for the destruction of existing governments." Havana, he added, had been engaged in this type of policy since 1978, when it first departed from its 1967 policy of disengagement. Therefore, "we must communicate to Cuba that the cost of escalating its intervention in the region will be very high."[16] On April 3, 1982, the Office of East-West Policy and Planning in the Commerce Department's International Trade Administration published a report, "Cuba Faces the Economic Realities of the 1980s." After recognizing some improvements under the revolution in the fields of education and public health, the report was critical of the Cuban economy, pointing out its failures due to its adapting to the island an inefficient Soviet economic model. The political and economic implications of this report were to endorse indirectly the administration's Caribbean Basin Initiative as much as to publicize the shortcomings of the Cuban economy.

Mexico, Cuban Peace Initiatives, and the Falkland Islands

Mexican President José López Portillo held talks with Castro in Cozumel, Mexico, in August 1981—the third meeting held by the two leaders in as many years, including a visit to Havana by López Portillo the previous summer when the Mariel boatlift was still going on, at a time when Cuban internal problems were receiving extremely negative coverage by Western mass media. The Mexican vote of confidence, publicly supporting Castro and the Cuban revolution, stood in marked contrast to Reagan's hostile approach to the Cuban regime. However, in spite of clear differences between Mexico's and the United States's positions on Cuba, Nicaragua, El Salvador, and Central America and the Caribbean as a whole, both López Portillo and Reagan seemed to be capable of warming up relations between Mexico and the United States.

As if testing the endurance of this new rapport, López Portillo and French President François Mitterrand joined in a common statement declaring that Salvadoran guerrilla groups and the left in general represented a "legitimate political force." Meanwhile, making the opposite point, the Reagan administration took another step in its get-tough-with-Cuba approach and denied in September 1981 entry visas to four Cuban officials. Ironically, the Cubans had been invited to a Washington seminar in which new ways to improve relations between both countries were to be explored.

On February 21, 1982, speaking at the Carlos Fonseca Amador Revolution Square in Managua, President López Portillo offered a peace proposal for Central America and the region. Recognizing that there were three "focal points of conflict in the area: Nicaragua, El Salvador and—let's face it—relations between Cuba and the United States," he offered Mexico's services as a "communicator" and as a "guarantor" of any outcome. His idea was that Mexico could become a "bridge" between the United States on the one hand and Cuba, Nicaragua, and the Salvadoran guerrillas on the other. López Portillo recognized that the "fundamental security interests" of the United States should not be endangered by a process of détente in the area. His proposal called for peace negotiations among all the parties involved in civil war in El Salvador. He also proposed a series of nonaggression pacts between Nicaragua and the United States and between Nicaragua and its neighbors. Almost immediately, Cuba, Nicaragua, and the Salvadoran FDR/FMLN forces came out in favor of López Portillo's proposal. Washington's reaction was mixed at best.

Then, in March, either as a genuine initiative or as a way to humor Mexico, the United States sent Ambassador-at-large Vernon Walters to visit Havana. Although the outcome of Walters's visit was reportedly negative, the Cubans followed with a peace initiative of their own in April. Havana seemed to want a "relative accommodation" with the Reagan administration, and it was sending signals in that direction. Knowing that the word would eventually get to Washington's foreign-policy makers, a group of U.S. foreign policy specialists was invited to Cuba for a series of briefings on Cuban initiatives toward the United States. In the words of one Cuba-watcher present at the meeting, William M. LeoGrande, "Never before have the Cubans moved so far so fast in order to begin a serious dialogue with the U.S."

Dropping practically all preconditions for negotiations with the United States previously insisted on by Havana, Cuba stated some rather interesting points: (1) It did not want to become a "victim" of East-West confrontation; (2) it disapproved of the Soviet invasion of Afghanistan; (3) it would like the Soviet Union to stay out of Poland; (4) it recognized some responsibility for the current situation in Central America due to its previous weapons shipments to Salvadoran guerrillas, but these had stopped more than fourteen months previously; (5) it would never abandon its right (and responsibility) to supply Nicaragua with arms, but currently it was not exercising this right because Nicaragua had enough arms as it was; (6) it was advocating that Latin American countries move not toward socialism (the objective conditions were not yet present) but toward democratic social change; (7) it was willing to negotiate present foreign policy problems in a multilateral context, even before relations with the United States had been normalized; and (8) it was willing to negotiate with Washington the long-standing bilateral issues, including financial claims for nationalized property, Guantánamo Naval Base, and others, prior to the lifting of the economic embargo.[17]

The Reagan administration—the real objective of Cuba's initiative—disregarded the whole episode as a meaningless gesture, another one of Castro's political propaganda shows.[18] This was a wrong interpretation, however, based on a faulty assessment of present Cuban intentions and reality. Castro wanted to reach some degree of peaceful coexistence with the Reagan administration. The rising tension in the region, the very real possibility of U.S. military action, and the realization that if the diplomatic momentum established by the López Portillo peace proposal was allowed to vanish the opportunity might not return, all seem to have convinced Cuba of the wisdom of its peace initiative. Moreover, Cuba moved rapidly into an interlocked de-escalation of the Cuban-U.S. problem: (1) It removed the problem from the East-West confrontation by putting significant distance between itself and Moscow; (2) it removed the problem from the regional confrontation by its assurances that arms transfers to El Salvador and Nicaragua had ceased; and (3) it agreed to a simplification of the bilateral process by accepting the Mexican peace proposal and by yielding on the lifting of the economic embargo as a prerequisite for negotiations.

As in 1975–1976 with President Ford, when Cuba intervened in Angola, and in 1977–1978 with President Carter, when Cuba intervened in Ethiopia, it is highly unlikely that Cuba would renounce its deeply felt commitment to revolutionary regimes and movements in exchange for an agreement with President Reagan. This conflict of interests has always been and remains the major obstacle to a Cuban-U.S. rapprochement. But even if this commitment is a nonnegotiable question, it does not have to be approached as a zero-sum game. There is enough room for each country's international commitments and interests, and some acceptable level of rapprochement could be worked out. Cuba's peace initiative was a way of saying that there already was a de facto situation in which Reagan's previous objections were being properly met (i.e., by having stopped any shipment of arms to El Salvador). If a "relative accommodation" between Havana and Washington became a reality, then the present de facto situation would turn into a permanent de jure relationship, putting an end to more than two decades of mutual hostility.

On the heels of Reagan's rebuff of Castro's peace initiative came the war in the Falkland/Malvinas Islands. Reagan's political support for and military assistance to Britain in this conflict isolated Washington not only from Argentina, heretofore its military ally, but from Latin America as a whole. After implying repeatedly that the 1947 Rio Treaty might have to be invoked in Central America because an extracontinental power (the Soviet Union) was interfering in the Western Hemisphere (Central America) through its surrogates (Cuba and Nicaragua), Washington was then siding with Britain and its Western European allies in a war that was understood by Latin American countries as an attack by a European state against a fellow Latin American nation. For Reagan, NATO's commitments meant much more than any Latin American alliance. The United States found itself voting against the OAS majority, which recognized Argentine claims of sovereignty over the islands even if it did not support their forcible occupation as ordered on April 2 by Argentine President Leopoldo Galtieri.

Suddenly Cuba, openly supporting Argentina for what it called its struggle against colonialism and imperialism, found itself in line not only with overwhelming Latin American sentiment, but with the OAS majority as well. At a meeting of foreign ministers of countries in the Nonaligned Movement in Havana, Castro gave a warm *abrazo* to Argentine Foreign Minister Nicanor Costa Méndez, welcoming him to militant Third World politics, while the new Buenos Aires–Havana political rapport was sealed with a $100 million trade agreement.

The profound shifting of Latin American political sympathies and allegiances over the Falklands dispute allowed Cuban Vice-President Rodríguez to declare, while attending a United Nations special session on disarmament: " 'A new relationship among the countries of Latin America' [has emerged] in which the U.S. influence will be curtailed and Cuba's long isolation in the region will begin to lessen."[19] Venezuela's friendlier attitude toward Havana since the war seemed to validate Rodríguez's statement. The war allowed Castro to even the score with Reagan even if Cuba had not had much to do with the war itself. Unfortunately, however, the troublesome journey toward an elusive rapprochement between Cuba and the United States was not advanced by this last development.

Conclusion

The new, unknown quantity in Reagan's foreign policy in late 1982 was the new secretary of state, George P. Schultz. Although similarly conservative, in personality he is regarded as the opposite of the temperamental, almost mercurial Haig. There is the possibility that Schultz, by reducing the confrontational emphasis and the antagonistic rhetoric of Haig and his subordinates, may be able to find some real possibilities for dialogue with Cuba, even if Reagan's Cuban policy is not changed in terms of its basic political and ideological assumptions. After such developments as the electoral victory of the extreme right-wing political parties in El Salvador and the war over the Falkland Islands and their far-reaching political consequences, Reagan's Latin American policy, including, of course, his Cuban policy, demands nothing less than a complete overhaul. It is also up to Cuba to seize upon the opportunity of what could be a new chapter in the foreign policy of the Reagan administration and come forward with new, creative peaceful initiatives. Without expecting overnight miracles, a different political reality may still emerge if the level of tension and the mutual hostility displayed so far is reduced. Under such new circumstances, discussing the possibility of a Cuban-American rapprochement may seem reasonable, a goal that lies within the realm of what is politically feasible. The prevailing conservative political trends in the United States today have imposed on Cuba the task of looking for ways that without compromising its revolutionary principles, may nevertheless lead to an improvement in its relations with the United States—not only because Cuba and the United States would benefit from a future rapprochement, but also because the future and well-being of Central America and the Caribbean demand it.

Notes

1. There have been instances since 1959 when it seemed as if Cuba and the United States were in fact heading toward rapprochement. There is

speculation that Kennedy was considering that option before his death in 1963, that President Ford considered it until Cuban support for Puerto Rican independence and intervention in Angola thwarted any improvement, and that President Carter did also. After a remarkable first year in 1977 in terms of reconciliation, Carter moved away from such an action after Castro's decision to intervene militarily in Ethiopia.

2. This was initially suggested by Roger W. Fontaine in an interview by Don Bohning, published in the *Miami Herald,* August 24, 1980, and included later as part of the Santa Fe Committee Document. In the spring of 1982 both President Reagan and Secretary of State Haig mentioned it as a policy alternative, depending on the direction taken by Castro.

3. *Granma Weekly Review,* July 27, 1980, pp. 1, 2. Castro favored President Carter over Reagan and said so publicly. His decision to pardon thirty-three Americans serving prison terms in Cuban jails just before the election was an unsuccessful attempt to influence the U.S. voter. *New York Times,* October 14, 1980, pp. 1, 6.

4. *Granma Weekly Review,* September 13, 1981, p. 1.

5. Ibid., September 27, 1981, pp. 2–4.

6. Ibid., November 1, 1981, pp. 2–5.

7. Associated Press, November 8, 1981.

8. The Reagan administration's first major report denouncing alleged Cuban and Nicaraguan complicity in smuggling weapons into El Salvador for the leftist guerrillas was the so-called White Paper (U.S. Department of State, "Communist Interference in El Salvador," Special Report No. 80, February 23, 1981), pp. 1–8.

9. "Reagan's Goal—Cutting Castro Down to Size," *U.S. News and World Report,* April 6, 1981, pp. 20–22; "Reagan Administration Policy Toward Cuba Takes Shape," *Cuba Update* (Center for Cuban Studies), Vol. 2, no. 2 (July 1981):1–2, 5–6; and "U.S./Cuba Relations: A Chronology of Important Events," *Cuba Update* Vol. 2, no. 3 (October 1981):1–8.

10. Max Azicri, "A Cuban Perspective on the Nicaraguan Revolution," in Thomas W. Walker, ed., *Nicaragua in Revolution* (New York: Praeger Publishers, 1981), pp. 345–373.

11. "Cuban Liberty, American License," *New York Times,* September 27, 1981 (editorial), p. 20EY. The potential for a "radio war" between the United States and Havana if Radio Martí went on the air was evidenced by Cuba's retaliatory action on August 31, 1982. Broadcasting news and music programs on five AM frequencies, Havana interrupted U.S. radio. Earlier, the Cuban government had threatened to disrupt U.S. radio if Congress approved the administration's proposal. *New York Times,* September 1, 1981, p. 11A.

12. Associated Press, July 29, 1981.

13. Barbara Crosette, "U.S. Linking Cuba to 'Violence,' Blocks Tourist and Business Trips," *New York Times,* April 20, 1982, p. A1.

14. Thomas O. Enders,"Tasks for U.S. Policy in the Hemisphere," *Current Policy No. 282* (U.S. Department of State, June 3, 1981), pp. 1–3.

15. "U.S. Interests in the Caribbean Basin," *GIST* (U.S. Department of State, Bureau of Public Affairs), May 1982, pp. 1–2. Both Cuban and U.S.

negotiating positions have shifted at times, with some issues being more constant than others. For Cuba the issues include: (1) ending the economic embargo and other forms of commercial pressure; (2) ending all subversive activities—i.e., stopping the organizing of mercenary invasions and the like; (3) ending the pirate attacks against Cuba from U.S. bases in Florida or elsewhere in the Caribbean; (4) ending all violations of Cuban air and naval space; and (5) returning the U.S. naval base at Guantánamo to the Cuban government. For the United States the issues include: (1) obtaining financial compensation for confiscated U.S. properties; (2) ensuring human rights; (3) removing troops from Angola; and (4) ceasing participation in any kind of violence in the Western Hemisphere.

16. Thomas O. Enders, "Strategic Situation in Central America and the Caribbean," *Current Policy No. 352* (U.S. Department of State), December 14, 1981, pp. 1–3.

17. Leslie H. Gelb,"Those Noises from Cuba Could Be a Signal or Just Static," *New York Times,* April 18, 1982, p. E3.

18. According to Wayne S. Smith, chief of the United States Interests Section in Havana from 1979 until his retirement from the Foreign Service in July 1982, "Having blown the [Cuban-American] situation out of all proportion by discrediting it as a major East-West test of wills, [the Reagan administration] was determined to demonstrate in no uncertain terms that it could 'stop communism in its tracks.' It wanted confrontation, not negotiations." Wayne S. Smith, "It Is Not Impossible to Deal with Castro; Realism is Required," *New York Times,* September 5, 1982, p. E17. Also see his "Dateline Havana: Myopic Diplomacy," *Foreign Policy,* no. 48 (Fall 1982):157–174.

19. Karen DeYoung, "Cuban Says Falkland Crisis Eased Isolation," *Washington Post,* June 21, 1982, p. A1.

11
Cuba and the Soviet Union:
Does Cuba Act Alone?

Robert A. Pastor

Imagine, for a moment, that the U.S. Air Force helped airlift 36,000 Colombian soldiers to fight in an African country. At the same time, the United States flew tanks, artillery, and other heavy military equipment directly to that country for use by the Colombians, whose wounded were evacuated to the United States for treatment. Two years later, about 12,000 Colombian soldiers would be airlifted to another African country by the United States to fight under the command of a U.S. general. And imagine that Colombia received more economic aid from the United States than did any other developing nation and that it received all its military equipment free.

Now imagine how the Cuban government would describe Colombia. Would Cuban officials or scholars suggest that Colombia was an autonomous actor in international affairs or that it was leading the United States into Third World missions of liberation? Not likely. Even when Latin American governments rail against U.S. foreign policy in public and in private, Cuba has no compunction about referring to them as "puppets of U.S. imperialism." If one used Castro's own criterion of what constitutes a "puppet" or a "proxy," Cuba would qualify. No country in Latin America has so slavishly followed the international line of the United States in the 1970s as Cuba has that of the USSR. However, as Castro knows better than any American, the principal purpose of using words like "proxy" is propaganda—to force the target to defend its independence and to alter its policies.

This chapter will not use Castro's standard; rather its purpose is to analyze the extent to which one can view Cuban foreign policy as independent.

History: The Three-Sided Bilateral Relationship

On New Year's Day in 1959, Fulgencio Batista lost power in the streets of Havana, and 32-year-old Fidel Castro picked it up. Since then, Cuban foreign policy has pursued a number of goals, but two have been central: maintenance and enhancement of the Castro regime and support for communist, anti-American revolution abroad.[1] The tactics employed by the Cuban government have been as flexible as the objectives have been fixed. Three distinct phases in Cuban foreign policy, which correspond to changes in the Cuban-Soviet relationship, can be identified: (1) revolution by improvisation, 1959–1967; (2) revolution in due course, 1968–1975; and (3) revolution by professionalism, 1975 to the present.

Phase I: Revolution by Improvisation, 1959–1967

Castro had not fully consolidated his revolution in Cuba in 1959 when he began launching expeditions to overthrow neighboring governments in Panama, Haiti, and (twice) the Dominican Republic. Some have argued that Cuba's aggressive export of revolution to Latin America and the Caribbean in the early 1960s was a natural reaction to U.S. hostility—a tactic "to break the diplomatic and economic isolation imposed on it by the U.S."[2] However, it is hard to see how the Cuban revolution was made more secure by creating new foreign enemies or provoking old ones; and indeed, although the United States tried since 1960 to isolate Cuba by Organization of American States (OAS) sanctions, it was Cuba, not the United States, that in 1964 catalyzed inter-American solidarity by getting caught exporting its revolution to Venezuela and elsewhere.

Unique among the world's leaders, Fidel Castro has repeatedly attached as much importance to extending his revolution abroad as to trying to make it work in Cuba. Put a different way, from 1959 to the present he has been unwilling to sacrifice his pursuit of world revolution in order to enhance the security of his regime. The United States gave him a clear choice several times. On November 18, 1963, President Kennedy pointed to Castro's export of revolution as the main obstacle to normalizing relations: "This and this alone divides us. As long as this is true, nothing is possible. Without it, everything is possible."[3]

Similar statements were conveyed to the Cubans during the Ford and Carter administrations and most recently by George Schultz on July 13, 1982, in his confirmation hearings: "If they change, we can change."[4] Castro's response has remained unchanged. In 1962 he said, "The duty of a revolutionary is to make a revolution,"[5] and he has reaffirmed that assertion at every possible opportunity.

In the early 1960s, Castro and his Argentine comrade Ernesto (Che) Guevara pursued the elusive revolution through Bolivia, Guatemala, Colombia, Peru, and Venezuela. Their adventures stemmed initially not from devotion to the world communist movement but rather from a romantic Latin American tradition of revolution, a sense of social injustice, and a deep-seated animosity toward the United States. Their *foco* strategy was aimed at replicating their experience in Cuba, making revolution by a small, well-organized group. It was Leninism mixed with Latin American impatience and youthful exuberance.

This strategy stood in contrast to the methodical and deliberate approach of the Soviet-line communist parties in Latin America, which had been working for decades to create the conditions whereby revolution would become possible. The Cuban revolution caught them—and the Soviet Union—by surprise.[6]

Scholars differ on whether Castro was pushed into the waiting arms of the Soviet Union by an embittered and belligerent hegemone (the United States) or leaped on to the unsuspecting shoulders of the Soviets as the best means of centralizing his control. All agree, however, that this two-sided relationship was driven and shaped by an unconnected third corner—the United States—and that the consequence of the replacement of U.S. hegemony with that of the Soviet Union was the elimination of alternative sources of economic and political power within Cuba and the systematic consolidation of a bureaucratic-militarized state.[7] The Soviets provided Castro with a legitimizing doctrine, a protective security shield, and economic aid and support to withstand the U.S. embargo and to help the Cubans extend their influence.

In this improvisational period, the Cuban revolution was something of a mixed blessing for the Soviet Union. On the one hand, it represented the first advance of communism since the Chinese revolution, and as the ideological and strategic struggle with the People's Republic of China grew more serious, the Soviets were eager to have the Cubans associate with their line. On the other hand, although the Cubans electrified the romantic left in Latin America, they also confounded the traditional communist parties. Castro did make a few attempts to enlist the support of Latin America's communist parties, notably in a meeting of the Soviet Communist party and Latin American communist parties in Havana at the end of 1964. But he and Guevara had little patience with the communist parties, and in the cases of Venezuela, Colombia, and Guatemala, the Cubans were not averse to criticizing the communists and supporting the guerrillas.[8]

The communist parties feared that the revolutionaries—whom they called "leftist opportunists"—would provoke a harsh reaction and jeopardize all that they had sought to build. The Soviets urged the Cubans to be cautious and to work with the communist parties rather than try to run over them, but the Cubans did not listen. "In the end," Cole Blasier concluded, "events proved Moscow and the orthodox Communists right."[9] Both the guerrillas and the communist parties were crushed throughout Latin America, and in October 1967 Che Guevara was killed in Bolivia. To a great extent, Cuba's freewheeling period of fomenting revolution died with Che.

In 1967–1968, relations between the Soviet Union and Cuba reached the breaking point. The Soviets first used an orthodox group of the Cuban Communist party led by Aníbal Escalante to try either to preempt Castro or to persuade him to cease his support for the armed struggle in Latin America. When Castro crushed that group, the Soviets turned to more conventional leverage, reducing shipments of petroleum to Cuba, which was—and remains—dependent on the Soviets for 98 percent of its supplies. Simultaneously the Soviets announced additional exports of petroleum to Brazil and Chile, two enemies of Cuba.[10] As Cuba had closed its U.S. and China options, Castro had no choice but to accept Soviet direction.

Phase II: Revolution in Due Course, 1968–1975

Castro's endorsement of the Soviet invasion of Czechoslovakia in 1968 and the Brezhnev Doctrine, which asserted the right of the Soviet Union to define the limits of permissible behavior for communist countries, signaled the end of the improvisational phase of Cuban foreign policy and the beginning of a more conventional approach. No better example of the domestication of Fidel Castro can be found than his endorsement of the Brezhnev Doctrine, the Soviet equivalent of the Platt amendment, which the United States had imposed on the new Republic of Cuba in 1901 and which granted the United States the right to intervene in Cuba's affairs.

One author described this period as representing a "Cuban retreat from Castroism," and in 1970 Douglas Bravo, a Venezuelan guerrilla leader, accused Castro of selling out to the Soviets. The charge was close enough to the truth that Castro responded passionately: "Cuba has not refused nor will she ever refuse to support the revolutionary movements. But this is not to be confused with support for just any faker [or for] destroyers of revolutions."[11] (This, of course, was the line of argument used by the communist parties of Latin America to criticize Castro during the first phase.)

In this second phase, while adopting a foreign policy more compatible with that of the Soviet Union, Cuba also tightened its economic and political relationship, driven by the failure of the 10-million-ton harvest and the decline of the entire economy. In 1972 Fidel Castro visited Moscow twice to negotiate Cuban membership in the Soviet-bloc Council for Mutual Economic Assistance (COMECON) and to sign five agreements, which have been described as the "point of no return" for Cuban economic dependence on the USSR.[12] Castro also pledged that Cuba would never accept "opportunism, neutralism, revisionism, liberalism, or capitalist ideological penetration"; in short, the Soviet Union could rely on Cuba.

Although Cuba did not retreat from supporting revolution abroad, it put away its trumpet and avoided antagonizing the communist parties. After Che's death, Castro shifted his attention away from Latin America and more toward Africa, Asia, and the Middle East. Cuba had supported African liberation movements since the beginning of its revolution, but in this second phase Castro began investing personnel and resources in training and supporting the various liberation movements.

A major emphasis, however, was on reestablishing normal diplomatic relations with its neighbors and seeking leadership of the Nonaligned Movement (NAM). Latin American countries responded favorably to Cuba's expressed interest in peaceful relations, and by 1975, Argentina, Peru, Colombia, Venezuela, Panama, Costa Rica, and the four main English-speaking Caribbean nations—Jamaica, Barbados, Trinidad and Tobago, and Guyana—had all reestablished diplomatic relations. The United States also privately began to explore relations in 1975 and publicly played an important role in removing OAS sanctions.

Cuba joined the NAM in 1961 principally to gain international support for its revolution and to raise the international costs to the United States of any interference in Cuba's affairs. In the second phase, Castro moved aggressively to align the NAM with the Soviet Union. In 1973, at the Fourth Nonaligned Summit in Algiers, Castro rejected the theory of two imperialisms—U.S. and Soviet—because of the "glorious, heroic, and extraordinary services rendered to the human race" by the USSR. "How can anyone call the Soviet Union imperialist?" Castro asked. "Let others lament the fact that the Soviet Union has become an economic and military power. Cuba rejoices. . . . Inventing a false enemy [the USSR] can only have one aim, to evade the real enemy [the United States]."[13]

Castro's attempt to steer the NAM toward the Soviet Union was resisted and denounced by a number of leaders, including Cambodia's Prince Sihanouk and by Col. Muammar al-Qadaffi of Libya, who said:

> We are against Cuba's presence in this conference of non-aligned nations. There is no difference between Cuba and any East European country, or for that matter Uzbekistan and the Soviet Union itself. The difference between me and Castro is that he is a communist and I am a socialist: he is aligned and I am not.[14]

Phase III: A Coordinated, Professional Approach to Revolution

The third phase of Cuban foreign policy began in September 1975 with the massive Cuban military intervention in Angola. If the first phase represented Cuban pursuit of an objective—communist revolution—shared by the Soviet Union by tactics that were not, and the second phase, Cuban acceptance of Soviet tactics, the third phase represented the culmination of the new and deeper relationship—a more coordinated and professional approach to extending communism to the Third World. In 1975 the first Congress of the Cuban Communist party approved a platform that acknowledged the subordination of Cuban to Soviet foreign policy.

In September 1975 the first detachment of 1,000 Cuban soldiers arrived in Angola to fight on behalf of the Popular Movement for the Liberation of Angola (MPLA), one of three Angolan factions seeking power. There had been up to 100 Cuban advisers in Angola for at least a decade and roughly 250 since the spring of 1975, but the September intervention represented the first use of Cuban combat troops on a major scale. Cuban soldiers arrived by ship and by airplane from Cuba, but most of their equipment came directly from the Soviet Union and Eastern Europe. After the South African incursion on October 23, some 2,000–3,000 Cuban reinforcements were airlifted; they arrived before the Portuguese formally lowered their flag on November 11 and Angola ceased to be a colony.

By January 1976, there were 10,000–12,000 Cuban troops using increasingly sophisticated Soviet weaponry, and the Cuban-backed MPLA was firmly in charge of Luanda and much of the country. Castro would later admit that at the height of Cuban involvement in the spring of 1975 there were 36,000 Cuban troops in Angola.[15]

The coordinated Soviet-Cuban effort was highly successful, not just in securing a friendly regime in a strategic area, but in effectively and, in the eyes of most Third World governments, legitimately using force in a regional conflict against the *bête noire* of the Third World, South Africa. Although the U.S. government saw Cuban involvement as a dangerous extension of Soviet influence, few in the Third World viewed it in that light. Cuba exploited its success by broadening its diplomatic relations in Africa (from eight nations in 1972 to thirty-one after Angola), by deepening its relationships in the Caribbean among groups and governments that were sympathetic with the black African struggle against South Africa, and by being elected host to the sixth summit of the NAM to be held in September 1979, thereby becoming chairman for the following three-year period.

Cuba also earned significant new amounts of economic and military aid from the Soviet Union for the operation. On April 14, 1976, the Soviet Union signed a new five-year economic agreement with Cuba that more than doubled Soviet economic and technical aid. The Cuban military also profited, increasing its political power in Cuba (two generals were appointed to the Council of State) and gaining a new generation of sophisticated military equipment from the Soviets. As a result of Angola, the Cuban military was transformed from one primarily defensive in nature to one with a significant offensive capability.

Just as Cuba chose military involvement in Angola rather than normalization of relations with the Ford administration, so too did it choose its next military involvement—in Ethiopia—in January 1978 despite clear messages from the Carter administration that such an act would make further progress toward normalization impossible. The Ethiopian operation was the result of complete coordination with the Soviet Union, and 12,000 Cuban troops fought under the command of a Soviet general.

Unlike the Angolan intervention, the Ethiopian operation generated considerable criticism in Africa. General Olusegun Obasanjo of Nigeria summed it up at the Organization of African Unity Summit in 1978 with a clear warning:

> To the Soviets, I should like to say that they should not overstay their welcome [in Africa]. Africa is not about to throw off one colonial yoke for another. They should see it to be in their interest not to seek to maintain perpetually their presence in Africa. . . . Let the Soviets and their collaborators heed this timely counsel.[16]

To Latin Americans, Cuban involvement in Africa was too distant to be a source of anxiety; many leaders joked that they preferred the Cubans to be in Africa rather than in Latin America. The Cubans did both. In March 1979 a group of radicals called the New Jewel Movement (NJM) seized power in Grenada in the first undemocratic change of government in the English-speaking Caribbean and requested Cuban support. There is some evidence that the Cubans assured the

NJM that if they were able to seize and hold power for a short time, the Cubans would soon come to their aid, as they did.

Some feared that Grenada was just the opening wedge in a new and more aggressive strategy in the Caribbean, but Cuba, by and large, continued to pursue correct state-to-state relations in the area. Radical groups, who had been encouraged by the Grenadian example, sought power through parliamentary channels but were beaten decisively in elections in every nation.[17] In only two cases did the Cubans overreach: in Jamaica, through the obtrusive meddling of their ambassador, and in Suriname, by trying to exploit the 1980 revolt of the sergeants (two years later, the Cubans were more successful influencing development in Suriname). In both cases, Cuban efforts were counterproductive, and their political comrades were defeated.

Cuba's approach toward Central America tended to favor armed struggle as the path to power because the region's politics were violent and because Castro felt he had some scores to settle against governments that had tried to overthrow him. Needless to say, Cuba observed political developments in Nicaragua in 1978–1979 with great interest, but it let Venezuela, Panama, and Costa Rica play the central role in helping the Sandinistas. Cuba stayed in the background, offering political and military advice to the military *comandantes* and supplying arms to the Sandinistas through a variety of means.

The victory of the Sandinistas emboldened Castro, just as his success in Angola had caused him to overreach into Ethiopia and his success in Grenada, to intrude into Jamaica. While cautioning the Sandinista leadership to go slow in implementing the revolution, he sought to accelerate the revolutionary process in El Salvador and Guatemala. Again, he used his considerable political influence to unify the various guerrilla groups, trying to create broad national fronts that would attract the middle class. At the same time, Cuba provided training, weapons, and advice to the guerrillas. Cuba also stepped up its support for guerrilla activities in Colombia and perhaps also in Venezuela and Peru and permitted its bilateral relationships with most of the governments in the area to deteriorate.

At the sixth summit of the Nonaligned Movement held in Havana in September 1979, Castro was so brazen in trying to steer the entire NAM toward the Soviets that he antagonized many of the participants. The most serious setback to Cuban aspirations for NAM leadership, however, was caused by the Soviet invasion of Afghanistan, a NAM member.

In the third phase, Cuba used troops in Africa, sophisticated political operatives in Central America, covert actions everywhere, arm-twisting diplomacy in the NAM, and training programs on a massive scale.

The Isle of Youth, on which a training center was opened in 1977, trained 26,000 children from Cuba, Africa, and Central America to make revolution; this typified the Cubans' long-term professional investment in revolution.

Summary

Cuban foreign policy has been singular in its pursuit of consolidating revolution at home and promoting it abroad, but tactics have changed as Cuban needs have deepened, as targets of opportunity have appeared, and as dependence on the Soviet Union has increased. In the first phase, Castro tried to duplicate his success in Cuba by pursuing revolution by improvisation at home and throughout Latin America. The Soviet Union patiently subsidized his experiment, but when repeated failures jeopardized Soviet-line communist parties, the Soviet Union forced Cuban policy into line.

In the second phase, Cuba tightened its relationship with the Soviet Union and the world communist movement, and it tried to align the Nonaligned Movement with the Soviets. It pursued revolution in due course, by investing in radical groups and liberation movements and legitimizing its strategy through broadening its diplomatic relationships. In the third phase, Cuba reaped the benefits. New "targets of opportunity" appeared in Angola, Ethiopia, Nicaragua, and Grenada, and Cuban capabilities and the Soviet-Cuban team were primed and trained to exploit them.

The Structure of the Current Relationship

One of the major intellectual contributions of Marxism to social science is the concept that human or institutional behavior is shaped, and sometimes determined, by economic and political structures. Let us therefore examine the structure—specifically, the economic, political, military, and attitudinal bonds that currently tie Cuba to the Soviet Union and affect the day-to-day relationship.

The economic relationship between Cuba and the Soviet Union has evolved from a few project agreements in the early 1960s, to membership in COMECON in 1972, to two five-year economic plans (1976–1980 and 1981–1985), which further integrated Cuba into the Soviet economic system. From 1960 to 1979, Cuba received the equivalent of $16.6 billion in aid from the Soviet Union.[18] Of this, about 35 percent (or $5.7 billion) was loans provided as balance of payments support and development aid, and 65 percent (or $10.9 billion) was subsidized prices for sugar and nickel that the Soviet Union purchased from Cuba and reduced prices of petroleum that it sold to Cuba. (In 1979, Moscow paid 44¢ per pound of sugar—five times the world price—for 3 million tons and sold 200,000 barrels per day of oil at $12.80 a barrel—or roughly one-third the OPEC price.)

The overall level of aid has quadrupled since 1974, partly in compensation for new Cuban activities in the world and partly because the world price of sugar has declined and that of oil has risen much more rapidly than Soviet prices. Soviet aid amounted to about $3 billion in 1978 and again in 1979, representing about one-fourth of the Cuban gross national product in each year. In 1972, the USSR terminated interest charges on Cuba's debt and postponed initial repayment until 1986. Cuba's debt reached $2.6 billion in 1980, of which $1.6 billion is hard-currency debt to Western commercial banks.

There have been three enduring strains in Cuba's economic development in the last twenty years. First, the economy remains very dependent on the export of sugar—probably the only country in the world more dependent on a single crop in 1978 (83 percent of exports) than in 1958 (78 percent). Second, it remains strikingly dependent on a single trading partner. In 1959, 68 percent of Cuba's trade was with its nearest neighbor, the United States; twenty years later, 66 percent of its trade was with the Soviet Union. Third, it continues to suffer a chronic trade deficit, currently financed by the Soviet Union.

Cuba is more vulnerable economically today than before the revolution because of its increased dependence on petroleum and hard currency. The probability that the Soviet Union will use this leverage in the years ahead if the Cubans prove recalcitrant on a particular issue is greater still because the Soviets themselves will be the object of considerable pressure internally and in Eastern Europe to use their oil for other purposes.

The military relationship has drawn much closer since the intervention in Angola. Cubans fought under Soviet command in Ethiopia while Soviet pilots substituted for them in Cuba. Cuba is the only country receiving Soviet military equipment free of charge, and it has been receiving massive quantities of it. Most recently in 1981, according to the U.S. State Department, Cuba received some 66,000 tons of military equipment, including the most sophisticated jet fighters, transports, and naval vessels—three times more equipment than in any previous year since 1962.[19] The State Department estimates a total of about 40,000 Cuban soldiers in a dozen African nations and 1,800 to 2,000 military and security personnel in Nicaragua. Although Cuba is not a member of the Warsaw Pact, Cuban leaders routinely participate as observers in Warsaw Pact military maneuvers. Cuba provides facilities for port calls by Soviet submarines, a massive intelligence-collection facility, an air base to deploy Soviet reconnaissance aircraft, and training facilities for tropical warfare for a 2,600-man Soviet combat brigade.

The political relationship between the two governments has been shaped by personal relationships and by the Cuban Communist party, which Fidel Castro calls "the revolution's finest expression and guarantee." As dependence on the Soviet Union increased, the Cuban Communist party grew in importance and in numbers—doubling its membership from 1970 to 1975 and again from 1975 to 1980.

On the question of how the Cuban and Soviet peoples have come to view each other, it is useful to distinguish between popular and elite attitudes. Cubans, as a people, are quite open, candid, and self-critical. However, despite the large number of Soviet advisers stationed there during the last twenty years, relationships between the Soviets and the Cubans remain cool and remote; most Cubans use every opportunity to poke fun at the Soviets. Soviet citizens, for their part, are disturbed by the boasts of their leaders that the Soviet government has provided so much aid to Cuba. They do not understand why their government continues to ignore domestic needs while giving so much to a distant little island.

The leaders of both governments acknowledge their respect for one another, both privately and publicly. The Soviets probably feel some vicarious thrill that Castro is carrying forward the revolutionary torch of Lenin. The Cubans feel personally distant from the Soviet leadership but always pledge their public support and avoid any private criticism. In his speech before the Cuban Communist party's first congress in 1975, Fidel Castro acknowledged the Cuban debt: "Without the decisive, steady, and generous aid of the Soviet people, our country could not have survived the confrontation with imperialism."[20]

Cuban dependence on the USSR for economic and military aid, support, and defense is staggering not just because of the magnitude of the aid and its importance to the Cuban economy, but also because Cuba lacks an alternative. As the Cuban government has no apparent interest in either ceasing its support for revolution or starting a new dependent relationship, a normal relationship with the United States is unlikely, even though popular attitudes in Cuba and elite attitudes in the United States might support bridging the chasm separating the two countries. The structure of the current relationship suggests that the Soviets will retain considerable power to compel Cuban foreign policy to remain within proscribed boundaries.

Process: Cuban-Soviet Interaction

To understand the role of Cuban foreign policy in the Cuban-Soviet relationship, it is important to understand not only the structure and the boundaries of the relationship, but also the process of interaction.

During the last twenty years, the only public disagreement between Cuba and the Soviet Union was during the missile crisis, when the Soviets agreed to withdraw their missiles and permit international inspection in exchange for a U.S. pledge not to invade Cuba. Castro strongly condemned the Soviet decision. No other incident could possibly say more about the different perspectives of the two governments, and the implications of this for Cuban foreign policy, than the missile crisis. The Soviet Union recognized its responsibility as a nuclear power to keep the world from tripping over the brink into nuclear holocaust, but Cuba, a small revolutionary government, would risk confrontation to avoid compromising with U.S. imperialism. In fact, the 1962 understanding was not consummated until 1970 because Castro would not permit international inspection of the missile sites. As late as October 1, 1979, in an interview with Dan Rather, Fidel Castro was not at all reticent in pointing to that incident as an example of when Soviet and Cuban policies diverged, nor has he concealed the fact that he would have taken the world over the brink in 1962 if the Soviets had let him.

Cuba remains more eager than the Soviet Union to take risks, more willing to assist national liberation movements in any and all ways, and more inclined to support any government—whether social democratic like the Manley government in Jamaica or right-wing like the military government in Argentina—provided that it is critical of or hostile to the United States. The Soviet Union shares both objectives but is naturally more reluctant about directly confronting the United States, more interested in maintaining its control of Eastern Europe, more protective of the international communist movement, and more niggardly about providing foreign aid.

In those areas in which Cuban and Soviet objectives and tactics converge, such as in Angola, Ethiopia, and the Middle East, one could predict that the Cubans would encourage the Soviets to do a little more, a little quicker while the Soviets would be more cautious and sensitive to the geopolitical implications of sending Cuban and/or Soviet soldiers into combat. In the case of Angola, for example, scholars who stress the independence of Cuban foreign policy have argued that the Cubans pressed the Soviets to undertake the operation rather than the other way around. That argument is plausible, for

Castro is undoubtedly more predisposed to risking an adventure. Moreover, the risks would be greater for the superpower if the Cubans were defeated and the Soviets watched passively. But once it became clear that the South Africans would withdraw, that U.S. involvement would be minimal, if anything, and that no other foreign military involvement was likely, the massive Cuban intervention seemed an effective and relatively low-risk operation. It needs to be recognized, however, that the Cuban effort would never have reached the magnitude it did without Soviet consent and logistical support, so that the suggestion that the Cubans did not even consult the Soviets is unrealistic. Moreover, the Cuban effort could not have succeeded if the Soviets had opposed it, or even if they had not supported it. Cuban Vice-President Carlos Rafael Rodríguez admitted as much: "Cuba and Angola did not have all the technical means for their men to fight the racist South African army . . . without the U.S.S.R., imperialism would have defeated the Angolan people."[21]

In Central America and the Caribbean, the Soviets have probably given the Cubans the most room to maneuver because the Cubans clearly know both the actors and the political landscape better and also because Fidel Castro has tremendous personal influence over the region's revolutionaries, which the Soviet Union could never duplicate. Occasionally the Soviets used the Cubans as intermediaries, such as in August 1981, when Cubans arranged a meeting in Panama between a senior Soviet Communist party functionary and Central American communist party leaders to discuss strategy in the region.[22]

The Cubans probably lobbied the Soviets to give more aid to Nicaragua, Grenada, and while Manley was in power, Jamaica, but the Soviets are not eager to subsidize other governments, as it is hard to see how these governments could benefit the Soviet Union any more than Cuba already does. The Soviets have been burned in Egypt, Indonesia, Ghana, and Somalia and are understandably reluctant to bankroll other governments that have not yet committed themselves totally to communism. Moreover, the Soviets probably see the Nicaraguan and Grenadian governments as Fidel's "offspring" rather than their own and are less certain of their survivability and therefore more reluctant to commit Soviet prestige. So it is perfectly understandable that the Cubans would press the Soviets to give more aid and political and military support, while the Soviets would hold back, on the one hand insisting on fealty to communism and on the other hand urging these governments not to antagonize the United States lest they become totally dependent on scarce Soviet aid. In short, Soviet strategy has to be much more ambivalent than Cuban strategy.

The Soviets are on occasion disturbed or perplexed about Cuban policy, but they are likely to interfere only when their direct interests are involved. For example, the Soviets were confused by Castro's behavior during the Mariel exodus, and they were also disturbed that Cuba so quickly destroyed the relationships it had built over a decade with Venezuela, Colombia, Ecuador, Costa Rica, Peru, and Jamaica. But there is no evidence that they communicated this concern to the Cubans.

On Poland and Afghanistan, in which Soviet and Cuban interests diverged, the Soviets did not even bother to keep the Cubans informed. In 1979 one of Cuba's principal foreign policy goals was to assume the leadership of the Nonaligned Movement in fact as well as in name and to try to steer the movement toward a "natural alliance" with the Soviet Union. After the summit, Cuba sought a seat on the United Nations Security Council in its capacity as chairman of the NAM, but the majority of Latin American states balked and joined the United States, Western Europe, and a number of Asian governments to block Cuba's bid. After more than one hundred votes in which Cuba was often quite close to winning the seat, the Soviets invaded Afghanistan, and within days the Cubans recognized that their position in the NAM was undermined and withdrew.

It must have been painful for Castro, who had the leadership of the NAM and the Third World almost within his grasp, only to be deprived of it by his patron—particularly as the Soviets did not consult him prior to their intervention or brief him afterward. One month after it occurred Castro was still puzzled about what had happened and why the Soviets had done it.[23] But when the United Nations General Assembly moved to condemn the Soviet Union for the invasion, Castro did not need instructions from the Soviet Union; he knew what position to take.

In a convoluted speech somewhat reminiscent of Castro's endorsement of the Soviet invasion of Czechoslovakia in 1968, the Cuban ambassador to the United Nations voted with the Soviet Union, but instead of endorsing the invasion, he attacked U.S. imperialism. That was as near as Castro could bring himself to criticizing the Soviet action, which had cost him dearly.

Privately, Cuban Vice-President Carlos Rafael Rodríguez would inform a group of U.S. academics in the spring of 1982 of Cuban displeasure over Afghanistan and Poland, but only on condition that he would not be quoted directly.[24] Publicly, in his speech to the Second Party Congress in December 1980, Fidel Castro defended the Soviet invasion of Afghanistan ("the USSR had to help save the process and preserve the victories of the April 1978 revolution") and intervention in Poland. "What happened there," Castro said in reference to Poland, "was partly a result of imperialism's subversive policy toward the socialist countries and its long-range design to penetrate, destabilize, and wipe out socialism in Eastern Europe, thus weakening and isolating the USSR and, if possible, destroying socialism throughout the world." But Castro went even further in endorsing the right and responsibility of the Soviet Union to prevent change in Poland and, by implication, to secure all communist regimes: "There is not the slightest question about the socialist camp's right to save that country's integrity and ensure that it survives and resists at all cost imperialism's onslaught."[25]

Partner, Proxy, Puppet, or Paladin?

How should one characterize the relationship between Cuba and the Soviet Union? Since the Cuban involvement in Angola, three quite different U.S. administrations have referred to Cuba as a "proxy" of Soviet policy, but most academics reject that term. "Cuba is not the Soviet Union's proxy in Africa," wrote political scientist William LeoGrande; "the two are partners, and though the partnership is asymmetrical, it is reciprocal nonetheless."[26] Cole Blasier, a noted scholar on both Latin America and the Soviet Union, wrote: "Castro has shown time and again, most particularly in the 1960s, that he is not a Soviet puppet, but a formidable negotiator, and useful ally."[27] And finally, Edward González and RAND has suggested that Cuba is really a "paladin," which denotes Cuba's autonomy "and her value as a separate global actor."[28]

Castro, of course, insists on his independence. In an interview in April 1976 about whether in sending troops to Angola he acted on his own or at the command of the Soviet Union, Castro insisted: "Cuba made its decision completely on its own responsibility. The U.S.S.R. . . . never requested that a single Cuban be sent to that country."[29] And in a typical response to a similar question by Dan Rather, on October 1, 1979, Castro threw the question back: "I am not going to respond to that ridiculous charge, but I will ask a question: Why, if we are a satellite country, is there so much attention paid to Cuba? And it is obvious that the U.S. government in the political field is paying practically more attention to Cuba than to the Soviet Union. So then we are unquestionably facing a strange case of a satellite."

Precisely. The reason that it has proven so difficult to attach a label to the Cuban-Soviet relationship is because it is unique; it is "a strange case of a satellite." Castro clearly believes that he acts on his own, and anyone who has spoken with him or knows anything about him cannot believe that he could take instructions from anyone. Although the expansionist character of Cuban foreign policy may serve Soviet interests, it also serves and is derived from three Cuban interests: (1) Egoism: Fidel Castro wants to transform not only Cuba but as much of the world as he can. (2) Nationalism: The extension of Cuban influence abroad clearly responds to the needs of a newly integrated nation; that is one reason why some Cuban-Americans who despise Castro felt a quiet pride over Cuba's adventures in Africa. (3) Ideology: The pursuit of "proletarian internationalism" clearly ties the internal with the international revolution and energizes both. But just because Cuban international activities respond to internal motives rather than external command does not mean that Cuba is an independent actor.

Cuba is neither a "puppet," a nation whose policies "are prompted and controlled" by the Soviets, nor a "partner" in the sense that denotes some rough form of equality. However, to the extent that a "partner" means "a player on the same side or team," as Cuba is with the Soviet Union, and with the understanding that the latter is the captain, the coach, and the owner of the team, the term could be considered more accurate. But this view suggests the Cubans do not call any plays themselves, which they clearly do; or that they would only accidentally go "off-sides," "clip," or "rough the kicker," which they clearly do on purpose and with considerable relish.

González's term "paladin" is clever if one identifies it with the "hired gun" of a popular television show. The dictionary definition, however, says that a "paladin" is "one of the twelve legendary knights of Charlemagne, therefore a determined advocate or defender of a noble cause." This does not appear to be what González had in mind, nor does it seem applicable. "Surrogate" or "proxy" means "one who is appointed to act for another; a deputy; a substitute," but this too is inadequate since it suggests that the Cubans are acting only in the Soviets' interests, whereas they are clearly acting in their own as well. It suggests that the two nations' foreign policies are virtually interchangeable, although the previous discussion on the evolution of Cuban foreign policy and the process of interaction with the Soviets makes it clear that the Soviet Union and Cuba have two foreign policies, not one. They share some important objectives—extending communism and containing the United States—but because of different national perspectives and interests, the leaders of the two nations do not see the world in identical ways nor do they approach it in the same way. Cuba might very well be more of a *demandeur* in its relationship with the Soviet Union, as the burden of maintaining international peace sits more lightly on Castro's shoulders than on those of the Soviet leadership, and because the Cubans are offering Soviet resources rather than their own.

The combination of Cuban manpower and Soviet resources has proved an effective tool for furthering the two nations' interests in the world. The Soviet Union cannot undertake the kinds of activities and operations in the Third World that the Cubans do routinely without provoking global tensions and perhaps a response from the United States or the People's Republic of China. The irony is that the United States is inhibited from confronting Cuba because Cuba is perceived as an independent, Third World nation struggling against the most powerful nation in the world.

The Cubans do make tactical foreign policy decisions themselves, but strategic decisions such as those that involve Cuban troops require Soviet consent. Scholars or policymakers are hard-pressed, however, to find an area in which Cuban and Soviet foreign policies have significantly diverged since 1968—certainly not in Angola, Ethiopia, Central America, the Caribbean, or the Nonaligned Movement. In areas where Cuban interests might lead them in a different direction—like Afghanistan, Poland, or China—the Cubans have dutifully supported the Soviet position.

It has been argued that Cuba is a small country with a big country's foreign policy.[30] No other developing nation maintains more diplomatic missions, intelligence operatives, and military advisers and troops abroad than does Cuba, not even the oil-producing states that can afford it. The gap between its internal resources and its external capabilities is filled by the Soviet Union, not because of altruism, but because the Soviets are assured that what the Cubans do abroad will serve their purposes. That does not mean that the Soviet Union gives instructions—it generally does not have to, as was shown, for example, by the vote on Afghanistan. Soviet instructions are not necessary because Cuba is pursuing a set of interests that coincide with those of the Soviet Union.

The Soviets do not tell the Cubans what to do, but they do let the Cubans know what they cannot do, and the Cubans accept that. As Fidel Castro himself put it at the first Cuban Communist Party Congress in 1975 and reaffirmed at the second in December 1980: "The Communist Party of Cuba considers itself a modest but reliable detachment of the international communist movement."[31] Cuba is not alone, but it is quite an actor.

Notes

1. For an alternative discussion of Cuban foreign policy, which identifies five objectives, see Jorge I. Domínguez, "Cuban Foreign Policy," *Foreign Affairs,* Vol. 57, no. 1 (Fall 1978):83.

2. William M. LeoGrande, *Cuba's Policy in Africa, 1959–80* (Berkeley: University of California Institute of International Studies, 1980), Policy Papers in International Affairs, No. 13, p. 1.

3. U.S., President, *Public Papers of the United States: John F. Kennedy,* January 1–November 22, 1963 (Washington, D.C.: Government Printing Office), p. 876.

4. *New York Times,* July 14, 1982.

5. Second Declaration of Havana, cited in William E. Ratliff, *Castroism and Communism in Latin America, 1959–1976* (Washington, D.C.: American Enterprise Institute and Hoover Institution on War, Revolution and Peace, 1976), p. 205.

6. Jerry Hough described the Soviet reaction to Castro's triumph as an "absolutely unexpected event"; their Institute of Latin America was first established in 1960. See Jerry F. Hough, "The Evolving Soviet Debate on Latin America," *Latin American Research Review,* Vol. 16, no. 1 (1981):127.

7. On the thesis that the United States pushed the Cubans, see, for example, Maurice Zeitlin and Robert Scheer, *Cuba: Tragedy in Our Hemisphere* (New York: Grove Press, 1963). For a brief but cogent discussion of the thesis that the Cubans were the pushers because "it was impossible to conduct a revolution in Cuba without a major confrontation with the U.S.," see Jorge I. Domínguez, *Cuba: Order and Revolution* (Cambridge, Mass.: Belknap Press of Harvard University Press, 1978), pp. 137–149.

8. Ratliff, *Castroism,* p. 27. Also see Cole Blasier, *Soviet Relations with Latin America in the 1970's* (Cambridge, Mass.: National Council for Soviet and East European Research, 1979), Part 4, pp. 8–20.

9. Blasier, *Soviet Relations with Latin America,* Part 4, p. 17.

10. Domínguez, *Cuba,* pp. 161–162.

11. Ratliff, *Castroism,* pp. 38–39.

12. Carmelo Mesa-Lago, *Cuba in the 1970's: Pragmatism and Institutionalization,* rev. ed. (Albuquerque: University of New Mexico Press, 1978), pp. 18–21.

13. *Medjunarodna Politika,* Vol. 24, no. 563 (September 20, 1973):16–17, cited in Rosita Levi, "Cuba and the Non-Aligned Movement," in Cole Blasier and Carmelo Mesa-Lago, eds., *Cuba in the World* (Pittsburgh: Pittsburgh University Press, 1979), p. 150.

14. Ibid.

15. Castro's admission was in his speech to the Council of Ministers at the National People's Government Assembly, December 27, 1979. For a good description and analysis of the Cuban involvement in Angola, see LeoGrande, *Cuba's Policy,* pp. 13–34; Nathaniel Davis, "The Angola Decision of 1975: A Personal Memoir," *Foreign Affairs,* Vol. 57, no. 1 (Fall 1978):109–124; and Edward González, "Institutionalization, Political Elites, and Foreign Policies," in Blasier and Mesa-Lago, *Cuba in the World,* pp. 23–33.

16. John Darnton, "Nigeria Asks Soviets Not to Overstay," *New York Times,* July 20, 1978, p. A1.

17. See Robert Pastor, "U.S. Policies Toward the Caribbean: Recurring Problems and Promises," in Jack W. Hopkins, ed., *Latin America and the*

Caribbean: A Contemporary Record, 1981–82 (New York: Holmes and Meier, 1983).

18. This section on the economic relationship borrows heavily from the statistics in Lawrence H. Theriot, "Cuba Faces the Economic Relations of the 1980's," a study prepared for the Joint Economic Committee of the Congress, March 22, 1982, by the U.S. Department of Commerce. See also Cole Blasier, "COMECON in Cuban Development" (pp. 225–256), Carmelo Mesa-Lago, "The Economy and International Economic Relations" (pp. 169–198), and Jorge F. Pérez López, "Sugar and Petroleum in Cuba-Soviet Terms of Trade" (pp. 273–296), in Blasier and Mesa-Lago, *Cuba in the World.*

19. For more detail, see the interview with Alexander Haig, *New York Times,* February 8, 1982. Carlos Rafael Rodríguez confirmed in a speech to the United Nations on June 16, 1982, that Cuba had "almost doubled" its military capability in 1981.

20. Cited in Blasier, "COMECON in Cuban Development," p. 229.

21. Cited in Nelson Valdés, "Revolutionary Solidarity in Angola," in Blasier and Mesa-Lago, *Cuba in the World,* p. 105.

22. U.S. Department of State, Bureau of Public Affairs, "Cuba's Renewed Support of Violence in Latin America," December 14, 1981, p. 3.

23. For a brief account of the meeting on January 17, 1980, between President Castro, Peter Tarnoff of the State Department, and the author, from which this observation and others came, see Jimmy Carter, *Keeping Faith: Memoirs of a President* (New York: Bantam Books, 1982), pp. 479–480.

24. Seweryn Bialer and Alfred Stepan, "Cuba, the U.S., and the Central American Mess," *New York Review of Books,* May 27, 1982.

25. Fidel Castro, *Main Report to the Second Congress of the Communist Party of Cuba,* December 17, 1980, published in *Cuba Update* (Center for Cuban Studies, New York), Vol. 2, no. 1 (March 1981).

26. LeoGrande, *Cuba's Policy,* p. 68.

27. Blasier, "The Soviet Union in the Cuban-American Conflict," in Blasier and Mesa-Lago, *Cuba in the World,* p. 37.

28. González, "Institutionalization," p. 37.

29. Cited in Valdés, "Revolutionary Solidarity in Angola," p. 110.

30. Domínguez, "Cuban Foreign Policy," p. 83.

31. Castro, *Main Report,* p. 41.

12
How Exportable Is the Cuban Model? Culture Contact in a Modern Context

Antonio Jorge

The main purpose of this chapter is to examine the inherent possibility and actual probability that Cuba will meet with success at exporting one aspect or another of its political-economic institutions and behavior to various countries. As we shall see in the course of the argument, the exportation *in toto* of what one might call the Cuban model is not feasible, because of both the historical peculiarities of the Cuban case and the highly singular characteristics introduced by the presence of Fidel Castro as progenitor and forever *máximo lider* of the revolution. Nonetheless, the political features of Cuba's model of governance are to some extent transferable to certain kinds of nations and leaders because they relate in an immediate fashion to the latter's need and ambition for political power and social change. The economic structures are more difficult to transplant in part, because they have been so often and radically modified by the revolution's swerving political-ideological course.

The theoretical questions of the conditions surrounding the transfer of institutions have been examined in the literature dealing with the influence of developed societies upon developing ones. Such questions are less tractable to analysis when other variables such as ideology, economic constraints, and balance of power issues are added to the discussion. Nevertheless they are worth serious attention. The interplay among political and socioeconomic goals in the bounded arena of conflicting interests and groups defies the simplicity of a mathematical model as well as the predictive ability of the social sciences. There is, furthermore, the somewhat ironic touch introduced by intellectual ideological dependence, which is a pervasive and ineludible influencing factor, less detectable and more difficult to expunge perhaps than conventional economic dependence. Ultimately the phenomenon of dependence may do more than shape the economic structure, it may even subtly condition the mind. As a consequence, one ends up confronted by a variety of situations, each one characterized by a different mix of objective and subjective factors.

Cuba's Impact on the Nations of the Caribbean

A perusal of the development of political thought, parties, and movements in the Caribbean testifies to their rich diversity.[1] However, one bold generalization that may withstand close scrutiny is the following: There is a detectable, although obviously not unanimous, tendency in the English-speaking Caribbean to respect and preserve representative democracy and its embodiment in the so-called Westminster model. Obviously, there are exceptions, Grenada being a glaring one and Guyana a less openly admitted instance. However, with equal assurance and with ample empirical support, it can also be affirmed that the Spanish-speaking nations of or bordering on the Caribbean have had the opposite kind of historical experience in their political life.

In this context, the Cuban efforts to export their political and economic recipes encounter considerable, if not insurmountable, difficulties, as they clash with long-established traditional values and institutional preferences. The Cubans, however, are eminently flexible. They will enter into a great variety of agreements with other countries, regardless of ideology, as long as there is some potential political advantage to be gained. Edward González has noted that: "*Fidelismo* is essentially classless, elitist and action-oriented." And quoting from *Granma,* "[Cuban] support does not necessarily have to be expressed exclusively in favor of guerrilla movements but [can be extended to] any government which sincerely adopts a policy of economic and social development and of liberating its country from the Yankee imperialist yoke; no matter by which path that government has reached power, Cuba will support it."[2] In effect, Cuba has a radical anti-American position, informed by the principle that any net loss inflicted on the United States automatically constitutes a gain for Cuba. Thus, Cuba seeks to actively multiply the geographical loci of confrontations with the United States in hopes of both creating new allies and simultaneously debilitating its main adversary.[3] One might say that Cuba represents the supply side of the revolution. The demand for it, on the other hand, may be actual or potential. Cuba tries hard to satisfy the first and foment the second. However, here is where the idiosyncratic traits of some Caribbean nations pose a real problem to the successful export of revolution, particularly along Cuban lines. Cuba is, for example, often used by West Indian leaders as a bugbear and *bête noire* for their foreign policy feints and as a domestic hedge against radical opposition. This is not to say that the ideological influence is nonexistent, which is certainly not the case, given that Cuba's impact on the Caribbean is not based simply on economic accomplishments or prowess.

On balance, it would be hard to deny that Cuba exercises a practical political influence through its manifold involvement in a good many nations: in their political and social organizations, military capability and operations, economic development and technology transfer, and support-mobilizing, populist, redistributional, and human resource–oriented programs and activities. Clearly the actual nature and extent of the Cuban involvement constitute the most important factor (the ulterior aims and intentions of the recipient nations are also important) that will precisely account for the weight exercised by Cuba in each particular bilateral situation. Naturally, one would tend to think that the two variables are directly related. Practical influence and ideological affinity normally go hand in hand as the extent, sensitivity, and number of selected areas of cooperation grow *pari passu.* That is, the kind of activities Cuba engages in with other nations and the Cuban impact on those societies will be strongly influenced by the ideological preferences and climate of the latter. Clearly, the correlation is not a perfect one and need not operate in every case. As mentioned before, wily politicians may slyly use Cuba for their own purposes in their complex and many-layered domestic and international maneuverings. That is, to the extent that Cuba's aid is purveyed to nations possessing their own political culture and sophisticated statesmen, the possibility that the interaction will become a maxi-min game from the Cuban standpoint and a negative-sum game from an objective perspective rapidly increases. Cuba may in some particular instances want to follow the strategy of maximizing high probability–low yield outcomes, although in effect this may be used to advance the objectives of the other party without any net benefit accruing to Cuba at the end of the process. Relations with some of the more politically conservative regimes in the English-speaking Caribbean, like Barbados or Trinidad and Tobago, can be classified in this particular category.

Another important variable to be taken into consideration in evaluating the Cuban impact on diverse nations is the size of the recipient society relative to the volume of aid. Again, the kinds of aid extended and the real motivations, aspirations, and ideological commitments of the recipient party are, of course, to be taken very much into consideration in the study of each case.

Grenada could serve to exemplify some of the previous statements. It is a microstate with a feeble and fragile economy, espousing an array of structural reformist tendencies coalescing in a mildly incoherent, partially revealed, and circumstantially adapted action program.[4] In this particular instance, Cuban aid is both qualitatively and quantitatively important, although by itself it is not sufficient to compensate for a decidedly strong adverse reaction on the part of the United States. Ultimately, Soviet aid to this tiny nation will tilt the balance as Grenadian relations with the United States deteriorate. In accordance with recent declarations of Grenadian Prime Minister Maurice Bishop, "The Kremlin had granted $1.4 million for the purchase of 500 tons of steel, 400 tons of flour and other essential goods. The Soviets also gave Grenada a 10-year credit of $7.7 million to buy equipment." Moreover, as part of a five-year trade agreement, Moscow agreed to "stable prices for deliveries of nutmeg and cocoa," two of Grenada's main crops.[5]

Cuban governmental assistance in fields of health, construction, and infrastructure, as well as others, is received by the Grenadian government more enthusiastically than by that of Guyana. The latter has a far less monolithic internal political situation and wishes to maintain close economic ties with the United States and international financial institutions. Further along the scale, relations with, say, the government of Barbados have been more businesslike and diplomatically correct, not to speak of the unquestionably distant attitude of the new government of Jamaica.[6]

Cuba's foreign policy perspective and judgmental criteria are founded on a mix of ideological international ambitions and concrete objectives, their relative weight, and the time dimension associated with policy implementation and goal attainment. Elements that rank high in Cuba's decisions about rendering assistance to Caribbean nations include manifest or underlying ideological or sociophilosophical affinities, even if subterranean or latent at the moment in question; the implied willingness to confront and challenge U.S. interests not only domestically but also internationally; the probability of closer cooperation in a wide range of endeavors, including diplomatic support for Cuba's foreign policy; the intention of transforming society in accordance with norms, precepts, and strategies that could be termed socialist, in some of the Marxist palingenesis acceptable to the established Soviet-Cuban orthodoxy; and lastly, life expectancy of the incumbent governments.

The preceding view of the fundamentals of Cuban foreign policy accords well with what some have termed Cuba's inclination or tendency to "principled pragmatism"—that is, a curious mix in which efficiency and expediency are given ample range within limits determined by ideological considerations. Keeping this in mind helps us to understand many of the apparent paradoxes of Cuba's external initiatives. For one thing, it shows that it is possible to reconcile seemingly opposed interpretive views of Cuban actions. In effect, there is no contradiction between Cuba's strong ideological inclinations, to the point of indulging in highly risky and economically costly foreign endeavors, and its effective application of instrumental intelligence to the pursuit of its chosen objectives. As Norman Matlin has pointed out: "The notion of the incompatibility of pragmatic and ideological goals seems obvious only to pragmatists."[7]

With the foregoing in mind, it is clear that Cuba was more interested in developing close relations and was disposed to offer more aid (of a highly visible, redistributional, and populist nature, geared at producing the maximum short-term impact in favor of his reelection) to Manley's Jamaica than to Burnham's Guyana. Although Manley has committed himself less than Burnham to implementing profound structural socioeconomic changes in society, Cuba correctly anticipated that, given the opportunity, Manley would advance in the direction of a form of socialism recognizable as such in terms of Western evaluative canons. His aspirations and loyalty to what he called democratic socialism were genuine and represented exactly what he wanted to bring about if circumstances made it politically feasible.[8] Burnham's checkered career,[9] his belated enthusiasm for a somewhat ambiguous cooperative socialism and cooperative republic,[10] the highly suspect nature of his political actions, his past opportunistic domestic and international policies, and of course, Cuba's true empathy for and confidence in Cheddi Jagan made him nothing more than a valued associate, not a fraternal ally.

These conjectures point in the direction of a dynamic and complex Cuban foreign policy in which subjective factors more often than not outweigh purely static, objective considerations in determining the amount and categories of assistance available to other Caribbean countries. The reading of a leader's intentions and motivations, his historical consistency, and his adherence to some basic shared views count for much. On the other hand, a record punctuated by sharp utilitarian veerings may, in the eyes of Cuba, detract from the value of a present policy that could not be categorized as anything short of radical.

Cuban ties with Guyana have involved commercial and technical assistance and were more developed than those established with, say, Trinidad and Tobago. They covered such areas as the purchase of rice, lumber, and other goods by Cuba and technical cooperation in the sugar and fishing industries. In the case of Jamaica, Cuba directly helped in building health and educational programs by supplying trained personnel. Agreements for technical cooperation in a wide variety of fields were reached between Cuba and the Manley government. They ranged from the fishing to the sugar industry, including foreign trade, tourism, transportation, and communication. The Cubans assisted in the construction of prefabricated housing and microdams.[11] They also helped to train the members of the prime minister's guard. Additionally, the Cuban Revolutionary Armed Forces (FAR) have established professional military relations with Guyana, Jamaica, and Trinidad and Tobago, among others.[12] According to Edward González, "Cuba's Caribbean activities most likely will continue to take the form of government-to-government programs and multilateral ventures for regional development. Additional cooperative programs include the possibility that the Cuban leadership will render conventional military assistance programs to Caribbean governments if such aid is requested."[13] Although Cuba does not dispense military aid nowadays as freely as it used to during the 1960s, it is very far from having abandoned the principle of international solidarity. As a matter of fact, since 1973 there has been a selective recrudescence of Cuban adventurist military policies.[14] The extensive spectrum of Cuban involvement covers several continents and a considerable range of activities.[15]

The pace of Cuba's military and subversive involvement has accelerated even further since 1978. There has been a return to the hard line of revolutionary armed struggle followed during the 1960s. Cuba's strategy at present consists of bringing together the various revolutionary leftist groups and factions in a given country and then actively proceeding to help and sustain the new unified movement in its attempts at gaining power by violent means. Cuba seeks in the process to establish new revolutionary allies that will roughly share its own political vision and abet its international policy. On June 26, 1982, Castro stated that the experience of several Latin American countries, such as Guatemala, El Salvador, Chile, and Bolivia, proved that there was no other "formula," no real alternative, to "revolutionary armed struggle." This declaration, patently, is an *ex post facto* attempt to justify Cuban actions in Africa, the Caribbean, and other parts of Latin America.

In its new approach, Cuba offers support to latitudinarian national liberation movements and does not insist on the ideological orthodoxy or purity of those collaborating in the political-military fronts engineered under Cuba's auspices. These vanguard movements receive widespread cooperation and are carefully helped along in their revolutionary mission, in contrast to the simplistic *foco* approach to revolutionary struggle of the early and middle 1960s. The cohesive and more sophisticated Cuban model in use at present includes propaganda, technical assistance, training courses, ideological formation, and logistical support, as well as other components, coalescing into a well-integrated aid package. Cuba has been particularly active in Central America, where it seeks to exercise maximum influence upon the Nicaraguan revolution, as it also actively promotes the downfall of the governments of El Salvador and Guatemala.

Thanks to a massive influx of Soviet aid, which has surpassed the $3 billion mark annually and which constitutes about 25 percent of the Cuban gross national product (GNP) (plus an untold amount of free military hardware), Cuba can devote considerable resources to its subversive activities in widely scattered parts of the world. By pushing with the Third World the thesis, by now severely strained, of the natural alliance with the Soviet bloc, Cuba simultaneously ingratiated itself with the Soviet Union—thus increasing the priority of its claims to economic aid and political support by the latter—and also advanced its own power objectives, prestige, and ideological values.

In Central America, Cuba was instrumental in organizing the Nicaraguan Sandinista National Liberation Front (FSLN) and after 1978 actively helped in training and arming its guerrilla forces. It shared major responsibility in organizing and fielding the so-called internationalist brigade that in 1979 fought in Nicaragua. Cuban military advisers participated in the mid-1979 final offensive of the Sandinistas. At present, Nicaragua serves as a training and launching base for guerrilla forces active elsewhere in the area. It also conveniently acts as a conduit to introduce weapons into other countries. El Salvador is a good example of the latter kind of involvement. Since about the fall of 1980, Cuba has helped Salvadoran radicals and provided them with limited aid and training. These efforts were considerably stepped up after the overthrow of the Somoza regime in Nicaragua. Cuba played a principal role in the 1979 and 1980 unity talks and subsequent agreement leading to the creation of the Unified Revolutionary Directorate (DRU). Cubans helped in designing the military activities of the DRU in the summer of 1980 and participated in the decision to initiate a general offensive in January 1981. After the failure of this military operation the guerrilla leaders traveled to Havana to revise their political-military categories.

Cuba influenced, and high representatives of its government were present at, the November 1980 ceremonies in Managua to announce the unity agreement among four Guatemalan extremist organizations that led to the establishment of the Guatemalan National Revolutionary Command (CGR). Since then the Cuban government has been instrumental in providing training and technical assistance to a large number of the estimated 2,000 guerrillas in Guatemala. Again, arms have been provided to the insurgents, sent from Nicaragua and transhipped through Honduras. In the case of Honduras, from the latter part of the 1970s up until the present, Cuba has provided military training to members of the Honduran Communist party (PCH) (who, in turn, were part of the internationalist brigade that fought in Nicaragua). Cuba is aiding Honduran revolutionaries to develop their potential for insurgency, but it has up to now concentrated mainly on utilizing the country for disseminating weapons to the revolutionary movements in the area.

Cuba has also rendered help of one kind or another to many other extremist groups and political factions throughout Latin America. Extensive documentation exists on the involvements and on the peculiarities of each case. Chile, Colombia, Argentina, Uruguay, and even Costa Rica are examples. They all neatly illustrate the constancy and perseverance of Cuba's underlying foreign policy purposes and aims. However, amid the tactical flexibility and chameleonic versatility a firm, invariant trend line can be distinctly discerned. Its Weberian motivational interpretation, in my view, is the following: Castro wants power and plays for keeps.[16]

The Cuban-Nicaraguan relation is a clearly defined one and responds to what are more clearly and sharply drawn ideological preferences on the part of the Sandinista government.

> Within a week after the triumph of the revolution, senior Nicaraguan officials traveled to Havana, where they were hailed as the guests of honor at Cuba's annual 26th of July celebration. The guerrilla leaders of the *FSLN* remembered that it was Cuba that had been their longest and most reliable friend in the struggle against Somoza. Nicaragua's relationship with Cuba blossomed quickly as Cuba sent several thousand teachers, hundreds of medical experts, and scores of technical advisors (including some military personnel) to help Nicaragua's reconstruction.[17]

In May 1980, Nicaragua acknowledged it was housing a small contingent of Cuban military advisers.[18]

Since then it appears that the level of Cuba's commitment has increased considerably:

> The *sandinistas* have allowed Castro to send 5,000 or more Cubans to work in Nicaragua. Many are based in sensitive areas near the Honduran border or in the tense Atlantic coastal region from which Nicaragua's Miskito Indians have been forcibly resettled. The United States contends at least half of the Cubans in Nicaragua are involved in military and security affairs. The others are teachers and medical personnel.[19]

Another Cuban innovation that has found ready application in the Sandinista society is the notorious defense committee. As was to be expected, it performs the same categories of functions that it does in Cuba, namely, political and military.[20] In part, thanks to it, Nicaragua, very much like Cuba, has been divided into a bimodal society, one in which the state recognizes two kinds of citizens: revolutionaries and counterrevolutionaries.[21]

One should not be surprised in the least—quite the contrary—if the Cuban influence in Nicaragua keeps on increasing by leaps and bounds. It would be only logical, the fundamental reason being that both in their institutions and their organization, as well as in their functioning, the two societies are growing closer together. There is a noticeable convergence in ideological persuasion, structures, modus operandi, and even in intangibles such as political and revolutionary style. Despite the many historical differences between the two revolutions, their intense political-ideological affinity and shared *Weltanschauung* will finally impose itself.

This seems to be a serious position to take. After all, ideas must count for something, especially if held with some passion by those in power. Certainly, in the modern pluralistic and confrontational world there is much room for the bizarre, the subjective, and the improbable, whether we call it Cuba or Nicaragua. Paradoxically, Marxist ideas are powerful not because of necessity or cogency but because of willful imitation. The ultimate irony is that of modern Third World leaders, reputedly Marxists, who as unwitting victims of Keynes's dictum are slaves of their own favorite defunct economist's views. In the end, they make everyone a victim of their own hubris and ignorance, not even managing to serve well their self-chosen master.

One may well believe that the Sandinistas have learned from the costly experience of the Cuban revolution. They may even have become convinced of the values of gradualism. Relative moderation may be the motto of new revolutionaries.[22] Probably all this is true. After all, Lenin and Mao had their moderate periods and policies.

Rumor has it that Castro himself has counseled prudence and patience to the *comandantes,* as he previously did to Salvador Allende. Nonetheless, a dispassionate examination of the Sandinistas's political structures,[23] and the economic ideology and plans of the revolution,[24] should suffice to convince one, on the basis of available evidence, of the unmistakable similarities and accelerated convergence of the Cuban and Nicaraguan societies. Disingenuous disclaimers (intended as placebos) aside, values, structures, and behavior must mean something. Nor can we disregard cultural ancestry. In the end, Daniel Ortega and Tomás Borge resemble Fidel Castro more than Eric Williams, Michael Manley, or even Forbes Burnham could ever do. Cultural anthropologists should not be all that lightly dismissed out of hand.

On the Irrational Nature of the Cuban Economic Model

In "The Transferability of Cuba's Revolutionary Development Model," Archibald R. M. Ritter made reference to the emerging Cuban socioeconomic model of the 1970s as one that was in the process of evolution and whose ultimate characteristics had not yet jelled.[25] Nonetheless, some of its traits were quite distinctive and clearly defined. The most significant one was its "de-marketization," a term meant by the author to denote the replacement of the market system by central planning. The degree of hierarchical control in the Cuban new "Economic Management System" was very high indeed and was essentially in conflict with attempts at granting more autonomy to individual firms. In reality, decentralization in that context would be applicable only to the delegation of supervisory tasks and not the substance of economic decisions themselves. These would remain unaffected by the administrative changes in process. This model superseded the earlier "basic dynamic model," which was primarily redistributive in nature and concerned itself with growth only at a subsequent stage. Even then, the impact of the model on the latter variable was to result indirectly from the improvement in human resources that it was designed to attain.[26]

It is interesting to compare Ritter's perception of the Cuban economic model with that of Arthur MacEwan, who has recently contributed a Marxist perspective on Cuba's economic development during the revolutionary period.[27] After contrasting the economic organization of the 1960s with that of the 1970s, noticing the changes in the incentive system and degree of decentralization, he concluded that prices and profits are not market determined, nor do they guide the investment process. Actually, profits just constitute an index of successful compliance with the economic plan. In the Cuban context, prices and profits are simply instruments for ensuring the short-run operation of the plan in accordance with its preselected political goals. These indexes are so rapidly divorced from any true economic function that there is no attempt to use them to instill rationality in the economic process or to endow the system with either static or dynamic economic efficiency. Their role is to assume that political decisions for the period in question are properly observed and implemented. It is in this context that I would disagree with Carmelo Mesa-Lago's view that the New Cuban System of Economic Management and Planning stresses efficiency.[28] The system may use market instruments but that per se does not guarantee the introduction of economic rationality or the pursuit of efficiency. Even if one were to assume that in Cuba the planner's determined price structure is both theoretically consistent and real, i.e., capable in fact of producing stable equilibrium situations for all of the economy's markets, it still would be composed of accounting or some variety of shadow prices and not of true scarcity and preference indexes. Even if all the systems' equations were to be satisfied by an appropriate set of uniquely determined values, the role of prices would be exclusively that of accounting units computed on the basis of chosen *numéraire.*

They would not perform any of the allocative or indicative functions associated with truly economic criteria of success. That is, money would provide only a convenient yardstick for the monitoring of the fulfillment of the physical plan. Obviously, even if the plan were to be perfectly consistent it could still be woefully inefficient, even in terms of the planners' preferences, not to mention its utility to the individual economic agents themselves. The plan is plagued by all sorts of inconsistencies, as one has come to expect in such situations. In any case, monetary measures have no identifiable function related to the generation, implementation, or verification of economic rationality and calculation in such a setting. It is futile to insist on injecting economic rationality and efficiency criteria into a physically conceived central plan. In effect, there is a radical opposition between the philosophical principles and technical norms underlying the Western orthodox economic concept of efficiency and the corresponding assumptions informing the usage of this concept in centrally planned systems.[29] Clearly, there is an unbridgeable chasm between the nominalist theory of society and individually directed economic activity and its Marxist opposite. In the latter, the economic subsystem is not a means to the realization of freely chosen individual ends but a historical evolutionary instrument for the eschatological transformation of man and society.

In the classical liberal society, an economic system is envisioned in which business units fulfill their social function simply by behaving in a profit-maximizing fashion in a competitive environment. Through the striving of the firms to best serve the interest of their owners, and the effort of all other factors of production to serve theirs, the commonwealth is best served. As a result of the working of the system, the aggregate utility or satisfaction enjoyed by the individual members of society reaches whatever constrained maximum the circumstances permit. Therefore, it follows that economic rationality is fully respected, economic calculation is applied throughout, and efficiency is optimized.

By contrast, the Marxist viewpoint would model one's conception of the proper function and purpose of economic institutions and organizations, and of the very nature of economic phenomena, in a totally antithetical manner. Definitions of such basic terms as economic rationality and efficiency would be radically influenced by it. In that kind of context, the instrumental role of economics in society would grow enormously—so much so that it may expand to the point at which economic functions would become indistinguishable from non-economic ones. Although economic functions would still be a means to something else, namely, the remaking of man and society, in actual practice its indivisible continuum with the rest of society would create a situation in some respects not unlike that of primitive societies. The similarity would consist in the fact that, ultimately, the very nature of the situation excludes the possibility of applying the logic of the economic calculus to social processes involving the use of scarce economic resources. Although in preliterate societies, in contrast to contemporary revolutionary societies like Cuba, economic activities are often final ends in themselves and not means, the remote character of the ends in the latter makes for the same kind of economic immeasurability in both. No cost-benefit calculations are possible for complex, distant evolutionary processes circular in nature and characterized by an unknown functional interdependence among a multitude of variables. There is really no sense in which one can meaningfully use terms like economic rationality and efficiency in such instances. And it is in this sense that Cuba has no economic model *qua* "economic" model to export. Eastern European societies have ended up looking like the Soviet Union economically; no society has ended up looking like Castro's Cuba economically.

The Cuban economic model has, however, exhibited a good deal of variability and change. Planning techniques, the degree of centralization, the nature of incentive systems, the relative emphasis on sectors and projects, the scope of private ownership and activities, even general conceptual developmental strategies and approaches—

all have rapidly succeeded one another in the Cuban scene in the short time since the advent of the revolutionary regime. One could say that Cuba has exhibited as checkered a career in the economic model area as has the USSR since the October Revolution. Nonetheless, it is clear that even though sharply vying ideological tendencies have swayed economic doctrine and policy in the Soviet Union and Eastern Europe, these countries, in contrast to Cuba, followed on the whole a more conventional economic model. The following quote neatly exemplifies the difference:

> In economies of the Soviet-type—i.e., in economies in which non-labor factors are massively nationalized—expansion in productive capacity, maximal growth rates in certain basic industrial outputs and in total output as well, were proclaimed as the driving forces of the state's economic policy, virtually from the very establishment of these regimes. The frequently proclaimed goal of reaching and surpassing the most advanced capitalist countries was viewed as an economic and military necessity even before these economies recovered from the World Wars, a Civil War, or both. The desire of their policymakers to elevate their countries on the world per capita income scale acquired additional urgency from the fact that almost all of these countries were extremely backward. They adopted a strategy of development predicated on a high investment rate, rapid expansion in the productive capacity of certain sectors, use of capital-intensive technology in the top priority industries, and massive development of technicians and skilled industrial workers, combined with a low priority for agriculture and consumer's goods industries.[30]

The contrast with the Cuban experience is all too manifest. Although Castro's Cuba has been rocked by intense ideological disputes that were invariably reflected in the economy's course, the resultant of these forces operated differently than in the Soviet Union and Eastern Europe. The differential factor was of enormous importance, namely, the plantationlike, open, and dependent nature of the economy, coupled with its close integration with the United States. The superimposition of these *sui generis* characteristics on the elements shared by all Soviet-type economies makes Cuba a very special case. The Soviet Union and, *a fortiori*, the Eastern European countries were variously categorized, with some notable intranational sectoral and regional exceptions, as traditional backward economies at the respective times of the ascent to power of Soviet-like Marxist regimes.

The chasm between Cuba and these societies should not be minimized or simply reduced to the superficial descriptiveness rendered by the hackneyed and much-misused statistical indexes for the measurement of economic underdevelopment. A backward Eastern European society in the post–Second World War period was an entirely separate and dissimilar reality from a Hispanic Caribbean society at the beginning of the 1960s.

The Cuban economic model, if distinctive, is so not because of its incorporation of Soviet-style economic traits. In that respect it is only quantitatively different from less structured or less technically proficient models in other economically underdeveloped and politically quasi-totalitarian Third World societies. What establishes Cuba's singularity is its mix of formal Soviet-type economic characteristics with its persistent monocultural, plantationlike, open, and dependent economy, closely associated in the recent historical past with the U.S. economy and, at present, even more tightly integrated with the USSR and the Eastern bloc.[31]

Quite a different dimension of the irrationality problem is posed by the unchanging leadership style of Fidel Castro. To the extent that his highly personalistic approach to the exercise of authority results in the conception and implementation of important singular decisions and policy courses, the basic question of the degree of autonomy of the economic system in Cuban society remains a crucial one. Power to define high-priority actions (whose implementation substantially affects, directly or indirectly, the growth of economic resources and their allocation cannot definitely be abstracted from the institutional nature, logical character, and capacity for efficiency of an economic system. The nature and impact of many of Castro's frequent interventions into the working of the economic system, either via economic-ideological considerations, special economic projects or plans, or major changes in political policy, has been amply documented by avowed sympathizers of the Cuban revolution as well as by more neutral academic observers.[32]

Much has been made of the so-called institutionalization process of the Cuban economy, which gradually began to evolve at the start of the 1970s.[33] The thrust of it, one is led to believe, is toward the technicalization, professionalization, and rationalization of the economy. Irrational and aberrant behavior, contrary to the cold norms of efficiency and planning, are supposedly on their way out. The technocrats and pragmatists, it is presumed, have gained the upper hand and they are not constitutionally inclined to suffer revolutionary fools gladly. One is told that the heroic times are over and that the reign of Bentham has arrived. After all, utilitarianism is the omega point of convergence theory. Modern social utopianism will not renounce the rationalist dream of a liberal-socialist symbiosis. Given this scenario, the only decent thing for Castro to do is to meekly comply or, at least figuratively, to exit from the stage. But, alas, he is not willing to play the part assigned to him.

Actually it seems that the speculations of some of our more prescient academic savants have come to pass. Castro has managed to conserve a considerable amount of real power and retains the role of generator and promoter of major policy changes and initiatives.[34] He has once again parlayed his charisma into power and has successfully utilized his very considerable capacity for internal political maneuvering. Through the skillful placement of loyal friends and associates, the co-optation of key elite groups and the expedient dissemination of decision-making faculties among them, Castro has been able to maintain his premier position and to frustrate the gestation of counterbalancing coalitions.

Paradoxically, his calculated risks in undertaking highly sensitive and potentially dangerous political-military actions abroad have not only strengthened his hand domestically as well as internationally, but they have also allowed him to advantageously renegotiate the Cuban position vis-à-vis the Soviet Union and its allies and to enhance his image in the Third World. Castro has proved that there are courses of action that, unsuspected by the political neophyte, lie open to economic exploitation for the benefit of the initiate. Obviously, there is more than one way to increase the influx of foreign resources and to generally better one's bargaining stance in the international economic arena.

We thus come by a roundabout way to the conclusion that Castro cannot be dismissed from the Cuban planning exercises. He continues to be a key variable in the system and still holds an autonomous role in it. His actions affect the inner working and parameters of the economy in a way no truly institutionalized situation would allow. To the extent that a man can assign to himself and his nation the kind of international tasks and responsibilities that Castro does, with all of the attendant consequences and repercussions one cannot in any normal meaning of the term speak of the institutionalization of the Cuban revolution.

To speak of economism or economically directed thought or behavior at the macroeconomic level in Cuba flies in the face of reality. It is as absurd as to apply those kinds of criteria to the empire builders of history or to the ascetic personality or to the mystic soul. At the passing of Castro, if the regime continues, a qualitative change will take place. Cuba will metamorphose into a much more conventional nationalistic state, with a markedly inward-looking approach and, by extension, a substantially greater concern for economic rationality and the utilitarian calculus.

For all of the above reasons, the Cuban "economic model" *qua* singular and differentiated entity cannot be exported. The economic reality, needs, and aspirations of each country, in conjunction with its political goals and objectives, will dictate results that will differ in each case. These outcomes have only the remotest possibility of resembling the Cuban configuration of relationships between means and ends.

There may be resemblances, of course, at the more generic typological levels among institutional, organizational, structural, and behavioral patterns, in the same way in which we refer to the homologous characteristics existing among specimens of the same genus: capitalism, socialism, corporatism, and others. However, the specific differences are likely to be as profound and visible as the coincidences themselves. Fortunately, in all likelihood, the Cuban condition can be applied only partially. A multitude of factors endogenous to the potential imitators, accompanied by variations in the exogenous forces attending the inception and development of the Cuban revolution, would strongly point in the direction of diversity and against uniformity.

On the Nature of Cuba's Political Model

Cuba differs from other countries characterized by comparable situations of socioeconomic underdevelopment insofar as it has adopted the trappings of a contemporary totalitarian state. At present, totalitarianism is coextensive with, and can only be completely fulfilled by, subscription to variants of the Soviet model. Despite their many individual divergences, Soviet-type systems possess certain generic similarities, some purely negative in character.[35] These will become more marked and functionally distinctive, depending not only on the simple confession of verbal affiliation or mere empathy with "Marxism-Leninism" by a given regime but also, more to the point, on its actual degree of political-economic integration and alignment with the Soviet bloc.

This differentiation is relevant to all political regimes, but it applies with special force to those governing in developing or insufficiently developed countries. In effect, although a goodly number of so-called modernizing regimes in the Third World exhibit a notorious proclivity to dictatorship and political violence, nay, to totalitarianism, only those counting on the active commitment and technical assistance of the Soviet bloc can actually succeed in instituting bona fide totalitarian systems. Technical proficiency born of long experience and unbounded freedom of experimentation is largely responsible for the nefarious virtuosity of Soviet-type regimes in the establishment and governance of totalitarian states. Non-Soviet-type regimes would be at a decided disadvantage in this field. *A fortiori,* this would apply to the case of underdeveloped countries. They would simply lack the means and the necessary experience for the protean task of organizing the governing of society along totalitarian lines.

The appeal of personal charisma and the mesmerizing attraction of modernization and developmental programs constitute a powerful political concoction. The emergence of numerous personalist and one-party regimes in Africa, Asia, and Latin America, which freely indulge in the naked use of power for the purported advance of populist causes, is altogether too common a reality to need elaboration. That many of these leaders and power elites profess their allegiance to socialism is well-nigh meaningless, given the diversity of antinomic spirits pullulating the socialist pantheon.[36] For our purposes, the *differentia specifica* lies in the extent to which any of these societies concretely adopt the institutional-organizational and functional-behavioral traits of a Soviet-type system.

The Cuban political model is particularly interesting because it combines extreme traits of independent provenance: charismatic leadership as conceived and exercised in the milieu of underdevelopment; a monistic big power irredentist yearning; international, nay, intercontinental messianic proselytizing ardor; and faithful adherence to Soviet political doctrine and irrepressible zeal in the observance of its eschatological, solidary dogma. These elements combine in a uniquely conflict-proliferating formula. As a consequence, the model's own structure and inherent logic, further reinforced by the influx of massive Soviet aid, is apt to produce excessive externalizations and atypical manifestations in both the domestic and the world arenas.

The Cuban political model thus contains not only dissimilar but actually disparate elements. These internal contradictions help to explain, in conjunction with the maximalist tendencies of the Cuban leadership, many of the erratic moves and apparently irrational and self-defeating measures of the revolution. The explosive blend of strong charismatic rule exercised in the context of totalitarianism, curiously embedded in the traditional Iberian *caudillo* tradition[37] and further mediated by the pining of Third World nationalism for modernization and development, finds its most refined expression in this model. If we add to the preceding, *ressentiment,* the great intervening variable that the prescient Alexis de Tocqueville already saw looming and that has become one of the most signal characteristics of our time, the assemblage of factors will be complete. Inequality, exploitation, abuses, assorted affronts, evils, and indignities are conjured up by the voice of a Faustian redeemer who speaks of apocalyptic confrontations between North and South in a modern day *Götterdämmerung*.

The predominance of the political over the purely economic in a restricted or narrow sense is an outstanding characteristic of a great many underdeveloped countries in our time. It is obvious that in the midst of real or announced profound structural transformations, the economic subsystem would more than ever assume an instrumental role in society. Third World nations could perhaps be arranged along a spectrum in accordance with the scope or degree to which their economies subserve traditional Western individualistic goals, or contrariwise, in accordance with the extent to which they are utilized as a weapon or means for the reshaping of people and society.

The Cuban model would have to occupy a polar position in the relative disposition of societies in our scale. Castro's personal vision of the proper domestic destiny and international role of Cuba requires maximum fluidity of institutions, organizations, and resources. The greater the flexibility and metamorphic capacity of human and nonhuman resources, the more degrees of freedom in experimenting with the intermediate means-end relationships of policy. And that is what power and social action are about, after all. When all is said and done, actual means count more than professed ends. We do not live final ends, we just talk about them.

Castro's obsession with his own brand of millennialism transcends the modest territorial boundaries of Cuba. His hypertrophied calling as a prophet and conquerer have acquired universalistic overtones. Because of this, the economic aspects of Cuban society have been totally subordinated to a variety of political objectives, which take precedence over the purely prosaic and utilitarian demands of everyday living. For Castro, revolution is the final output and the Cuban economy an intermediate product.

In the political realm, Cuba is a totalitarian state of Stalinist filiation and *caudillo* sociohistorical ancestry—a regime using technically sophisticated repressive measures and an integral coercion, superimposed on a thoroughly collectivized, centrally planned and operated economy; violently espousing the Leninist antineocolonialist line; mercilessly and unrestrainedly rebuking and reviling the United States for all of the real and imagined evils, failures, and miseries of the Third World; and unreservedly committed to supporting all actual and potentially sympathetic political movements throughout the globe.

Thus, the kaleidoscope view of an improbable society: It is a society that has reoriented its economic dependence toward the Soviet Union. It is a country that remains basically underdeveloped and that has made very few strides in its efforts to institute growth over the last two decades. It is a state that keeps asking its members for more sacrifices into the indefinite future for the sake of socialist solidarity and the construction of a new communist world that is to arrive *ad kalendas Graecas.* It is a nation that despite its paucity of resources frequently undertakes costly political-military ventures abroad at enormous direct and indirect costs to its society. It is a regime that shows more impatience at the purported evils of an international order, in its view devoid of any redeeming features, than its political progenitor and mentor country does. And finally, it is a small revolutionary society unremittingly bent on telescoping history and inaugurating a universal chimera by dint of subjectivism.

The Cuban model, *qua* developmental model, has not materialized as a coherent and cohesive archetypical articulation or formulation capable of export to anxious buyers in international markets. Rather Cuba as an individual actor appears as a ready and willing abettor and supporter of assorted discontent and disgruntlements throughout the Third World, always on the lookout for potential rewards for its moves. These last may range from active ideological solidarity, to formal or informal limited cooperative agreements, to mutual undertakings in one or another area or field, or simply to a decrease in the level of hostility with another country.

Likewise, the means employed by the Cubans in their self-imposed internationalist mission range over the whole scale of imaginable common endeavors: from literacy and health campaigns, technical assistance in project building, security training and ideological indoctrination, to military involvement and active fighting with dissident national factions and foreign nations. Clearly, commercial agreements, economic cooperation, cultural and educational endeavors, and all forms of international political cooperation in regional and world forums and organizations are also to be included in the voluminous external agenda of this little country.

Recapitulating, we may say that in the political order Cuba possesses the repressive efficiency of its post-Stalinist ancestry, coupled with the peculiar sociohistorical and cultural authoritarian and charismatic traits of the Latin American *caudillo* tradition. Cuba has incorporated some basic Soviet-type economic, institutional, organizational, and functional features, in amalgamation with its basic monocultural, plantation-oriented, open, and dependent character, deeply embedded in a messianic politization mold that renders the model's goals and policies inherently unpredictable, largely voids its very nature, and certainly makes it cumbersome, if not impossible, to export.

Seen in that light, there may be no prototypical substance or contexture to the Cuban model. It may simply constitute a variant or a mutant whose fortuitous historical conformation and limited potential for adaptability do not presage its successful reproduction as a recognizable entity with a clearly defined identity of its own. Obviously, this does not mean that some of the more generic traits of the model, which in any case are not originally its own, may not be adopted by other nations. Many political and economic circumstances will make that outcome probable. But such adoptions do not establish much with respect to the model's exportability.

Notes

1. See Anthony P. Maingot, "The Difficult Path to Socialism in the English-Speaking Caribbean," in Richard R. Fagen, ed., *Capitalism and the State in U.S.–Latin American Relations* (Stanford, Calif.: Stanford University Press, 1979), pp. 255–301. Refer to p. 257 for the author's thesis regarding the political cultures of Guyana, Jamaica, and Trinidad and their orientation to state-directed populism.

2. Edward González, *Cuba Under Castro: The Limits of Charisma* (Boston: Houghton Mifflin, 1974), pp. 214n, 215.

3. See Thomas O. Enders, "Cuban Support for Terrorism and Insurgency in the Western Hemisphere," U.S. Department of State, March 12, 1982.

4. Although the Bishop government may see the Grenada revolution as "clearly prosocialist in spirit and intent, as demonstrated by the revolution's social programs [sic]," this belief may be interpreted in the latitudinarian fashion in which the term "socialism" has come to be understood in today's parlance. In any case, the Grenadian version of socialism does not seem to exclude the presence of strong private and cooperative sectors in the economy. See *Grenada: The Peaceful Revolution,* A report by the EPICA Task Force (Washington, D.C., 1982), especially pp. 74–80. The report's statement that "the revolutionary government has only made gradual changes in the Grenadian economy so far" (p. 75) coincides with Maingot's view as expressed in "The Caribbean: The Structure of Modern-Conservative Societies," in Jan Knippers Black, ed., *Latin America: A Multidisciplinary Introduction* (Boulder, Colo.: Westview Press, forthcoming), p. 29n. There he noted that "by 1982 [the New Jewel Movement, which came to power in 1979] had not undertaken any significant socialization programs."

5. *Miami Herald,* July 29, 1982, p. 5.

6. On the point of diversity in the Caribbean and different attitudes toward Cuba, see Jacqueline A. Braveboy-Wagner, "Changes in the Regional Foreign Policies of the English-speaking Caribbean," in Elizabeth G. Ferris and Jennie K. Lincoln, *Latin American Foreign Policies: Global and Regional Dimensions* (Boulder, Colo.: Westview Press, 1981), pp. 223–236, especially pp. 230–231. Also, on the autochthonous character of economic policy and

reform programs in the area, holding that the nationalization process has its own logic but no clear strategy and that the needs of the area ("the laws of economics") dictate a pro-Western policy, see Maurice A. Olde, "Towards Understanding the Dynamics of Nationalization in the Caribbean," in Basil A. Ince, ed., *Contemporary International Relations of the Caribbean* (Trinidad: University of the West Indies, 1979), pp. 102–120, especially pp. 108–109.

7. Norman Matlin, "The Myth of Mastery, A Methodological Critique of 'The New Cuban Presence in the Caribbean,'" *Caribbean Review*, Vol. 9, no. 4 (Fall 1980):22–29, 50–54.

8. For Manley's own views, see the *Miami Herald*, June 20, 1982, p. 5E.

9. On this topic, see Thomas J. Spinner, "The Emperor Burnham Has Lost His Clothes," *Caribbean Review*, Vol. 9, no. 4 (Fall 1980):5–8.

10. For a detailed description of Guyana's economy, its evolution and present structure and situation, including economic policy and developmental strategy, see Kempe R. Hope, *Development Policy in Guyana: Planning, Finance, and Administration* (Boulder, Colo.: Westview Press, 1979), especially pp. 59–93, 97–99, 143–145, and 184–191. This work demonstrates the close relationship between the country's economic strategies and policies, and the ideological meanderings of Burnham.

11. See Ronald E. Jones, "Cuba and the English-Speaking Caribbean," in Cole Blasier and Carmelo Mesa-Lago, eds., *Cuba in the World* (Pittsburgh: University of Pittsburgh Press, 1979), pp. 131–143, especially pp. 137–139.

12. See Edward González, "Institutionalization, Political Elites and Foreign Policies," in Blasier and Mesa-Lago, *Cuba in the World*, pp. 1–33, especially pp. 20–21.

13. Ibid., p. 32.

14. Ibid., pp. 19, 20, 24, 26, 29, and 31.

15. See Jorge I. Domínguez, "The Armed Forces and Foreign Relations," in Blasier and Mesa-Lago, *Cuba in the World*, pp. 61–72.

16. For a detailed account of Cuba's activities, see Enders, "Cuban Support for Terrorism," and idem, "Cuba's Renewed Support for Violence in Latin America," Special Report No. 90, U.S. Department of State, December 14, 1981.

17. William M. LeoGrande, "The United States and the Nicaraguan Revolution," in Thomas W. Walker, ed., *Nicaragua in Revolution* (New York: Praeger Publishers, 1981), pp. 72–73.

18. Ibid., p. 75.

19. Shirley Christian, "The Sandinistas' Plans Go Awry," *Miami Herald*, July 18, 1982, p. 4E.

20. See Stephen M. Gorman, "Sandinista Chess," *Caribbean Review*, Vol. 10, no. 1 (Winter 1981):17.

21. For an impressionistic view of life in Nicaragua at the present, refer to Robert A. Rankin, "'1984' Alive and Well in Nicaragua," *Miami Herald*, July 18, 1982, p. 3E.

22. See Max Azicri, "A Cuban Perspective on the Nicaraguan Revolution," in Walker, *Nicaragua in Revolution*, pp. 345–371, especially pp. 345–348.

23. See Gorman, "Sandinista Chess," pp. 15–17.

24. The Nicaraguan economy has undergone considerable change. The changes have not been greater in order to avoid massive disruption of the economy, which would worsen the already delicate political situation. The immediate objectives of "Plan-80" (Programa de reactivación económica en beneficio del pueblo) were to promote rapid economic recovery while instituting redistributive programs. The main restriction was the need to avoid major macroeconomic disequilibria in the transformation process. Nonetheless, the government has already proceeded to nationalize large sectors of the economy. It is contemplated that the contribution to the GNP of the public sector will almost triple (from 15 percent to 41 percent). The authorities, among other things, fix the prices of many goods, confiscate underutilized capacity, and impose high taxation rates on income and property. Obviously, the intended transition to a "new economy" is going to be a most difficult one. The creation of a "New Sandinista Economy . . . which would permit a 'just, free and fraternal human life in our country,' " implies the construction of an entirely different society. See E.V.K. Fitzgerald, "The Economics of the Revolution," in Walker, *Nicaragua in Revolution,* pp. 203–220 (quotations from p. 214); and, Thomas A. Walker, *Nicaragua: The Land of Sandino* (Boulder, Colo.: Westview Press, 1981), pp. 58–62.

25. See Archibald R. M. Ritter, "The Transferability of Cuba's Revolutionary Model," in Blasier and Mesa-Lago, *Cuba in the World,* pp. 316–319.

26. Ibid., pp. 314–316. Ritter distinguished between the original Cuban redistributive model and the model of the 1970s. The evident political advantages of the first, both in Cuba and in Allende's Chile, have been abundantly proved. As to economic consequences of the model and its suitability in a growth-oriented society, very serious doubts must be raised at the purely theoretical level as well as on the basis of historical experience. See Felipe Pazos, "Comentarios a dos articulos sobre la revolución cubana," *El Trimestre Económico,* Vol. 29, no. 113 (1962):1ff.

The second model has been too closely tailored to fit Cuba's conditions and needs. It is not of much use in its totality to any other developing society. However, for reasons that are well established in the development and planning literature, some of the model's general characteristics may be easily adopted by other nations. Among them are nationalization of basic industries; government planning or control of investment and of the external sector; formulation of the overall developmental strategy and resource mobilization effort; and many other related tasks. Politically, it is clear that substantial control of the economy becomes an almost essential condition during processes of far-reaching social change.

27. See Arthur MacEwan, *Revolution and Economic Development in Cuba* (New York: St. Martin's Press, 1981), Chapters 14, 22, and especially 25.

28. See Carmelo Mesa-Lago, *The Economy of Socialist Cuba* (Albuquerque: University of New Mexico Press, 1981), Chapter 2.

29. Refer to P.J.D. Wiles, *The Political Economy of Communism* (Cambridge, Mass.: Harvard University Press, 1962), Chapters 3, 4.

30. Nicolas Spulber, *The State and Economic Development in Eastern Europe* (New York: Random House, 1966), p. 6. See also, for an elaboration of the same point, Robert W. Campbell, *Soviet Economic Power* (Boston: Houghton Mifflin, 1966), Chapter 2, especially p. 9 and pp. 25–27, section entitled "Economic Growth a Basic Obsession."

31. Clearly, very fundamental questions about the metasociological as well as the socioeconomic implications of Soviet-type development for Third World countries are raised by the Cuban experience. See Charles K. Wilber, *The Soviet Model and Underdeveloped Countries* (Chapel Hill: University of North Carolina Press, 1969), Introduction.

32. The reader is referred to K. S. Karol, *Guerrillas in Power* (New York: Hill and Wang, 1970), and to René Dumont, *Socialisms and Development* (London: Andre Deutsch, 1973), especially pp. 84–88, for an account of Castro's unipersonal role as *máximo lider* of the revolution and how it has introduced inefficiency and irrationality into the economy. An account that takes into consideration the many facets of the revolution and the peculiarities of Castro's own personality is rendered in González's *Cuba Under Castro,* Chapters 8 and 9, especially pp. 197–206.

33. See Carmelo Mesa-Lago, *Cuba in the 1970s* (Albuquerque: University of New Mexico Press, 1974), chs. 1 and 2; idem, *Economy of Socialist Cuba,* Chapter 2, pp. 27–32; and González, *Cuba Under Castro,* pp. 225–236.

34. See González, "Institutionalization," particularly pp. 7, 11, 12, 16, 17, 19, and 20. In an essay that displayed remarkable foresight in the analysis of the elements most likely to influence the future course of Cuban policy, Jaime Suchlicki made the same point. See "An Assessment of Castroism," *ORBIS,* Vol. 16, no. 1 (Spring 1972):53–54.

35. For an excellent analytical classification of institutional variants in Soviet-type economics, see P.J.D. Wiles, *Economic Institutions Compared* (New York: John Wiley and Sons, 1977), Chapters 1, 3, and 20; and idem, *The Political Economy of Communism* (Cambridge, Mass.: Harvard University Press, 1962), Chapters 1 and 2.

36. See Helen Defrosses and Jacques Levesque, eds., *Socialism in the Third World* (New York: Praeger Publishers, 1975). Also Introduction to the revised editions of Paul E. Sigmund, ed., *Ideologies of Developing Nations* (New York: Frederick A. Praeger, 1967).

37. Castro's *caudillo* manifestations are too well known and almost stereotypically represented by the personage to require documentation. Nonetheless, some well-known references to the Latin American *caudillo* phenomenon in general and to Castro's embodiment of it may be of interest. See, on the first point, Howard J. Wiarda, "The Struggle for Democracy and Human Rights in Latin America: Toward a New Conceptualization," p. 241, in Howard J. Wiarda, ed., *The Continuing Struggle for Democracy in Latin America* (Boulder, Colo.: Westview Press, 1980). On Castro, see Claudio Velez, *The Centralist Tradition of Latin America* (Princeton, N.J.: Princeton University Press, 1980), p. 300n.

13
On the Limits of the New Cuban Presence in the Caribbean

Gordon K. Lewis

Just as the Russian revolution reshaped world politics after 1917, so the Cuban revolution of 1959 has reshaped Caribbean politics. There is the new ideology of Cuban social justice, based on the socialist principle of organized production for community consumption. There is the new *fidelista* principle that the United States and Cuba are two separate cultural entities destined to eternal conflict, not unlike the old *arielista* vision of a Catholic Latin society pitted against a Protestant North American society. There is the new Cuban doctrine of "revolution for export," not unlike the Trotskyite doctrine of "world revolution" of fifty years ago. There is the regional appeal of the Cuban message—just as the pilgrimage to Moscow was the done thing with the old left of the 1919–1939 period, so today the pilgrimage to Havana has become a necessary tour for the new left of the modern period.

No one can underestimate the massive appeal of the Cuban event for the rest of the Caribbean. It is as much a cataclysm as the Haitian war of national liberation in the period between 1791 and 1804. As the St. Domingue slave rebellion shattered the myth of white supremacy, so the Cuban revolution has shattered the myth of U.S. supremacy.

For historical reasons, the Cuban revolution was born in violence; its authoritarian structure—the 1976 constitution closely follows the Soviet constitution of 1936—follows the Soviet model of rigid one-party state directions; and as in the Soviet Union, there is a law of power that dictates that the dictatorship of the proletariat becomes the dictatorship of the Communist party and the dictatorship of the party becomes the personal dictatorship of the party's secretary-general.

I do not say this in morally critical terms, for all those elements are rooted in a Cuban past in which the democratic and constitutional tradition was notoriously weak. But I also note that in much of the Caribbean that tradition, by contrast, has always been strong and deeply rooted on native grounds. It means the multiparty system, freedom of thought and speech, a free press, and the rule of law.

It is argued by much of the Caribbean left that all this belongs to what is called in the English-speaking Caribbean the imported "Westminster model." The argument seeks to persuade us that it should be abandoned. It is a specious argument. Freedom of thought, for example, cannot be dismissed as merely a bourgeois invention. Historically, it predates modern bourgeois society by two thousand years. Maybe the idea of polite parliamentary debate is English; but its larger meaning—summed up in Whitehead's phrase that civilization means the replacement of force with persuasion—goes beyond that single institutional form. To dismiss everything as the hated "Westminster model" is to throw out the baby with the bathwater. Uncritical acceptance of Cuban aid can only mean the road to the totalitarian society.

I argue thus because much of the Caribbean left is set within the mold of hard-line Stalinism: They claim Soviet Russia and Cuba are the only socialist societies; multiparty competition is simply a bourgeois delusion; the Americans are Fascists, so that the leader of the Puerto Rican Socialist party can advance even the absurd claim that U.S. rule in Puerto Rico is as repressive as Nazi German rule in wartime occupied France.

Nor is this a criticism made only by democratic socialists like myself. There are many voices in the Caribbean today that argue forcefully for a marriage of socialism with democracy. Some are social liberals, like Carl Stone in Jamaica and Selwyn Ryan in Trinidad. Others are Marxists, like Clive Thomas in Guyana, or like the Trinidadian Tapia group, social reformers anxious to reconstruct the neocolonial economy along decentralizing lines.

This line of argument is based on what H. G. Wells once aptly termed the "theory of the suppressed alternative." The U.S. and the Cuban ways are not the only ways. There was a third force of democratic socialism existing in the Caribbean long before 1959. "Marxist theory," wrote Thomas, "has always been explicitly based on the creative interaction of socialism and political democracy. No serious understanding of history can ever show that the advance of political democracy and the obtaining of individual and collective freedoms have been the product of bourgeois generosity. The workers have won through struggle every limited democratic right they have ever had. . . . Political democracy and freedom therefore cannot be put to stand counterpoised to socialism."[1]

David de Caires has pointed out further that the Soviet authoritarian model, arising out of special historical conditions alien to the Western experience, and certainly to the Caribbean experience, has been uncritically accepted as the official custodian of the Marxist tradition, with fatal consequences. "Because of this," he added, "any political party in the Caribbean which describes itself as Marxist-Leninist inevitably raises certain anxieties about its democratic intentions. How can the theory of the vanguard party fit in with the system of multi-party democracy that still survives in most of the Caribbean Commonwealth?"[2]

The Cuban Connection

If this line of analysis is correct, it means certain things with reference to the Caribbean and the Cuban connection: (1) The Cuban revolution has been, and remains, the most powerful force against what Juan Bosch has aptly termed U.S. *pentagonismo.* As such it deserves the support of every Caribbean radical. (2) Cuban help, therefore, is to be welcomed. But as Cuban advisers arrive in Jamaica and Guyana and Grenada—and probably other territories where the seeds of a Grenada-style coup d'etat are present—they must be made to understand that they come on *our* terms and not on theirs. (3) Those terms relate to the rich variety of ideology existing in the Caribbean. Marxist ideology has to be married to nationalist ideology.

Indeed, it is curious that so many Caribbean groups accept the Cuban-Soviet model at a time when that very model is under severe scrutiny throughout the socialist world itself. That is the meaning of the debate on Eurocommunism. It is the meaning, to use a Caribbean example, of Aimé Césaire's famous letter of 1956 chastizing the French Communist party for overlooking the special conditions of French Antillean colonial society and assuming that French party commissars could dictate tactics and strategy to colonial comrades who were seen, even by the French communist mind, as "backward" children to be educated by the metropolitan *savants.* There is, in sum, no immaculate conception of socialism.

All this has important consequences for the foreign policy of the emerging Caribbean states. Historically, the Caribbean has been a helpless pawn in the dangerous game of big-power rivalry. In the sixteenth century it was Spain against its Protestant rivals. In the twentieth century there is a clear and present danger that it will be the United States against the Soviet Union. Independence will become meaningless if the region becomes once again the spoils in the cold war between Moscow and Washington. That danger is enhanced if Cuba becomes a surrogate of Soviet policy in the Americas; and every indication is that it has so become. That is a frightful gamble, on any showing.

What would happen if the Havana regime decided at some point to reach accommodation with Washington? There are precedents: the infamous Soviet-Nazi pact of 1939 and the present-day rapprochement between China and the United States. The men who run the Kremlin are no more sentimental than the men who run the Pentagon. If they decide, at some moment, that it is necessary to appease Washington, and if Havana follows suit, what would happen to all those groups and regimes in the Caribbean that have accepted the party line that the United States is the eternal enemy? Quite brutally, they would be left out in the cold.

Or, again, what happens if Havana decides to back one Marxist group in Guyana against the other, thus creating a sort of Ethiopia-Eritrea situation? In such a situation, only the Guyanese people would stand to suffer. Or if, yet again, a Cuban-supported regime in, say, Grenada were one day to decide that the Cuban yoke was too unbearable, would Havana move to crush the nationalist spirit as the Soviet Union crushed Hungary in 1956 and Czechoslovakia in 1968, or as the British crushed Guyanese Marxism in 1952, as the Americans crushed the popular movement in Santo Domingo in 1965? Merely to mention the possibilities is to apprehend the awful risk that is involved in allowing other people, however well intentioned they may be, to make your foreign policy for you.

What the Caribbean badly needs is a sort of Monroe Doctrine that would declare, unequivocally, the neutrality of the region. That, of course, was the prime issue in the recent Havana-centered meeting of the Nonaligned Movement. If we follow Dr. Castro we run the risk of converting ourselves into Soviet surrogates. If we follow Marshal Tito we at least make certain that, in crude terms of realpolitik, we can balance one great power against the other. And, in idealistic terms, we guarantee that we retain intact our own creole, indigenous conscience. A stance of neutrality will enable the different Caribbean countries to maximize their choices in the international patron-client game.

No one, admittedly, should underestimate the vast difficulties involved in such a choice. As Frank Moya-Pons has pointed out, the Caribbean lacks a common Caribbean consciousness. In the absence of a rational world economic order, the Caribbean economies still rely upon their respective metropolitan markets for the sale of their raw tropical products and act as receiving societies for their continuing emigration patterns. There is political and racial fragmentation. Linguistic divisiveness continues so that—to take an odd example only—even those English-speaking Caribbean intelligentsia who support Cuba rarely bother to learn Spanish.

Cultural dependency continues: In higher education the Puerto Rican graduate student goes to the United States just as the French Antillean student goes to France. All in all, the picture of heroic Caribbean masses rising up in revolt against colonialism and imperialism is, sadly, a myth rather than a reality. As Moya-Pons concluded, there is not a single holistic Caribbean community, with common interests and aspirations; there is a series of separate Caribbean societies often fatally hostile to each other.[3]

Yet, paradoxically, there is a strength in this weakness. The very diversity of the region makes it difficult for any one power to take it over. U.S. policymakers see it, simplistically, as a "trouble spot." Yet it would take decades of Americanization to overwhelm Barbadian anglophilism or Martiniquean francophilism, as even after eighty years, Puerto Rican society remains intractably Spanish-speaking and in many areas solidly Hispanic. In Trinidad, where the penetration of U.S. culture is widespread, Trinidadians are not over-awed by it, and it would be difficult to discover any Trinidadian who would concede that his great bacchanal event of Carnival had anything to lose by comparison with that of Rio or New Orleans. In Santo Domingo and Haiti, suspicion of the U.S. "way of life" still survives, going back to the U.S. occupation of those republics in the 1920s and 1930s.

Correspondingly the Cuban revolutionary appeal is limited. Cuban short-term aid to its Caribbean neighbors is obvious. It can provide tractors, heavy equipment, medical teams, language teachers, agronomists, forestry experts, military advisers. There is even intellectual cooperation: There is an English-language section in the annual literary prizes presented by the Casa de las Américas. All this is admirable, if only because Cuba, by historical experience and geographical location—and unlike the United States—is a bona fide member of the Caribbean family.

But the long-term aid is a different matter. For Cuba, as much as any other Third World economy, remains trapped within a trade-dependency and debt-dependency situation. There is little that its influence can do to alter drastically a world system in which the less developed economies become increasingly obligated to an international loan-banking and world trading regime dominated by the more developed economies. Havana possesses precious little leverage to facilitate major reforms such as fairer terms of debt amortization and more equitable exchange terms in world commerce. Indeed, it is oil-rich Trinidad, rather than Cuba, that plays the new role of Caribbean banker; and recent complaints from the small-island finance ministers demonstrate that the Trinidad government is as much prepared to insist on hard Yankee trades in return for its loan aid as the former imperialist masters. All in all, the future historian of the Cuban revolution and its Caribbean significance may have to conclude that its influence, for good or ill, has been ideological rather than practical.

Notes

1. Clive Thomas, "Bread and Justice," *Caribbean Contact* (Barbados), April 1976, p. 15.
2. David de Caires, "Marxism and Human Rights," *Caribbean Contact,* November 1979, p. 12.
3. Frank Moya-Pons, "Is There a Caribbean Consciousness?" *Américas,* Vol. 31, no. 8 (August 1979):33.

14
Toward a New U.S. Presence in the Caribbean

Franklin W. Knight

The United States and the Caribbean states—mainland as well as island Caribbean—are not enjoying one of their best seasons. If the situation was difficult and confused during the tenure of U.S. President Jimmy Carter, it is even more so under that of his successor, Ronald Reagan. In the popular press and among a considerable number of those who fashion public opinion the impression has been propagated that the Caribbean is on the verge of a new round of political and social explosion.[1] Yet one has only to recall the alarm with which the planter-historian from Jamaica, Bryan Edwards, addressed his colleagues in the British Parliament in 1793. "The times in which we live," he declared, "constitute an awful period in the history of the world; for a spirit of subversion is gone forth, which sets at nought the wisdom of our ancestors and the lessons of experience."[2] The apprehension Edwards expressed pertained specifically to a certain class whose political fortunes seemed jeopardized by the French revolution. But the economic and social jeopardy continued as the tumultuous events of the nineteenth century cast a long shadow over the imminent changes in the Caribbean. Political restlessness and revolutionary change are integral constants of Caribbean reality and history.[3]

Americans are especially concerned about the recent changes. That is readily understandable. What is not readily understandable, however, is the old, unimaginative message repeated *ad nauseam* and echoing the shallow arguments made about Southeast Asia since the Vietnam war: The Americans are losing touch; U.S. power is being challenged;

entire local societies are in jeopardy; every political change, regular or irregular, is a harbinger of a communist takeover.

But this U.S. concern for the political and ideological manifests a troubling double standard. When Joe Clark's Conservative government fell in Canada in December 1979 after being in office for only six months, *Time* magazine reported that a "well-informed" official of the government of the United States said that there was nothing to worry about. When the United States changed presidents three times in six years during the 1970s there seemed nothing to worry about—even though one of those changes took place without an election.

This understanding attitude toward Canadian or domestic political change is not extended to states in Latin America or the Caribbean. When the Cubans replaced the corrupt government of Fulgencio Batista in 1959 with an apparently honest and idealistic one, the United States supported a massive attempt to overthrow it. The most overt action failed disastrously at the Bay of Pigs in mid-April 1961, when 1,200 of the 1,300 invaders surrendered to the Cuban army after a short and futile attempt to establish a beachhead. When the thirty-year-old dictatorship of Rafael Leonides Trujillo in the Dominican Republic abruptly ended with an assassin's bullet in 1961, the local political process was subverted by external intervention. The United States dispatched 23,000 troops in 1965 ostensibly to "protect American lives and property."[4] Of course, as General Earl Wheeler admitted when he assigned Lieutenant General Bruce Palmer, Jr., more was at stake. "Your announced mission," he confided, "is to save American lives. Your unstated mission is to prevent the Dominican Republic from going communist. The President [Lyndon Johnson] has stated that he will not allow another Cuba. . . . You are to take all necessary measures . . . to accomplish this mission."[5] At the time of the supervised elections of 1966, which ensured the victory of the conservative Joaquín Balaguer over the liberal populist Juan Bosch, the United States still had 9,000 troops in the Dominican Republic, along with 2,000 others from Brazil and other Latin American states.

When the New Jewel Movement of Grenada replaced the repressive government of Eric Matthew Gairy on March 13, 1979, there was a frantic response and alarm that the small eastern Caribbean state was "going communist." The Carter administration forbade its ambassador to the Eastern Caribbean to travel to Grenada. The Reagan administration refused to assign an ambassador to Grenada or to accept the credentials of Grenada's nominee to Washington. The minor revolt of Rastafarians in St. Vincent got more U.S. press coverage than the island's achievement of independence in 1979. The Jamaica elections of 1980 attracted considerable attention largely because Prime Minister

Michael Manley had attempted to introduce "democratic socialism" and closer relations with Cuba. By contrast, the first election in Trinidad after twenty-five years of Eric Williams went almost unnoticed in November 1981. Caribbean states attract attention only when their actions are perceived as contrary to the interest of the United States.

Why is the United States so concerned about change in the Caribbean? Why, in the relatively short span of two hundred years has the country gone from the trend-setter in sociopolitical change to the virtual unilateral opponent of such change in the Americas? It is strange to find the United States, which fired the "shot heard round the world" in 1776, thereby sanctioning the idea of political revolution, intervening to prevent or reverse revolutions in Cuba, the Dominican Republic, Grenada, Jamaica, Guatemala, Nicaragua, and El Salvador.

The United States's relations with the rest of the hemisphere manifest the profound shortcoming of a program without a policy—without a thoughtful, flexible, long-term policy toward Latin America and the Caribbean. Even when the United States articulates such a policy, as President Reagan attempted to do in his speech to the assembled diplomats of the Organization of American States on February 23, 1982, the rhetoric and the reality prove tantalizingly irreconcilable.

From the historian's point of view, the United States often acts contrary to the interests of the Caribbean states, and some of these actions might very well be inimical to the long-term interests of the United States itself. This was true when the United States tried on several occasions to play big brother in Cuba, Haiti and the Dominican Republic. A former U.S. ambassador to the Dominican Republic, John Bartlow Martin, expressed a similar idea when he wrote in *U.S. Policy in the Caribbean* that, regarding the Caribbean, the United States has "a policy without content." Martin thought, with a great measure of justification, that if the United States "cannot move more effectively and helpfully in the Caribbean, we can hardly expect to do better in Asia or Africa."[6] Reagan's ambassador to the United Nations, Jeane Kirkpatrick, has described U.S. foreign policy as inept and ill-conceived. Effective and helpful actions, however, depend on the guidelines supplied by a sophisticated and consistent policy. How can this type of policy be initiated, and how can things be reversed?

A New Policy

The formulation of a genuinely new policy requires three interrelated processes: a complete change in the prevailing mental attitude toward the states and peoples of Latin America and the Caribbean;

political actions that respect the autonomy, sovereignty, and independence of each state regardless of size; and a set of economic actions that attempt to help not only the governments of the region, but also the masses of the separate states.

The two most popular general notions of the Caribbean are startlingly contradictory. One represents the region as an idyllic playground with windswept palm trees delineating white sand beaches of extraordinary beauty where ever-smiling natives stand ready to pamper their foreign guests. Such was the view portrayed by national tourist organizations eager to lure visitors to their shores. In the late 1970s the Jamaica Tourist Board distributed a beautiful poster of a marvelous tropical island isolated in a calm, variegated sea with the calculatedly evocative words: "In a world of bad air, poisoned water and litter, there are still a few virginal places. Enjoy. Quickly." The second notion suggests that the Caribbean is a danger zone on the point of explosion. The reality is closer to the second than the first. But political revolution of a violent sort is not yet at the door. The Caribbean has a range of grave problems of all sorts, but the region is no closer to political explosion and communist domination than is the United States. Although the region as a whole is undergoing considerable social changes, to characterize these changes as negative, nihilistic, ominous occurrences is patently absurd.

It is imperative that in the present preoccupation with the direction of political change the significance of diminutive physical size not be lost. Size is a serious constraint and an unavoidable influence on the actions of most of the Caribbean states. It is sometimes difficult for the United States to understand the full implications of the basic inhibitions of a small land area and a small population on the daily affairs of a modern mini-state, or the resulting differences in world view.

Nowhere was this difference in perception more clearly manifested than during President Ronald Reagan's "working holiday" in the Eastern Caribbean in April 1982. Continuing the direct attacks on Grenada and Cuba that had clouded his February address in Washington at the Organization of American States meeting, Reagan told a gathering of heads of state: "I think all of us are concerned with the overturn of Westminster parliamentary democracy in Grenada. That country now bears the Soviet and Cuban trademark, which means that it will attempt to spread the virus among its neighbors." This type of thinking clearly irked his host, Prime Minister Tom Adams of Barbados, who was forced to reply: "It is quite important to note that within this region, there is very little cause at the moment, to think that Grenada could represent by its example a superior way of either economic or political development to the other islands. . . . How can a country like Grenada threaten Barbados with five times its per capita income, very well distributed, spending more per capita on education and health than virtually any communist country . . . and virtually any other developing country?'"[7] Barbados, with a population of 279,000 on 166 square miles of land, only about 150 miles from Grenada, demonstrated more sanguine sophistication about the political and ideological changes of its neighbor than the superpower United States of America.

That the Caribbean states deserve special handling by the United States is obvious—although there is no obvious way to define the Caribbean. Apart from being small—and that is a major problem over which they have no control—the Caribbean states possess few natural resources, and even fewer of global economic importance.[8] Trinidad, the most fortunate of the island states, has petroleum reserves estimated to last until about 1990 at the current rate of exploitation. Its natural gas reserves should last considerably longer. Jamaica and Haiti have extensive bauxite deposits, but unlike fellow producers Guyana and Suriname, lack enough local energy to convert the ore beyond the stage of alumina. The Bahamas has extensive deposits of aragonite, a calcium carbonate mineral once used widely in bottling soft drinks but no longer considered an important item of international commerce.

As a region of individual mini-states, the Caribbean does not wield major political clout. Only Cuba has the equivalent of a global foreign policy and has served a term as head of the Nonaligned Movement, with nearly one hundred members. The Bahamas chose not even to join the Organization of American States. Many of the others find providing the economic and human resources for a viable international policy a major strain. Indeed, even among the most economically viable states the domestic problems are enormous.

In the past, the principal rationale for special concern on the part of the United States arose because the Caribbean was depicted as of tremendous strategic importance for the military defence of the United States. In an age of computerized rockets, intercontinental ballistic missiles, and potential nuclear warfare, this strategic argument has lost most of its plausibility. With the treaty to return the Panama Canal to Panamanian sovereignty already concluded, the strategic importance of the Caribbean is further diminished. But the recognition that the islands and states no longer serve as potential bastions of military defense should not be construed as meaning that they are no longer of importance to the United States.

Taken individually, with very few exceptions, the Caribbean states—especially those Eastern Caribbean states such as Antigua, Dominica, St. Vincent, St. Lucia, and Grenada—appear like so many San José de Gracias, the marvelous little town beautifully portrayed by Luis González in *Pueblo en vilo, Microhistoria de San José de Graciá*—a town that in the author's view was significant because of its insignificance.[9] Similarly, these Caribbean states, no matter how small, are visible scenes where real people are confronting concrete problems. They are trying to help themselves and to solve their own problems. They may use external assistance to solve these problems, or—as the examples of the Mariel flotillas of 1980 and the Haitian boat people have demonstrated—those problems will grow to become the problems of the wider American and world community.[10]

From the U.S. point of view, the Caribbean peoples are neighbors profoundly affected by any action or inaction the United States takes in the realization of its global pursuits. No one suggests that the United States should exercise either benign neglect or unilateral action with regard to the Caribbean. No one suggests that the United States can solve any or all Caribbean problems. No one suggests that a unanimity can be achieved between the interests of the United States on the one hand and of the several Caribbean states on the other. But it is important that an informed and intelligent policy be sought that strives to establish a workable compromise between the goals, rights, and legitimate aspirations of the United States and of each nation state of the Caribbean. Moreover, it ought to be recognized that the relations of a mighty world power like the United States with these neighboring mini-states provide an important index of its relations with a great part of the wider world. If the United States can move from the legacy of domination and conflict to a new era of peaceful coexistence and cooperation, it will have demonstrated that not only can it do great things, but it can also do little things of great importance—and that it can do both equally well. Changing traditions is never easy, but it is of paramount importance that the architects of U.S. foreign policy be aware, as was Alfred, Lord Tennyson, that "the world advances and in time outgrows those laws which in our fathers' days were best."

The proliferation of mini-states in the Caribbean is a painful reality that must be accepted. Political confederation appears to have lost its appeal in the contemporary world. The implications of this centrifugal development must also be accepted. Greater numbers of states with voting privileges participating in international organizations and agencies present a new arena in which conventional power politics do not always work well. Not all the Caribbean island states have the same interests. Countries such as Grenada, St. Vincent, Dominica, St. Lucia, and Jamaica cannot—and do not—have the same preoccupations as Venezuela, Mexico, and Colombia. The small island states do not fit easily in a general policy designed for Latin America, or for the Third World, or for the less developed countries, however many qualities they may share with the most representative states of those larger denominations.

In confronting this new reality of an expanding number of new, small states, the United States must be aware that this increased number also increases the possibilities of dissension and differences. Each Caribbean unit sees itself and the world with a slightly different focus. Each has a slightly different set of priorities that cannot be expected to be consistently congruent with those of the United States. The governments of these states must be expected to act in what they perceive as their best interests, however singular such a perception may be. The state that hallowed the words "all men are created equal" can do no less than accept the consequences of the pursuit of internal political goals. From the U.S. point of view some of these states may seem to be neither democratic in the choice of their governments nor capitalist in the orientation of their economies. But the choice is theirs. They should make it without external threats; and they and others must learn to live with the consequences. Anything that infringes on the hard-earned sovereignty of these states is an unwarranted interference in their domestic affairs.

Reagan's impolitic statements in Barbados clearly reveal that the United States still does not understand the Caribbean. The new political leaders of the Caribbean states do not share the old phobia of communism that still complicates the foreign policy of the United States. Most of these leaders do not feel that the inevitable choice is servile subordination either to the United States or to the Soviet Union. They do not believe that ideological differences negate political, economic, or diplomatic interchange. To them it is possible—and often desirable—to be equally friendly with Cuba, the Soviet Union, the People's Republic of China, the United States, or any other member of the United Nations. They find it illogical, inconsistent, and incomprehensible (if not downright hypocritical) that the United States should not only refrain from having diplomatic relations with Cuba but should also attempt to restrain the Cubans from free and open intercourse with their Caribbean neighbors. If the United States had no relations with any socialist government then its position would be more understandable. But Caribbean politicians find Cuban communism no more unacceptable than Soviet or Chinese communism. A president of the United States who can travel the thousands of miles to Moscow and Peking ought to be able to go the hundreds of miles between Havana and Washington.

The Caribbean is not the best locale to play an anti-Cuba card, at least not in the crude form of an implacable hostility based on ideological grounds. For from the internal Caribbean perspective, ideology is not the foremost political concern. All the political leaders in the Caribbean are, to a very great extent, political pragmatists. They have no choice if they are to survive in their local habitat and make headway against growing internal problems, which their limited assets exacerbate. The new Cuban presence in the Caribbean stems not just from the fact that it has resisted U.S. hostility for twenty-three years. The appeal of Cuba lies far less in its espousal of socialism than in its successful resolution of some long-standing problems that are common to all the Caribbean states, and indeed to much of the world. Apart from socialist intellectuals, most Caribbean political practitioners point to Cuban achievement in sports, education, medicine, culture, art, population control, and mass mobilization with a certain amount of envy mixed with pride.

But there is another point to be made. It is a serious mistake to believe that invidious support of certain factions in the Caribbean will ensure a political scenario permanently harmonious with the interests of the United States. The divide-and-rule tactic of playing favorites or creating showcases has not worked in the past. There is no reason to believe that it will work in the future. President Reagan could not contribute to either Caribbean harmony or additional U.S. goodwill by selecting Edward Seaga of Jamaica and Tom Adams of Barbados as his favorites while excluding George Price of Belize, neglecting George Chambers of Trinidad, and attacking Maurice Bishop of Grenada and Fidel Castro of Cuba. The formal political opposition in those Caribbean states in which such an opposition exists cannot afford to be less nationalist than the government. Edward Seaga might have a different rhetoric—and a different economic program—from Michael Manley, but their goals are similar and their differences are more of degree than of kind. The accession to power of Cheddi Jagan in Guyana, Errol Barrow in Barbados, or Basdeo Panday in Trinidad would not alter dramatically the present direction of political or economic change.[11]

Increased political violence cannot be taken as indicative of greater political instability. Providing military support or selling arms to presumably friendly governments will not guarantee political stability or administrative efficiency. Military intervention probably secured orderly political succession in the Dominican Republic in 1965, but it did not create political democracy. Indeed, President Carter had to warn the military to allow Antonio Guzmán to accede to the Dominican presidency and not to intervene to negate the 1978 election results. Governments that do not have a popular base, or that demonstrate an indifference to the majority of the population (and in some cases, a determined minority) run the risk of being replaced by the ballot box if possible, by bullets and bloodshed if necessary. U.S. support of the status quo on promises that some individuals or groups will either observe human rights or be uncritically friendly to the United States is neither thoughtful nor efficacious. Reducing general principles to a set of specific issues or labels undermines the flexibility necessary to assist peoples despite the conduct of their governments.

The new policy with respect to the Caribbean must try to put things in perspective. The political choice at any given moment of the people of Cuba, or Puerto Rico, or the Dominican Republic, or Jamaica, or Barbados will not of itself change the course of world history. The separate political choices, too, will not necessarily affect one another. As Tom Adams pointed out to a visiting U.S. delegation, the political system of Grenada, with its population of 100,000 (of whom 50 percent are below the age of 18), is hardly likely to have any effect on Trinidad, with its population of 1 million, or on Jamaica, with a population of 2 million. A policy that is predicated on the analogy of a falling domino structure is neither imaginative nor intelligent. A policy that accepts the inherent variety of the peoples and politics of the Caribbean will, in the long run, respond effectively and with reciprocal benefits to all the parties involved. Such a policy is both feasible and necessary.

A Policy of Cooperation

In order to establish a new policy of cooperation, the United States must endeavor to demonstrate that its primary concern in the Caribbean is not only the support of "friendly governments," but also the welfare of the majority of people in the region. A policy that seeks to help the people of the Caribbean ought to formulate programs that will address three vital concerns by providing diversified aid so that the trickle-down effect reaches the lowest economic stratum; by reducing or eliminating chronic unemployment and underemployment; and by encouraging a return to the agricultural base that offers the best hope of small islands to control their manifold problems. All three goals are intimately connected, as President Reagan acknowledged in his address to the Organization of American States.[12]

Foreign aid constitutes one of the most controversial issues in the Caribbean. However it is administered, it presents some degree of conflict between donors and recipients. In the Caribbean, foreign aid provides a major source of hard currency and subsidizes the provision of vital sources of food, clothing, and other items that form the basis of general material indexes of development. Foreign exchange, especially U.S. dollars, are crucial for the increasing proportion of commerce dominated by food imports. By the mid-1970s the major societies of the Caribbean had developed the pattern of virtually being fed by the United States. Jamaica, Trinidad and Tobago, and Guyana imported between 77 percent and 92 percent of their cereals and wheat flour from the United States. Food items accounted for 6.6 percent of total imports in affluent Trinidad and Tobago; 22.5 percent in Barbados; and nearly 40 percent in Jamaica in 1973.[13]

In the public mind, the scale of aid and its potential for effecting social change are grossly exaggerated. Between 1963 and 1973 the amount of public and private support from seventeen countries that are rich and nonsocialist—Australia, Austria, Belgium, Canada, Denmark, France, West Germany, Japan, Italy, the Netherlands, New Zealand, Norway, Portugal, Sweden, Switzerland, the United Kingdom, and the United States—increased from $8.57 billion to $24.43 billion. Initially this seems like a lot of money. Divided among the poor of the world in 1973, it amounted to an annual expenditure of $13 per head—hardly the type of expenditure to make a tremendous impact on the daily lives of the recipients. Foreign assistance channeled through a government bureaucracy has an even smaller effect than might be expected.

The countries of the Caribbean need aid, but they need aid designed to achieve a number of integrated goals: reducing population; increasing food production; providing roads, jobs, transportation, housing, health care, and all the essential services the community and its citizens require. This type of cluster program can be attempted most successfully by a combination of bilateral aid, multilateral aid, private banking organizations, and in some cases, capitalist and socialist cooperation.

Unemployment and underemployment are major problems that have virtually defied resolution in the Caribbean. The establishment by the United States of a *gastarbeiter* (or regulated foreign worker) program modified along the practice of some of the Western European countries would be a dramatic step in alleviating the labor problem of the Caribbean states. It would have a number of advantages for both the Caribbean and the United States. Instead of steadily increasing expenditures to pursue and prosecute illegal aliens, the United States could use some of that money for more worthy causes. Controlled labor would be more dignified for the workers and probably more productive. The overall impact on U.S. employment, wage structure, or social services would be minimal. Remission to the home countries would boost their foreign exchange reserves. And, of course, foreign workers would continue to promote consumer sales.

Assuming that work permits would be given only to those with secured employment, it is difficult to envisage how the scheme could lead to the greater exploitation of workers—a criticism that prevails currently about the employed undocumented aliens. A documented worker program would no more hurt the United States than it did Germany, Switzerland, France, or Sweden. It would not inundate the United States with Hispanics and Afro-Caribbean peoples. A documented workers program would not be an open invitation to a new wave of immigration. It would be a labor recruitment program, no more and no less. It would operate when the United States required these foreign workers for as long as they were needed.

Liberalizing the terms of trade to facilitate the entry of Caribbean agricultural and manufactured goods into the U.S. market would be a third way to assist these neighboring peoples. This is a key provision of President Reagan's Caribbean Basin Initiative; he described it as "the centerpiece of the program."[14]

Although currently some 87 percent of Caribbean commodities enter the U.S. market under some preferential trade terms, the expansion of free trade promises more advantages. Opening U.S. markets might stimulate local agriculture and enable local governments to achieve at least two important aims. The first would be to work against the internal migration from the rural areas to the cities and arrest the increasing disaffection from the land and agricultural labor. This would modify the alarming figures for the employed and partially employed, the greater number of whom are in the cities. The second aim is to increase local food production. Not only do Caribbean governments import wheat flour, rice, and fish, which are components of the basic diet, but they also import potatoes, beans, onions, and other vegetables that could be grown locally.

The Caribbean Basin Initiative

The Caribbean Basin Initiative has recognized and targeted the economic area, and it has gone a bit further to designate the Caribbean as a special region with which the United States will have virtually free trade. But whether the bill to implement the initiative will, as it states, "promote economic revitalization and facilitate expansion of economic opportunity in the Caribbean Basin region" is anybody's guess.[15] The odds are not in its favor. It can be argued that the additional sum of $350 million earmarked for fiscal year 1982 is inadequate given the twenty-eight entities theoretically entitled to receive this aid. But the way the Reagan administration hopes to divide the aid—with the greater proportion targeted for El Salvador, Honduras, and Jamaica—makes it likely that the purpose is more political than economic. And if the prevailing rationale for support is military and political, then basic infrastructural changes to promote sustained economic development will be neglected.

But the most serious handicap of the Caribbean Basin Initiative is its extraordinary reliance on private-sector benevolence, supply-side economics, and the financial recovery of the United States. No matter how successful, private enterprise and individual initiative alone cannot supply the jobs and social services and execute the social programs required to lift the Caribbean countries from their present malaise. The public sector is a major and an important part of Caribbean economic life. What the Caribbean Basin Initiative ought to attempt is the harmonious yoking of public and private sectors to achieve public good as well as private profits. And it ought to achieve that without irrevocable damage to political independence and national sovereignty.

Notes

1. See Richard Millet and W. Marvin Will, eds., *The Restless Caribbean. Changing Patterns of International Relations* (New York: Praeger Publishers, 1979).
2. Quoted in J. H. Parry and P. M. Sherlock, *A Short History of the West Indies* (New York: St. Martin's Press, 1971), p. 160.
3. Franklin W. Knight, *The Caribbean. The Genesis of a Fragmented Nationalism* (New York: Oxford University Press, 1978).
4. The most thoroughly documented account of this period is Piero Gleijeses, *The Dominican Crisis. The 1965 Constitutional Revolt and American Intervention* (Baltimore: Johns Hopkins University Press, 1978).
5. Abraham F. Lowenthal, *The Dominican Intervention* (Cambridge, Mass.: Harvard University Press, 1972), p. 116.
6. John Bartlow Martin, *U.S. Policy in the Caribbean* (Boulder, Colo.: Westview Press, 1978), p. xii. Martin's analysis of U.S. foreign policy is excellent, and his recommendations are sound. For details, see pp. 277–292.
7. As reported in *Caribbean Contact* (Barbados), June 1982, pp. 8–9.
8. See Ransford W. Palmer, *Caribbean Dependence on the United States Economy* (New York: Praeger Publishers, 1979).
9. Mexico City: El Coleegio de México, 1968.
10. See "The Caribbean Exodus," *Caribbean Review*, Vol. 11, no. 1 (Winter 1982).

11. See "The Role of the Opposition in the Caribbean," *Caribbean Review,* Vol. 7, no. 4 (October-November-December 1978):22–41.

12. See text of President Reagan's speech to the OAS, February 24, 1982. The congressional version is called the Caribbean Basin Economic Recovery Act.

13. These statistics are taken from Palmer, *Caribbean Dependence,* pp. 36–37.

14. See text of Reagan's February 24, 1982, OAS speech.

15. 97th Congress, 2nd Session, H.R. 5900.

About the Contributors

Luis E. Aguilar, professor of Latin American history and political development at Georgetown University in Washington, D.C., has taught at universities in Cuba and the United States. Among his books are: *Pasado y ambiente en el proceso cubano; Cuba: Conciencia y revolución; Cuba 1933, Prologue to Revolution; Operation Zapata;* and the edited volume, *Marxism in Latin America.* He was a member of the Cuban Revolutionary Institute of Culture in 1959–1960.

Max Azicri is professor of political science at Edinboro University of Pennsylvania. He is the author of many studies on Cuban politics and society, as well as comparative studies of the Cuban and Nicaraguan revolutions.

Demetrio Boersner is professor of the history of international relations at Universidad Central de Venezuela, Caracas. Among his books are *The Bolsheviks and the National and Colonial Question, 1917–1928; Socialismo y nacionalismo; Venezuela y el Caribe, presencia cambiante;* and *Relaciones exteriores de América Latina: Una breve historia.*

H. Michael Erisman is associate professor of political science at Mercyhurst College in Pennsylvania. He is coeditor of *Colossus Challenged: The Struggle for Caribbean Influence* (Westview Press, 1982) and editor of *The Caribbean Challenge: U.S. Policy in a Volatile Region* (Westview Press, forthcoming). He is currently working on a book entitled *Castro and Cuban Globalism: The Politics of Restrained Nationalism.*

Henry S. Gill is research fellow in international politics at the Institute of International Relations at the University of the West Indies. He has written extensively on Latin America and the Caribbean.

Antonio Jorge, professor of political economy at Florida International University, Miami, has taught at universities in Cuba and the United States. Among his books are *Competition, Cooperation, Efficiency and Social Organization: Introduction to a Political Economy* and the coedited volumes *Integración y cooperación económica en América Latina* and *The External Debt and the Economic Development of Latin America.* He was chief economist in the Cuban Ministry of Finance from 1959 to 1961.

Franklin W. Knight is professor of history at Johns Hopkins University, Baltimore. He has taught at the State University of New York (Stony Brook) and the University of Texas (Austin). He is author of *Slave Society in Cuba During the Nineteenth Century; The African Dimension in Latin American Societies;* and *The Caribbean: The Genesis of a Fragmented Nationalism.*

William M. LeoGrande, former director of political science in the School of Government and Public Administration at the American University, Washington, D.C., is currently working for the Senate Democratic Policy Committee on a Council on Foreign Relations fellowship. He is author of *Cuba's Policy in Africa 1959–1980* and has written widely on Cuba and Central America.

Barry B. Levine, professor of sociology and anthropology at Florida International University, Miami, has taught at universities in the United States and Latin America. He is author of *Benjy Lopez: A Picaresque Tale of Emigration and Return* and coeditor of *Problemas de desigualdad social en Puerto Rico.* He is editor and cofounder of *Caribbean Review.*

Gordon K. Lewis, professor of social science at the University of Puerto Rico, has taught at various universities in the United States. Among his books are *Puerto Rico: Freedom and Power in the Caribbean; The Growth of the Modern West Indies; The Virgin Islands: A Caribbean Lilliput; Notes on the Puerto Rican Revolution; Slavery, Imperialism and Freedom;* and *Gather with the Saints at the River.* A forthcoming book is *Main Currents in Caribbean Thought 1492–1900: The Historical Evolution of Caribbean Society in Its Ideological Aspects.*

Anthony P. Maingot, professor of sociology and anthropology at Florida International University, Miami, has taught at universities in the United States and the Caribbean. He has written extensively on the Caribbean and Latin America and is presently working on a manuscript entitled *The Caribbean as Modern Conservative Societies.* During 1982–1983 he served as president of the Caribbean Studies Association.

Robert A. Pastor is a faculty research associate at the School of Public Affairs, University of Maryland, College Park, where he directs a research program in Caribbean Basin Studies. He was senior staff member responsible for Latin American and Caribbean affairs on the National Security Council during the Carter administration. He served as executive director of the Linowitz Commission on U.S.–Latin American Relations in 1975–1976. He is the author of *Congress and the Politics of U.S. Foreign Economic Policy.*

Steve C. Ropp is associate professor of government at New Mexico State University, Las Cruces. He is author of *Panamanian Politics: From Guarded Nation to National Guard.*

Aaron Segal, professor of political science at the University of Texas, El Paso, has taught at universities in the United States, Latin America, and Africa. A past editor of *Africa Report,* he is the author of *The Politics of Population in the Caribbean; The Politics of Caribbean Economic Integration;* coauthor of *The Traveler's Africa;* and editor of *Population Policies in the Caribbean.* He is currently working on a manuscript entitled *Cultural Splendor and Political Poverty in Haiti.*

Index